Also by Mark Hughes

Speed Addicts

Lewis Hamilton: The Full Story

Crashed And Byrned:
The Greatest Racing Driver You Never Saw
(with Tommy Byrne)

MARK HUGHES

UNSTOPPABLE

THE ULTIMATE BIOGRAPHY
OF MAX VERSTAPPEN

HEADLINE

First published in 2023 by
HEADLINE PUBLISHING GROUP

1

Cataloguing in Publication Data is available from the British Library

Hardback ISBN: 978 1 4722 9904 8
Trade paperback ISBN: 978 1 4722 9908 6

Designed and typeset by EM&EN
Printed and bound in Great Britain by Clays Ltd, Elcograf S.p.A.

Headline's policy is to use papers that are natural, renewable and recyclable
products and made from wood grown in well-managed forests and other
controlled sources. The logging and manufacturing processes are expected
to conform to the environmental regulations of the country of origin.

HEADLINE PUBLISHING GROUP
An Hachette UK Company
Carmelite House
50 Victoria Embankment
London EC4Y 0DZ

www.headline.co.uk
www.hachette.co.uk

For Heather

CONTENTS

INTRODUCTION

Max Verstappen roared into F1 like a whirlwind, imposing himself as a would-be great barely before the racing world knew what was happening. For many fans, the Verstappen name was a throwback to the 1990s and early 2000s, when Max's father, Jos 'the Boss', had brought colour and occasional controversy to the sport with his forthright personality and aggressive style, but had never played a part in the outcome of a race. It had never really happened for Jos in F1; his star faded before it had properly risen, and he ended up just making some noise to fill in the gaps as the crowd waited for the leaders.

But almost from the moment Jos disappeared from F1 view, the second Verstappen offensive was underway. If there could have been an experiment in how to create the perfect racing driver, it would probably have looked something like the making of Max Verstappen. Because Max wasn't just the son of Jos: he was also the son of Sophie Kumpen, one of the very best kart racers in the world in her time. She raced against Jenson Button, Giancarlo Fisichella, Jarno Trulli and an able but slightly less stellar racer than those guys, Christian Horner. On her day, Sophie could beat the best of them. She was formidable, talented and smart.

But is there such a thing as a speed gene? Was Max to the world championship born? Was it that double dose of racing DNA that got all of his neurons and synapses firing just right from birth, bequeathing him not only the fiercely competitive personality but also the preternatural feel for the physical limits of tyres on tarmac necessary to turn him into a champion? Or was the real gift that Max was brought up at the kart track – raised, with the smell of burnt rubber and two-stroke fuel in his nostrils, by one of the toughest, most demanding and at times downright scariest Competitive Dads ever to stalk a race circuit?

Hundreds of thousands of hours of scientific study have gone into trying to figure out if sport genes exist *at all*, whether experts in any field are essentially born or made, and what mix of nature and nurture is required to bring any innate potential to full, world-beating fruition.

David Epstein, in his 2014 book *The Sports Gene: Talent, Practice and the Truth About Success*, did a landmark job of pulling together the available evidence. 'The result of expertise study . . . can be summarised in a single phrase that played like a broken record in my interviews with psychologists who research expertise: "It's software, not hardware." That is, the perceptual sports skills that separate experts from dilettantes are learned or downloaded like software via practice.'

That research was based around field athletics; the equivalent research has not been made to determine whether it holds true in motorsport. But there has been some research made to aid the selection process of fighter pilots, much of which would seem to have parallels to the motor racing world. What was found there would seem to correlate more closely to the 'hardware' theory – that the skills are innate and there are considerable differences between individuals in natural aptitude even before the lifetime of training begins.

Both can, and probably are, true. There are differences in 'natural' ability *and* the '10,000-hour rule' applies. A phrase popularised by journalist Malcolm Gladwell in his bestseller *Outliers*, the 10,000-hour rule was based on a 1993 paper by Florida State University psychologist Anders Ericsson and his team, studying world-class violinists in the Music Academy of West Berlin.

This 'rule' suggests that effortful, structured activity aimed at overcoming and eradicating weaknesses and mistakes, while regularly having your performance mercilessly scrutinised to find areas to improve on, for an accumulated 10,000 hours by the age of 20, is the difference between elite and non-elite.

This kind of graft is not enjoyable – it is sustained only by the most determined and motivated – but it is, according to Ericsson, essential to enable elite sportspeople to build up detailed, complex cognitive models that allow them not just to rely on raw reaction skills but to anticipate and respond to opponents' moves in a pre-conscious way.

So did Max have an inherent 'natural' ability? A kid of four who climbs into a kart, slides it around the track and is soon lapping faster than kids who have been doing it for years very much suggests that.

Did he put in his '10,000 hours'? Absolutely. And then some. With Jos for a father, it could never have been any other way. Though Jos had risen through the ranks all the way to F1, he remained fully immersed in the sport's entry level of karting; he was one of the racing world's biggest experts in that field with the deepest knowledge and making his living from that. So when four-year-old Max demanded that he be given his own kart (he threw such tantrums when he was told to wait for a year or two that Sophie insisted to Jos it would be easier for all concerned if it happened sooner, not later), Jos was happy to oblige.

But when, a couple of years later, Max asked to start racing, having already shown a clear aptitude for the sport, Jos insisted it had to be done properly. They were not going to play at it. In reality, being born into the heart of the sport's entry level, Max would probably not have ever seen any other way than to be fully committed. Within this environment, both the desire to race and the approach drilled into him once he was doing so, could be taken for granted.

•

How do we go about de-coupling the ambition of Jos playing out through his son, putting right the wrongs of his own career, and that of Max himself? There had, after all, been a certain buzz around Jos when he'd arrived in F1, this wild guy from the Dutch travelling and scrapyard community who had been something of a sensation in karts and the junior categories of car racing.

Even for the most gifted and ambitious of drivers, even those with the head start of family wealth, motor racing is an often-bemusing world which takes time to properly understand. Just buying your way in won't grant you the knowledge and smarts needed to maximise opportunities: there are endless traps, landmines capable of derailing even the most promising of careers. The acquisition of that knowledge only begins once the kid is racing and even for quick, shrewd learners it can take years. But for Max the way would be prepared by someone who had been through it himself, someone who was ready to apply himself 100 per cent to managing his career, avoiding the mis-steps he'd made himself. It was a 10-year project that would make the Verstappens an inevitable, unstoppable force.

In the nitty-gritty of racing, the hard work and huge knowledge which must be acquired are informed not only by the essential craft but also the attitude. The racing attitude is not for everyone. It's an obsession which allows only the smallest of spaces around the margins – for other interests, for relationships outside of racing, for understanding the world outside of the racing bubble. It's a full-on performance attitude: responses to stimuli and solutions to problems have to be a) right and b) acted upon with no delay. Focused doesn't even begin to describe it. It has to be all-consuming. Thinking of ways to be yet faster, stemming from yourself or your car, has to occupy your being pretty much all the time. There are layers and layers of discoveries to be made but they are not revealed without the compulsion and the graft. Coming away from a race track feeling that you left performance out there that could have been accessed is intolerable, totally unacceptable. That's okay for hobby racers. It's maybe okay for those kids indulged by their parents to just enjoy the racing and the kudos. But it's not okay for those on the path.

'I have worked with many great drivers,' says Kees van der Grint, the Bridgestone tyre engineer who worked with Jos from karts to F1 and who witnessed at close hand the early rise of Max, 'but the way they approached things was not normal, even by racing standards. It was extreme. The determination of these people not to compromise on anything was unbelievable. I don't believe, at that age, that Max had much input in the decisions. This was all decided by Jos. But they give everything. Everything. Like back to the track after a test to get some rain running in case it rains on race day, the approach to making the engine or the kart faster, the hours they spend, the work involved. I have not seen anything like this.'

Even when Jos was an F1 driver his heart remained in karting. He ran teams, he prepared and sold engines. Giedo van der Garde won the 2002 karting world championship with a Jos Verstappen engine, for example. Even between grands prix he was to be found in the karting paddocks of Europe or his workshop, grafting still, as Van der Grint recalls: 'Even when Jos was racing in F1, and before Max was racing, you could have a problem getting him to a test day if it clashed with an important kart meeting. His focus was always on karting.' So from a competitive perspective, there could not have been a more perfect environment for young Max. Dad was already operating there and knew every nook and cranny of competitive advantage, so Max's chances at racing's starting point were immediately maximised.

Although Jos' short fuse is occasionally evident in Max in moments of strain, his underlying character is more even-tempered and it takes more to stress him than it does his father. More Sophie than Jos. That sometimes made Jos believe Max wasn't taking it as seriously as he demanded and was the cause of a few incidents between the father and the child. But beneath the relaxed, open demeanour with the ready smile and the easy quip, Max's attitude is that of an unspoilt racer. Flip the visor down and he becomes, as his Red Bull team boss Christian Horner describes him, 'A thoroughbred. He is strong-willed, he can be very sharp obviously when emotions are running high. He doesn't hold back.

'But you know you get 100 per cent from him and his mental resilience is the strongest I have ever seen. His ability under pressure is phenomenal. And the more pressure you put on, the better he delivers. Just phenomenal.'

Despite the head start in life, Max has the gift of hunger and application. He has the council estate grit because that's what Jos put into him, by example and occasionally more directly. The way he did that won't be found in any parental guidebook and could occasionally stray into what has been criticised as abuse.

Take the incident, now racing folklore, at Naples in 2012 when a silly error by Max on track led to Jos being so furious that he left his 15-year-old son at a service station. There was also the time Jos made him walk the several miles from the circuit back to the hotel after another incident on track. Walking in his race suit and carrying his helmet, Max was picked up by a passer-by and given a lift back to the hotel. Upon seeing him arrive earlier than expected, Jos asked how he'd done it so quickly. When Max told him, Jos insisted on taking him back to where he'd been picked up, dropping him off there and making him complete the punishment. Jos' way of making his points wasn't gentle, quiet or subtle. Max was enlisted to the cause – the cause of making him the best racing driver he could possibly be – and Jos knew only one way. Compromise or bruised feelings didn't come into it.

But for that to work, Max needed to be more than only vastly talented. It also demanded a very special personality, combining the assertiveness and drive required to be a successful racer but not the often-associated rebellious qualities. It required the resilience to withstand the extremity of Jos' approach but without replicating his faults.

For Jos' heavy hand to have the desired effect required Max's complete buy-in, but that part wasn't necessarily so extraordinary given that he never knew anything else. The extraordinary part was how Max retained his own distinct identity, despite the 24/7 tutelage of so extreme a character as his father.

'Max is the diplomat,' said his mother Sophie on *RTL Boulevard*. 'He always wants to make things right.' Given Jos' dominant personality and Sophie's feisty intelligence, it's easy to imagine there might have been quite a lot for young Max to try to make right for the first 11 years of his life before his parents separated.

Talk to him today and there's no apparent damage; he's relaxed and sociable, with a ready smile. The most special part of his personality, the most critical part, is that he is not cowed by anything. He fears no one and reputations mean nothing to him and never have. He's straight-talking and on track he's always the dominant one in any tango. But there's been zero rebellion. Not as far as anyone knows. Just wide-eyed, straightforward, matter-of-fact openness, very characteristically Dutch in that way, taking forward the life and career Jos helped to shape. He hasn't left his dad behind and floated away on a sea of dollars and fame. Jos is still right there by his side, a partner in his success, maybe even an equal one, though the separation of the boy from the father away from the track seems to have been completed quite seamlessly.

Jos and Raymond Vermeulen, the manager Jos found for his own career years ago and still his trusted consigliere, quietly take care of business while Max is out there taking the opposition apart, only then to return to normality which for Max, since late-2020, is partner Kelly Piquet and Penelope, her daughter from a previous relationship.

'Kelly is of course a little bit older,' said Sophie on *RTL Boulevard* in 2021. 'She has a little child. They have created some sort of a little family and I think that Max maybe missed that when he was young and I think such stability has also helped him this year as he knows that someone is waiting for him at home. She also comes from a race family so she understands everything. When you see how sweet he is to her child but also for his sister, for me, he has his heart in the right place.'

Max has seemingly created the serene home life he never had as a child but surely craved, given how tempestuous his parents' marriage was. Some idea of just how bad things got can be gained from the fact that Sophie had a restraining order placed upon Jos in the wake of their break-up in 2008. In the post-marriage arrangement, Max stayed with Jos – not least because they were by then locked together in their karting endeavours anyway – while Max's sister Victoria stayed with Sophie. Max has remained close to them all, a loving son and brother.

His sincerity was quite obvious when he said in an interview a few hours after winning his first world title that he viewed it as a family success. 'You achieve your life goal and it feels really incredible, not just for me but my whole family. They also had to live for me. My dad was away a lot; it probably cost the marriage. Also, my sister; she missed me, she missed her dad because he was always with me. All of this now, it brings back a lot of . . . it hasn't been for nothing. That's something which is very special.'

'I think Max knows how sad I've been that I had to miss him when he was younger,' said Sophie in the Verstappen's own *Whatever It Takes* documentary series of 2020, 'and I think he wants to make up for lost time.'

Victoria lived through this split too and while Max's successes have enabled her to pursue her own interests – which have included kart racing – they have, as Max suggests, also come at a cost to her. She talked of that in *Whatever It Takes*: 'I understand why Dad spent all his time with Max. It's incredible that they've made it to F1. But it has been difficult for me sometimes. I had times when I didn't feel important, when Max was the only one they talked about.'

Max also talks of leisure time spent with his mother and sister at kart tracks. 'We race together in karts sometimes. With my mum and my sister there's always competition. They're within a tenth [of a second] of each other and my sister gets angry because she thinks she's better. I last raced my dad when I was 13 and we were doing similar lap times. I enjoyed it.'

'When they were kids, Max always gave Victoria the sticker or colour book to keep the peace,' Sophie told *RTL*. 'He always thinks of her. That's two hands on one stomach. It typifies his character: that good, that sweet. Max will always want to solve things first by talking, he is a sensitive person. He gets that fierce racing from Jos. The gentle lake of me. But make no mistake, eh. Under the helmet, he is a tiger.'

Sensitive enough to engender a good atmosphere around him but not particularly reflective, Max doesn't give the impression of devoting much time to contemplation. So the deep psychological questions about his childhood relationship with his father just wouldn't resonate. There would be no deeper answers within him than the 'it is what it is' shoulder shrug 'and I'm very appreciative for it'. His reality. Which is all that matters. His story is that he saw the racing going on around him and demanded he join in. Jos met that 'urgent request' (as he later phrased it) but in so doing drilled and coached him like no one has ever been drilled and coached before. Not in this sport, anyway. There are perhaps parallels with the Williams sisters or Andre Agassi in tennis.

The boy born into the circus, he's the one up there now on the high wire, putting into practice all the lessons he was taught by the ringmaster across the karting paddocks of Europe. The ringmaster looks up with obvious pride, knowing his son walks the rope better than he ever did, but taking satisfaction from having given him what – in his eyes – were all the tools necessary to fully succeed, a schooling way better than his own could ever have been.

But what sort of guy has a life spent in the racing laboratory made? Despite his incredible talent, he appears down-to-earth, maybe even a little vanilla in his attitudes and interests. Gen-Z's preoccupation with the mores of social justice seems to have passed him by; he doesn't give the impression of knowing or caring what is going on in the world around his bubble. He's a nice guy, a caring guy, a reasonable guy, but not one seemingly troubled by things beyond his immediate orbit. There is always this pull towards equilibrium. Not in the car, obviously. But everything outside of it is about making things as stress-free as possible, including for the important people around him. From a racing perspective, it's actually a perfect combination: fire and aggression in the car, easy-going balance outside of it. Perhaps this, even more than the raw material of racing talent, is the crucial genetic inheritance: the combination of Jos' fire and Sophie's calm. 'That's scientifically, maybe, the best mix there could be,' says Frits van Amersfoort, whose team ran both Jos and Max. 'You know, the sheer eagerness and animal side of Max comes from Jos, and the social side from Sophie. It's the perfect mix. I don't think in a laboratory they could have achieved the same, what these two people did!'

There's a burning focus to maximise himself every time he is in the car which, in Max's early days of F1, would sometimes spill over into moves that were not within the code of racing etiquette. Forcing Kimi Raikkonen to brake at 200 mph on the straight at Spa to avoid what would have been an aircraft-scale accident was the most extreme example. 'He needs to see a psychiatrist,' said legendary triple world champion Niki Lauda of the incident.

'Great, we can go together,' laughed Max when he was told

of Lauda's criticism. Not aggressive or defensive. Simply not bothered what anyone outside his circle thought, because he's totally secure in his own.

The usual rules were often rendered meaningless by his mercurial talent and the shrewd way it was marshalled by Jos. New sporting regulations had to be written as a result of some of Verstappen's more exuberant moves, just as they had been a generation earlier for Michael Schumacher's. One was a new sporting regulation stipulating a minimum age for an F1 driver of 18, imposed after Max had made his debut as the youngest ever at 17 years and 166 days. He was a veteran of 14 grands prix before he was even allowed to drive on the roads in Europe.

Max has no time for the way F1 has transformed itself in the social media age, for he is old-school despite being a digital native. He can do things with a car others can only dream of, he can race wheel-to-wheel in a way which makes him almost impossible to beat on equal terms. But he is defined within the terms of the sport, and is not the sort of character who will transcend it in the way Lewis Hamilton has or Ayrton Senna did. He's too straightforward for that, too uninterested in the world outside of racing. Because it's a world in which he's never lived. But within the bubble in which he has spent his entire existence, very few in history have ever flown so high.

1

MONACO

More than any other track, it was Monaco that showcased the off-the-scale potential of the boyish novice . . .

Winning the world championship in 2022 was far less stressful and controversial than it had been the year before. The final race, at the same Abu Dhabi venue, was a cruise and Max's 15th victory of the season, the title already having been clinched four races earlier. It was also a new record, Max having clocked up more race wins in one dominant campaign than former greats Jack Brabham, Graham Hill or Emerson Fittipaldi had in their entire long careers. From the Middle East, it was a flight home on the Dassault Falcon 900EX – the private jet he purchased from Richard Branson in 2020 – to Nice and then just a short helicopter hop along the coast to Monaco, his home since the day after his 18th birthday in September 2015.

I'd interviewed Jos earlier that year, when Max had not yet flown the nest despite now being an F1 driver. He still saw no reason why Max should leave their home in Maaseik,

Belgium. 'He gets all his laundry and stuff done here,' tough old Jos pleaded, as if that might have made Max rethink. Their journey from Max's childhood to F1 was complete, and 17-year-old Max was itching to spend some of his multi-million euro paycheque on a place of his own, where he could work out, rest and play in relative anonymity.

From the age of 11, Max had lived just with his dad, visiting his mum and sister between races, often getting out of school early to climb in the van and drive across Europe with Jos to the next race, and the next chance for Max to just do what he loved doing. That's how Max sees it today, at any rate.

'Whether Max liked it every day, I don't know. I doubt it. History is always a bit different from reality,' says Kees van der Grint. 'Now that they have had so much success, they can laugh about how they travelled for miles and miles where Max had to sit in the van. I'm not sure that every night Max was happy. But they deserve all the success they have because of this time. I don't think there was any pushing from Jos to do it but it was clear from Jos if we do it, we do it right.'

'I have always put everything aside for Max's career,' said Jos soon after Max had left home. 'Max was busy with his career and when he was in Formula 1, he departed to Monaco. And then you lose something and I do find that difficult.'

It had been an amazing adventure, from the karting kid to the hottest of F1 properties, his talent and Jos' expertise making for an unstoppable force. But now he was ready to lead his own life, even if professionally he'd remain totally under the guidance and direction of his father and Jos' commercial guy Raymond Vermeulen (who had found the Monaco apartment he was about to move into).

It was in the two-week gap between the Japanese and Russian Grands Prix that Max turned 18. Jos bought him a jet-ski as a leaving home present, while Sophie helped him shop for furniture. She had that maternal feeling that this was it: she was losing him to superstardom and this was the last normal thing they would do together as mum and son. A son already with 14 grands prix under his belt, such was his record-breaking youth as an F1 debutant. At Suzuka, he was still technically a child living with his dad, for all that his race in the Toro Rosso included trying for a 200 mph pass on Daniil Kvyat's Red Bull around the outside of Suzuka's legendary 130R corner, casually applying a little opposite lock as his right-rear tyre nibbled at the rubber marbles offline. Two weeks later at Sochi he was legally a man with his own Monaco pad.

That Monaco hosts the world's most prestigious grand prix around its sun-baked streets is almost incidental. For many F1 stars amassing a high income over a relatively short time, it is the low tax burden of the principality that makes it the obvious place to reside. Still, Monaco does have a particular resonance with Verstappen's career. In his first race there, in the 2015 Toro Rosso, he'd been quick but had crashed out dramatically, flying over the top of Romain Grosjean's Lotus.

There was Monaco 2016, the very next race after his victorious debut for the senior Red Bull team, when he glanced the wall exiting the swimming pool section in the first qualifying session, breaking a track rod and leaving him with no way of steering around the immediately following corner, the resultant crash obliging him to start the race from the back of the grid in a rebuilt car. There was the near-identical accident there in Saturday practice two years later which prevented him from taking part in qualifying at all. In both cases, he'd been among the fastest and looking a likely pole contender – and therefore a potential victor, such is the near-impossibility of passing around the streets. Two potential prestigious wins thrown away on a heartbreaker of a track.

Thursday practice of 2015 was his first ever experience of the track, a notoriously exacting and punishing place in which to attempt to thread a 1,000-horsepower monster through the narrow, wall-lined streets. In a Toro Rosso that was by no means a top car, the 17-year-old rookie was a sensational second fastest, just two-tenths behind Lewis Hamilton's Mercedes. When assessing the potential of new drivers, the peaks tell you far more than the averages. They tell of the calibre of performance that will be regularly unleashed when the driver has enough experience to unlock it rather than stumbling into it by some combination of instinct and raw skill. Thursday first practice 2015 was an important marker of greatness to come. In only his second season of car racing (as opposed to karting), he was second-fastest in an F1 practice session in a mediocre car around one of the biggest tests of driver skill on the calendar.

The 2018 incident was equally significant. Three years on from that startling rookie appearance around these streets, he came to Monaco having had some sort of incident in all five of the season's preceding races. It was as if, finding the Red Bull still to be significantly adrift of Mercedes in his third season there, he was trying to do the impossible by compensating with his driving, trying to make up the shortfall with a crazy high-wire performance that could never be sustained. Jos had privately advised him: he needed to back away from the edge a little, that it was too much. Others asking Max about it received short shrift. 'I won't be changing my approach,' he'd said coming into the weekend. 'I will never do that, because it has brought me to where I am right now.'

It had become something of a mantra as he went from one incident to the next. He'd been vying with teammate Daniel Ricciardo to be fastest when he'd crashed heavily on the Saturday morning at the swimming pool exit in that re-run of his 2016 incident at the same corner. Climbing out of the wreck, he glanced at one of the big live screens placed around the track to see Jos angrily banging his fist on the table. As Max returned to the Red Bull garage, perhaps expecting the usual 'don't worry about it' from the team, he instead found Helmut Marko turning away from him, unable to hide his frustration. Team principal Christian Horner told the TV cameras that Verstappen had to figure out a way of changing his approach, because this one just wasn't working. He'd later find Max slumped in his room in the team's base on the harbour and would try simultaneously to console him and suggest that change. The team worked crazy-fast to get the car repaired in time for qualifying two hours later but just as the final preparations were being made and with the session about to get underway, a crack was discovered in the gearbox. He'd be taking no part and his Monaco weekend – at one of just two or three tracks where the car would be genuinely fast all season, and where Ricciardo would go on to win from pole – was consigned to the dustbin.

Thereafter, despite protestations that he hadn't changed his approach, he did just that. He came close to finally confirming it when I interviewed him in 2019. 'I think it's little margins which can go really wrong or really well. But you always learn from your mistakes, and I definitely did – but to say that I completely changed the approach was not true. It was just fine-tuning a few things that makes the end result of the whole weekend a lot better. Just learning, adapting, trying to get better. I don't think I tried to drive harder or faster. Maybe just taking it a bit back and that's made me go a bit faster. I was maybe trying too hard . . . It's about picking your moments when to push and when not to.

'Also, you have to remember, because my progress to F1 was so fast, with only a year in F3 between karts and F1, I guess some of the mistakes I made in F1, others made in lower categories where there's not much media around. For me, I prefer to make them in F1 than staying in lower categories.

'My dad always told me: "Even when you think you are not going fast enough you are still by far quick enough." I felt that by driving a little slower I became better after those six races. Every single race I learn.'

It was the final piece of the jigsaw. After that humiliating experience, he became the great driver he had promised to be in that rookie practice session in 2015. Whatever he changed after Monaco 2018 gave him access to his ridiculous, improbable talent pretty much on demand. All he was waiting for now was the car.

He had a strong race to second at Monaco the following year, hassling the older-tyred Hamilton in the closing laps, the pair even making contact at the chicane for the final time. But it wasn't until the next race there in 2021 (the 2020 event was cancelled due to Covid) that he finally became a winner around his 'home' track, with a dominant performance. Aside from the prestige, it was a significant career benchmark: the result put him in the lead of the world championship for the first time in his career, his first taste of being the chased and not the chaser.

•

Fast forward to 2022 and Monaco was one of the few races that season which Verstappen, now the reigning world champion, failed to win – and the circumstances of that failure infuriated 'Team Verstappen' and imposed strains on the relationship with Red Bull. All triggered by teammate Sergio Perez's accident in the final seconds of qualifying.

The backdrop to that was how Perez had been much more competitive with Verstappen in the season up to that point than had been the case in their first season together at Red Bull the year before, when Perez had qualified an average of almost half-a-second slower and garnered less than half of Max's tally of championship points. He'd been taken on as a support driver, a role he'd performed satisfactorily in 2021, there to save the day when Verstappen had suffered a problem, such as in Baku when Max's tyre explosion while leading put him in the wall. But this guy, who'd been in F1 for over a decade but never before with a competitive car, clearly had aspirations to be more than a support act.

In 2022, with a car to which Perez was much more attuned and which Verstappen felt was limiting the full expression of his own skills, the Mexican was occasionally able to offer some real internal competition. In Jeddah for the second race of the season, he had set a stunning pole position and was only taken out of victory contention by the unfortunate timing of a safety car, something which paved the way for Verstappen's win there after a late battle with Charles Leclerc's Ferrari.

Tensions had been mounting within the team the week before the Monaco showdown thanks to a team instruction to Perez in the Spanish Grand Prix to allow Verstappen past after he had recovered from a trip through the gravel trap. Giving up his own hopes of victory, Perez had radioed magnanimously, 'I think it's very unfair, but okay.'

At Monaco, Perez was quick, as he invariably is around street tracks; quicker, run for run, in qualifying than Verstappen, albeit behind the Ferraris which were better-suited to the demands of the track. The problem for the Red Bulls in qualifying was in generating the required front-tyre temperatures by the start of the lap, something the Ferraris could do with ease. Verstappen and Perez were each trying to find ways around that, with an extra preparation lap before the attack lap or even two extra preparation laps. You need to know about this nitty-gritty to appreciate what happened between the Red Bull drivers here as they fought for their all-important Monaco grid positions.

In the more time-restricted final session, Perez had decided to do a multiple-lap first run, with two attack laps interspersed by a cooling-off lap. That would leave him very little time for his new-tyred second run, obliging him to do the final single attack lap without the extra preparation lap, meaning his front tyres would almost certainly be too cold. So he was heavily reliant on doing a good time on that multiple-lap first run.

Verstappen by contrast had opted for the conventional, equally spaced two runs, two separate single attack laps giving him the time to do the extra prep lap on the new tyres on each occasion. In theory, that would allow him to take fuller advantage of the way the track tends to be grippier at the end of the session, as more rubber has been laid down.

Perez's first run gave him a marginally faster time than Verstappen. But into the final runs Verstappen, with his extra prep lap, had already beaten Perez's first sector time from the first runs and looked on-course to leapfrog ahead. Unsurprisingly, given his under-temperature tyres, Perez's second run was not shaping up well and he was not set to improve. That became a certainty as he piled his car into the wall at Portier corner and was then collected by Carlos Sainz's Ferrari. The red flags for that incident ended qualifying and ensured that Verstappen didn't get to complete the lap which had been looking likely to eclipse Perez's earlier time – and maybe even that of Sainz. All of which put Perez third on the grid, Verstappen fourth.

Verstappen smelt a rat. It wasn't unheard of at Monaco for a driver to crash under suspicious circumstances after setting a good time on the first outing, thereby preventing rivals from taking advantage of a less-good final run. Michael Schumacher had been thrown to the back of the grid in 2006 for just such an offence. In 2014, Nico Rosberg had brought out the yellow flags on the final runs, preventing teammate and title rival Lewis Hamilton from improving. Without definitive proof, the stewards were forced to accept Rosberg's explanation that it has been a simple misjudgement. Unlike with Rosberg, Perez wasn't even called to the stewards to explain. But what the team – and Verstappen – saw on his telemetry and in-car footage left them in little doubt. They believed Perez had deliberately crashed, with an untypical full throttle application very early in the corner and little apparent attempt to control the resultant power slide.

Perez dismissed it without much conviction and would quickly move the conversation on. For an F1 driver to have stood so hard on the gas at the wrong point of the track, and to have not made any significant steering correction until so late, is unfeasible if it was not deliberate. 'It's just part of the sport and the speculation people like to make,' he said. 'To me, this happened so many races ago that it's totally irrelevant.'

•

Two things about Max Verstappen: his competitive zeal is extraordinarily intense, even by the standards of an F1 driver, and he tends to be binary in his assessment of situations – black or white, not grey. These are traits shared with his father. Someone who saw both in action at close quarters was Kees van der Grint. 'Once when Jos won one of the European kart championships and he had only to finish third or fourth in the final to take the title, Mike Hezemans was leading but Jos just drove over him. Literally over the top of him. He landed in a good place and won. After I congratulated Jos I asked him why, when it could have gone wrong. He said: "I don't care about the championship." He just wanted to be first. That's part of the Verstappen DNA and it's very hard to fight that. It's the same with Max. He has the judgement and maybe is not so rash on the track but inside he respects absolutely no one as a rival. He knows how good he is and if someone is in the way they do not get the benefit of doubt.'

It's one thing for that intensity to be triggered by a rival but when it was from within his own team – and from a driver he considers a support, not truly a rival – Max's indignation was immediately apparent and he didn't care to hide it. 'It is irritating,' he said in the paddock afterwards, 'and a pity of course that the one who put it in the wall was my teammate. But in the end, you don't get a penalty for that. So, if you know you have a good first run, then you can think: ah well, you know what, I'll park it and tactically send it into the wall. You could do that.'

He always talks straight like this when he feels strongly about something. There's no PR filter. And he clearly felt very strongly about this. He felt even more strongly about it the following day when Perez's better starting position won him the race. In Red Bull's race with the Ferrari drivers, Perez, as the team's leading man, was pitted from wet tyres to intermediates at a time to maximise his chances of overhauling early leader Charles Leclerc (and subsequently Sainz too). The timing of Verstappen's stop, as the car behind and thus not within as close a striking range of the Ferraris, was dictated by Perez's stops. Thus compromised, he came in third. Perez – who had just signed a two-year extension to his contract – partied hard with the team to celebrate his victory. The Verstappens, however, were not in a party mood.

Jos took to Max's website the following day to articulate his displeasure: 'To be honest I wasn't left with a good feeling about the race weekend in Monaco. And that's putting it mildly . . . As a father, I was also disappointed with the race. Max's third place was very disappointing. We all saw that it was a difficult weekend for him. It starts with the car, which simply doesn't have the characteristics for his driving style yet. Max has far too little grip at the front axle. And especially in Monaco, with all those short corners, you need a car that turns very quickly. That was just hard.

'Red Bull achieved a good result, but at the same time exerted little influence to help Max to the front. That he finished third, he owes to Ferrari's mistake at that second stop of Charles Leclerc. The championship leader, Max, was not helped in that sense by the chosen strategy. It turned completely to [Perez's] favour. That was disappointing to me, and I would have liked it to be different for the championship leader.

'Pérez actually won the race because of the earlier pit stop. The team can perhaps explain that as a gamble, but they had already seen, with for example Gasly, that the intermediates were the best option at that time.

'I would have liked them to go for Max, but of course I am not entirely objective. I think 10 points from Max have been thrown away here. Especially with the two retirements we've had, we need every point. Don't forget that Ferrari currently has a better car, especially in qualifying.'

Unlike Max, Jos had stopped short of mentioning Perez's qualifying but to be so publicly critical of the team on Max's own website was no small thing. It may have been partly the father's famed knee-jerk emotions but it was also Jos acting to pull Red Bull up short and with the implicit power to do so because of Max's phenomenal ability. Red Bull's Helmut Marko didn't waste any time in responding.

'I called him right away,' he told *De Limburger*. 'I said, "What is this, Jos?" Everyone can have their own opinion, including Jos, but he shouldn't publish it on his son's website. He said, "Yes, but I am the father", which is fine but don't do it in that way.

'Jos is great and that's why Max has come this far. When Max came to Formula 1, at the beginning it was sometimes not easy with Jos. He had an opinion about everything and still does, by the way. His comments create resentment within the team and give journalists something to write about. Anyway, Jos is Jos. He can sometimes get angry quickly and none of that is going to change.'

In other words, there was little Marko could do beyond expressing his displeasure. This was the same struggle for power and control that had existed between Red Bull and Team Verstappen right from the start and which clearly the winning of the 2021 world championship and the multi-year mega-contract that followed had not dissolved.

The events of Monaco 2022 are quite illuminating in this regard. They tell us about the complex, delicate relationship between Red Bull and Max and how even though they rely on each other totally for their combined success, in some respects it's still not a full marriage. They have been partners for many years and enjoyed good times. But there's still a distance – and it's put in place by the Verstappens. It's about control.

Red Bull has its famed junior driver programme, sponsoring young drivers throughout karting and in the junior car categories, looking for the next champion. Helmut Marko – an F1 driver of great promise in the early 1970s – oversees that search as part of his role. Part of that ladder of opportunity is the fact that Red Bull has a junior F1 team (then named Toro Rosso, now AlphaTauri) to bridge the gap between the junior categories and the top team, where drivers can either establish their credentials as a future world champion or be cast aside.

But through karting and F3, Verstappen was never a Red Bull junior driver despite his obviously immense potential. Jos had kept him independent absolutely for as long as necessary – by design, to keep his options open as long as possible. Only when Red Bull offered Max, who had completed only one season in car racing (in 2014 F3), a cast-iron F1 drive for 2015 with Toro Rosso did he enter the squad.

'There was a tug of love with Mercedes to get him and part of that was this competition between the two Austrian old boys,' explains Red Bull team boss Christian Horner in reference to Helmut Marko and Niki Lauda, the latter filling a Marko-like roving brief at Mercedes. The two had competed with each other since the late 1960s, to see which of them got to F1 first (it was the same race), which of them made it big first (it was looking like Marko until his accident), which of them might get a Ferrari drive (Marko had a Ferrari contract offer in his briefcase the weekend of his accident, but the drive eventually went to Lauda who won two world championships there). They became good friends but the rivalry remained. Two old warriors of the track, both disfigured by accidents in what was a lethally dangerous era of F1, would continue to score points off each other. Marko would frequently remind Lauda that he owed his career to Marko's accident, that he took all the drives Marko had been forced to vacate. Lauda would tell him he'd never have made it anyway. So it was as they vied to land F1's obvious next superstar for their respective teams.

'So [the Verstappens] were going backwards and forwards between us and them and I remember having dinner in Heidelberg at Hockenheim with Helmut and he said, "The only thing that we have for Max that Mercedes don't is a seat in Formula One." And that we should offer him a seat next year in Toro Rosso.

'Initially I thought that was a massive step, you know? Then you think, he has done it in Formula 3. So we thought, why not? The kid looks an outstanding talent, if he is good enough, he'll adapt. Mercedes were trying to position him in a GP2 team and they couldn't offer him a Formula One seat straightaway. And so that was our trump card. I think Helmut took delight not only in signing him because of the talent he was but also because it was a big middle finger to Niki!'

The importance Jos had placed on keeping Max's options open until this point was fuelled by perhaps the single most important factor in Jos' own F1 career not working out in the 1990s – he surrendered control to someone else (Benetton boss Flavio Briatore) and was put in a subservient role (to Michael Schumacher). This probably did immeasurable harm to Jos' psyche. He had been every bit as big a sensation in karts and junior car racing as Max would subsequently be. He was seen as the next big thing. Straight out of F3, Jos had been the number one in everything he'd done up to his arrival in F1, but here suddenly he was relegated into a support role and – even worse – a support role without even the same tools at his disposal as the number one. Perception is everything and his F1 career was defined as less than it might have been from that moment. Control was therefore always a massive part of Jos' strategy with Max's career.

So even as Red Bull gave Max the F1 ride straightaway, they were new to each other. The Verstappens had chosen Red Bull rather than Mercedes only because of what Red Bull was offering. Jos had leveraged Mercedes' interest brilliantly to get the 2015 F1 drive with Toro Rosso, allowing Raymond Vermeulen to negotiate a tough deal. Not in monetary terms, but in terms of control, something which Red Bull junior drivers notoriously did not have. Daniel Ricciardo, under Red Bull's wing since 2006 and making his F1 debut in 2011, had only become contractually free at the end of 2018. Any time in between he could have been dropped if his performances were deemed not up to scratch, as had happened to many before: Christian Klien, Jaime Alguersuari, Jean-Eric Vergne and others.

Max's Red Bull contract was nothing like that. It was almost as if Jos and Raymond were doing Red Bull a favour by lending Max to them – hence the immediate F1 race seat (plus a few Friday practice sessions in the remaining 2014 races) and the options open after that to defect if he were not promoted to the senior team by an agreed date.

'There was a junction within Max's agreement,' confirms Horner. 'By switching him with Daniil Kvyat we extended Max's agreement with us. We could do that because the two teams were under common ownership.'

It was brilliantly negotiated and tightly controlled by Jos and Raymond. They parlayed Max's talent and obviously enormous potential with incredible nerve and to clinical effect. This was a match of mutual interests, not some happy ending sealed with holy vows. The Verstappens were not necessarily going to be staying at Red Bull long term.

That cool headedness remained even as the partnership flourished: even after Red Bull promoted Max out of Toro Rosso to the senior team in 2016, just five races into his sophomore season (thereby contractually closing off the possibility of losing him at the end of 2017); even after he sensationally won his very first race with the senior team in Spain in fairy-tale fashion, the youngest ever grand prix winner at 18. Even after all that, he was still a gunslinger for hire and the Verstappens were not signing up to anyone's legion but their own.

That inevitably created a certain tension in the relationship, which rumbled on as Mercedes continued to dominate the sport and Lewis Hamilton rewrote the record books. For the next five seasons, Max Verstappen raced a car which was in no way comparable to the Mercedes, good enough only to snatch the odd victory when something had gone wrong at the silver team. For Max, quite possibly the fastest driver on the grid – and increasingly recognised as such – it was an exercise in controlling his mounting frustration, so that it didn't come through in his personal performances. In the power dynamic with the team, the Verstappens continued to have the upper hand, but what use was that when the team couldn't give him a title-calibre car?

•

A clause negotiated by the Verstappens for 2019 meant that if certain performance targets were not met by the team by a certain cut-off date, Max could be contractually free for 2020. There were rumours of renewed interest from Mercedes, of him being paired there with Lewis Hamilton to form a super-team, which would have been a devastating blow to Red Bull. Nothing came of it, not least because the performance clauses were met. But Team Verstappen were publicly quite open about looking around to see where Max's long-term future might best be served. The Mercedes rumours were at their height around the time of the 2019 British Grand Prix. I had been pestering Red Bull for an interview with Max and had received a firm 'no', the PR department surely concerned I'd be asking about him and Mercedes. But it was in Team Verstappen's interests to have their views out there and so they made the interview happen anyway. The windows of Max's Red Bull motorhome looked out over not just its own trucks at the back of the garages but also those of the adjacent Mercedes team. The big three-pointed star formed the perfect backdrop for the picture the photographer had in mind as Max sat down with his back to the window. Could he just angle his seat a little, the photographer asked. Max glanced over his shoulder to see what would be in the background, smiled and said, 'Sure'. Just games, but it did signify something of the dynamic between team and driver. Then, finally, a competitive car arrived in 2021, Max's sixth season at Red Bull. And with it came the first title, after that epic, season-long controversial battle with Hamilton and Mercedes. This finally seemed to convince the Verstappens that Red Bull was home, not just a temporary stop along the way, and at the beginning of 2022 a seven-year mega deal (actually a two-year extension to his previous deal but on totally new terms, starting immediately) was announced.

'Max was on the radio in Abu Dhabi [2021] saying can we do this for many, many years,' relates Raymond Vermeulen in the *Lion Unleashed* documentary on Max's career. 'That was the reason for Dr Marko calling me again and from "let's sit and have a coffee to see how we can work this out", we worked for a few weeks and the deal was done. It was a very natural conversation and negotiation, we made a deal, and this is a long-term deal so I think that is something that was important for Red Bull to have Max on board for their long-term future because they are investing heavily in their powertrains and other things. We felt very comfortable with signing up with Red Bull for the long term, so the deal was done pretty easily.'

Vermeulen, a real estate investor before he took over the commercial management of Verstappen Senior's career, has Jos' total trust. He became busy all over again – this time much more lucratively – when Max began racing seriously. Affable but a tough and shrewd negotiator, he has been instrumental in maximising the Verstappens' earnings.

The new deal unambiguously aligned Red Bull and Verstappen for the long-term whereas previously there were always feasible loophole clauses, notably for non-factory engines.

This is a typical contractual get-out clause for a driver. If he originally signed with a factory team – a team with an engine partnership with an automotive manufacturer as its engine supplier – and the team subsequently loses that status and becomes a customer team (which has to buy its engines), then very often the driver can be released before the contract has run its course. This had always been a sensitive point for Red Bull, especially given its often-acrimonious relationship with its previous partner Renault, which ended in 2018 after 12 years. Renault was replaced by Honda and although that relationship was infinitely better, at board level the Japanese manufacturer was not committed to F1 long term.

Mercedes and Ferrari – the only other teams of comparable calibre – didn't have this problem, as they made their own engines. It was time Red Bull did the same. So, at the end of 2020, Dietrich Mateschitz, the soft drinks billionaire from Austria who had founded the team, gave the investment green light for the creation of Red Bull Powertrains. Honda would remain involved at least for a time, but the team was no longer reliant upon them, no longer subject to the whim of a big corporation on the other side of the world.

In terms of Max's contractual situation, the closing off of that engine loophole combined with the fact that Mercedes and Ferrari had seemingly already instigated their own long-term succession plans with George Russell and Charles Leclerc respectively, surely brought Team Verstappen and Team Red Bull more permanently together.

There was speculation that the financial terms may even have bettered those enjoyed by Lewis Hamilton at Mercedes at somewhere between £40–50 million per year. 'I don't know if that's true,' answered Helmut Marko to the question, 'because I don't know Hamilton's contract. But it seems normal to me that Max will earn more as world champion. I am proud of what Max has achieved. It confirms that it was the right choice at the time to bring him to Formula 1. And it has also silenced all the scepticism that existed in the beginning.'

But Marko did admit to being relieved. 'A little, yes. In the long run, when we couldn't give him a championship car, I was afraid he might go somewhere else.'

Verstappen is central to Red Bull: it all revolves around him at an operational and support level, he's very happy in that role and that brings its own spiralling benefits. Before this deal, there was always the possibility that his Red Bull success would be the equivalent of Schumacher's at Benetton or Hamilton's at McLaren – impressive but less than the entirely different level the driver was capable of if everything was in full alignment, as each showed with their blockbusting era-defining runs at Ferrari and Mercedes respectively.

But even now that Max and Red Bull were contractually aligned for the foreseeable, it still wasn't the Ferrari/Schumacher love-in where the joins were almost invisible and not a raised eyebrow of public criticism ever crossed Schumacher's face. It wasn't even the slightly less serene but still very close relationship of Mercedes and Hamilton.

The fall-out from Monaco 2022 demonstrated that Red Bull could not take Max's commitment to the mutual cause for granted, mega-contract or no mega-contract. The balance of power had permanently changed over the years and there would be more evidence of that through the season. Post-Monaco, behind the scenes, the Verstappens demanded changes, and quick. Two races later, Max had a further developed car, tailored to fully exploit his freakish abilities – and which Perez found much more difficult, putting him firmly back in the support role. Thus, the foundation for Max's subsequent domination of the 2022 season was put in place in the aftermath of that Monaco weekend. Maybe it would have happened even without Jos throwing Max's weight about. But Jos isn't one not to take matters into his own hands and Team Verstappen's tolerance for anything other than full commitment to Max is now zero.

'When I think it's shit, it's shit,' said Max in typical Verstappen style to the *Guardian* in July 2021. 'When it's good it's good. That's how I interact with the team. That's what I say to the team: "You can say the same to me. When I am a dickhead you can tell me." When I fuck up, I fuck up. When I do good, I do good.

'I cannot always be super-polite and nice; that's not how I work. You need to be hard on each other, especially in tougher times or when you are not happy with certain things. It works both ways. They tell me, I tell them. You should be able to be criticised and take criticism.'

Team boss Christian Horner is a skilled operator and understands the delicate dynamic well. His first experience of walking that line came in Red Bull's first era of title success with Sebastian Vettel who didn't always react well to any challenge from teammate Mark Webber. The Australian, in turn, was capable of blowing up any internal conflict into a very public matter when he felt his own chances were being compromised. Yet Red Bull and Vettel still won four consecutive titles with Webber alongside. The Verstappens provide Horner with different challenges and the relationship is perhaps tougher, less emotionally close. But Horner harnesses their relentless energy incredibly well within the team to drive overall performance to an increasingly dominant level.

'He can be very sharp and cutting,' says Horner, 'when emotions are running high and a lot of engineers would wilt under that strain. He is demanding. The fuse is a little shorter than it was with Seb.' Of Jos, he says merely that while he is a 'passionate dad as a lot of the dads are. He no longer gets overly involved as he was wont to do in the early days at Toro Rosso. He has been as good as gold with us.'

It just works, he says. 'Max feels very comfortable in the environment. There is a belief and a passion and a shared philosophy of how we go racing and I think he enjoys that. He is very loyal and protective of the team.'

The closest Max had to a personal bond within Red Bull was probably with Dietrich Mateschitz. The 78-year-old team founder passed away in October 2022 after a battle with cancer but lived long enough to see Verstappen clinch his second title in Japan. He died on the weekend of the following race, in Austin, where Verstappen said: 'I find it really incredible what he has done. Luckily, I got to spend a little bit of time with him a few weeks back, which is now of course even more special. I really enjoyed that . . . The last time I saw him, the things we discussed, that made the day very special even then. And now that final encounter has gained even more depth. The news of his death is very difficult to take. I will remember him as a man of gentle character who took care of people with extreme love. He didn't seek the limelight. I got to know him as a racer at heart with an enormous passion for the sport. I mean, who else in the history of Formula 1 has ever started two teams?'

Mateschitz wasn't involved in the nitty-gritty of running those teams, typically appearing at no more than a couple of races per season. But his projection of freewheeling, high-risk adventure to market the Red Bull soft drink is part of the team's brand DNA. Red Bull, much more than any corporate automotive team, can wear a little bit of controversy quite comfortably. The Verstappens fit into this ethos well – it's even possible that Max derives some performance from it. This boy was always going to go racing if he wanted to and had the talent. It's led to a certain free-spiritedness in his approach, answering only to himself.

Perhaps more than any driver on the grid, maybe even more than Fernando Alonso, Verstappen is racing on his own terms. Red Bull's only intolerance – and it's a severe one – is lack of performance, which is not something Max has ever had to worry about. He oozes performance, it's locked into his own DNA, allowing him to be supremely relaxed in doing what he does – which only adds to the performance.

More than any other track, it was Monaco that showcased the off-the-scale potential of the boyish novice in 2015; the over-the-top attack mode of the early days at Red Bull in 2016; the crucial error in 2018 which triggered the re-set; the truly great driver that resulted to gain his first Monaco win in 2021; and finally, in 2022, the team turmoil that led the Verstappens to lay down their terms of total dominance within the Red Bull team.

As Max jogs around the streets of what is now home, he could doubtless reflect on each of those step-change moments. If he were the reflective type.

2

FATHER AND SON

'As a driver, Jos was as good as Max in my opinion . . .'
Kees van der Grint

Two weeks after flying home from the Abu Dhabi 2022 finale, Verstappen was in Bologna for the official FIA Awards, the ceremony at which the world champions from every category of motorsport are officially crowned. The F1 prize is obviously the most prestigious of all and here was Verstappen taking it for the second successive year. 'Your whole life you aim for the goal of being a world champion,' he said in his address to the 1000 guests gathered in the Fiera di Bologna exhibition centre, 'but this year we were more competitive and we won the drivers' and the constructors', so I would say this one is better than last year and more rewarding, but the first one is always more emotional.'

The previous year, although Verstappen had won the drivers' title, Red Bull had failed to prevent Mercedes from taking its eighth consecutive constructors' championship. This time the domination was overwhelming, suggesting a partnership in the ascendancy. In the much closer battle of 2021, the controversial Abu Dhabi showdown with Lewis Hamilton had left the latter so disillusioned that he had declined to show for the 2021 FIA prize-giving gala which, as runner-up in the championship, he was technically obliged to do. Hamilton harboured no ill-feeling towards Verstappen but felt that he had been robbed of the title due to a mis-application of the sporting regulations by the then F1 race director, Michael Masi. If the biggest prize in the sport could be decided in such a way, he reasoned, then why should he respect the regulation which demanded he attend the gala?

'I can understand how he felt,' said Verstappen of Abu Dhabi 2021. 'Everything was looking great for him, and then something like this happens. It's tough. The only thing I said to myself at the time was, he's won seven titles and won one of them when it looked like he was going to lose – and then the situation turned around again on the last lap. So I hoped he would understand.'

This was a typically defusing response from Max, very different from how his dad might have handled things. 'Jos is "bang", straight down the middle,' says Helmut Marko, 'not thinking, all instinct. Max is more thoughtful. His character and education are different to Jos'. His character is like his mother's.'

That Max is every bit as tough as Jos, however, is beyond question, and his aggression can flare, Jos-like, when pro-voked, both in the car and out. He has better control of his temper than his dad ever did, though. He can usually decouple the instinct from the action. But then that's not so surprising given their contrast in upbringing.

That tough, aggressive streak is what enabled Jos to propel himself from life in the scrapyard to the pristine garages of F1. It was an unlikely journey: even back in the 1980s when Jos began karting, motorsport was the preserve of the wealthy. It was not a world people from a modest background could realistically aspire to. But at its entry level, local karting, someone with an aptitude for mechanics and a tenacious spirit could find their way in, even if their prospects of progressing to something glitzier would be limited.

With his flamboyant skill at the wheel and a ferocious competitive zeal, however, Jos was soon driving for professional teams. With a bit of help from a key mentor and benefactor, he won the Dutch Junior championship of 1984 and in 1989 as part of the CRG factory team won the European championships in both the Formula A and ICA classes.

He then got himself a 'lucky' break, if it can be called luck when it happens to someone both prodigiously talented and doggedly determined, someone hustling like hell to get himself noticed. Jos' fellow Dutchman Huub Rothengatter, a failed 1980s F1 driver but highly successful businessman, happened to be a spectator at the world championship karting final in 1991. He also happened to have just done a deal with Philips and Marlboro, so was looking for drivers. Recalls

Allard Kalff, Dutch racer and commentator: 'Jos crashed with Fisichella. Fisichella just sat there saying, "Oh fuck I've crashed". But Jos? Jos just pulled his kart out and got himself going again. Huub spotted this. He said, "I want him." He took him to the grand prix at Estoril and said, "This is where we are going to end up if you do what I tell you." That's how they financed Jos' move into cars.'

Motor racing participation burns through money. But for the top guys the funding structure is different between karting and car racing in one crucial way: the recognised top few drivers in karting – and we're talking no more than maybe a dozen in the world – will be recruited by kart manufacturers and paid to race as factory drivers, because the better the results of that manufacturer, the more karts it will sell. Karters can graduate through all the categories of that sport supported and paid by the factory, so long as they keep winning. In the junior categories of car racing there are no factory teams. Factories such as Dallara make cars, which typically as a wannabe racer you buy and then get a specialist professional race team to run you in. But this still requires you to cover the cost of the racing plus enough profit to keep them in business.

No matter how giant your reputation in karting, this is the harsh reality of the move into car racing: from being funded, suddenly you have to pay. A lot. You need millions. It's where many a promising career has come to a shuddering halt. A few decades ago this came as such a rude shock to Ayrton Senna that he briefly retired from the sport and flew back home to Brazil complaining that budgets rather than talent decided who got the good drives. He was still only driving in Formula Ford at the time, then the lowest rung in the car racing ladder. Ordinarily, someone of Jos' background, without family millions but with a big, showy talent, might make the grade in karting but would be unlikely to progress from there. But now Jos had Huub.

With Rothengatter bringing in the money (a task in which he was later aided by Raymond Vermeulen), the combination of talent and take-no-prisoners approach which had made Jos the top kart racer of his generation paved the way for instant success in junior car racing in the early 1990s. He was 1992 Benelux GM Lotus champion (eight wins from nine races) in his first season and he followed that in 1993 with the German F3 championship (11 wins from 17) driving for Willi Weber's team, the launch pad for his graduation to F1. Without Rothengatter there would have been no F1 career for Jos. Without that, the world would arguably never have heard of Max Verstappen.

Rothengatter's story is therefore foundational to that of Max. Rothengatter's Formula Ford mechanic was a young guy called Frits van Amersfoort who recalls: 'I'm from a garage family. Zandvoort was our local track and when it hosted the Dutch Grand Prix in the sixties, the whole workshop, mechanics, everyone went each year, paid for by the company. In 1966 I was old enough, at 12, to come along on the practice day as the prices weren't so high on the Saturday. That was my first ever sight of a real F1 car. I saw John Surtees, Bruce McLaren, loads of other things. I was grabbed by the smell and the noise and being from a technical background already, I was infected by the bug and have been ever since.

'By coincidence Huub lived about five streets behind us. He was karting but we didn't know him. We met after he bought a Formula Ford Royale in the seventies and wanted it sprayed. I thought. "Ooh, a real race driver." That's how it started. Back then in Formula Ford you had a driver and a mechanic, that was it. Just like a go kart team of the time. And I became his mechanic.

'He was already a special character, very single-minded and opinionated. One year later he bought a March F3 car, a 763. We still have the car. I helped him with that a couple of times but I also had to finish school. Then Huub graduated from privateer into Racing Team Holland in F3, with Jan Lammers and Arie Luyendyk. So I had to let it go.

'But Huub was always there. He's a friend, a special friend. It all started through him that I formed my own team and ran other drivers. After Huub's F1 career went down the drain because he realised he had the talent to find the money but not the talent to be fast enough, he met Jos who was already a name in karting. And he looked for a team for him. In those days, we were doing Formula Renault. We tested Jos one day in that car but he didn't particularly like it. They wanted to do Opel Lotus. So we switched and in '92 ran him there. He was the rising star. Huub was his manager. That management went on over the years until Jos' F1 career had fizzled out.'

Just as that career was fizzling out, Max's karting was getting underway with Jos' supervision. Rothengatter saw first-hand the potential of the kid as he progressed all the way to the 2013 world karting title. There was nowhere to go from there but cars, which rendered Jos' karting expertise some-what redundant – and left a big hole where a budget had to be inserted. Regardless of karting superstardom, Max needed cash, and lots of it. This is where Rothengatter came back into the picture. He paid the £200,000 required to buy an F3 car from Dallara so that Van Amersfoort's team could run Max.

Something has gone badly wrong with the relationship between Jos and Rothengatter since then. They no longer speak and it dates back to that time. Rothengatter won't talk about it, only that this phase of his life he considers to be in the past.

Recalls Van Amersfoort, 'There were three grown-up guys [along with Vermuelen], already earning quite a fortune in their lives in motorsport, they were arguing, fighting about the percentage of the income of Max in the future. And that's something, for my feeling, that was wrong.

'[Jos and Huub] are too much alike. I still figure if those two would have had more human sense, it wouldn't have gone that way. But Huub was stubborn, Jos was stubborn, and Raymond was in the middle.'

•

Jos grew up in a mobile home. Grandad had a scrapyard, dad Frans a café, both in Montfort, Holland near the Belgian border, about a hundred miles from Amsterdam. Jos' childhood was spent shuttling between the two places. When Frans and Jos' mother split up, Jos stayed with his father, foreshadowing what would happen a generation later with Jos, Sophie and Max. Frans Verstappen was a totally uncompromising character himself: he would lock Jos inside as punishment for whatever new shenanigans he'd been up to. This tempestuous relationship would often descend into physical fighting – right up to 2016 when, as reported in *De Telegraaf*, Frans had to be treated in hospital after another bust-up with his son.

It's easy to picture the disenchanted young teen fleeing to Grandpa's scrapyard after the latest bust-up with Dad. There, he would ride motorbikes, work on their engines, bring scrap cars to life and drive them around under-age. You get the picture. Let's just say, there wasn't much in the way of social niceties.

Yet later, once Jos was karting, Frans would be there helping him, acting as his mechanic, dishing out advice – though not from a position of knowledge, like Jos a generation later. Sadly, though, Jos and Frans were estranged by the time Frans died of cancer in 2019, aged 72. Nevertheless, it is clear that the foundation of Max's career really goes back two generations, not one.

'It was a very complex relationship,' says Kees van der Grint of Jos and his father. 'I liked Frans, I was in contact with him throughout. I thought it was very sad how that ended. Because he did so much for Jos. He had to work hard in his pub and his scrapyard and he was mechanic for Jos whereas Jos was able to employ a full-time mechanic for Max. Doors opened when the famous "Jos Verstappen" was running Max. No doors opened for Frans when he was running Jos, but in his heart, I think Jos must know what Frans did for him. But it was a very difficult relationship because Frans was also a bit of a wild character.'

'Our family aren't easy to deal with,' Frans Verstappen said on Dutch TV in 2018. 'But I think that's common among athletes or ambitious people. I always go to the limit and am a perfectionist. Jos is the same. Max on the other hand has a different attitude.'

'My father approached everything with the all-or-nothing attitude,' said Jos in *Whatever It Takes*, 'and that's what he taught me and how I raced. Max has the same mentality but he's smarter.'

While Jos saw the attitude as a positive in his professional life, the flipside is that it has caused his personal life to be written out in constant clashes not just with his father but with his grandfather, his mother, his wives and girlfriends

– and of course, with Huub. As Van Amersfoort points out: 'There's always something going wrong in his life. Why, I don't know. You would have to ask a psychologist, I think. I'm not going to judge that.'

Young Jos raced at Genk, Belgium, only about 30 miles from his home in Montfort. There he was taken under the wing of Paul Lemmens, who had created the track in 1980 and whose GKS team would go on to run many champions. Lemmens gave him a job in the track's workshop. This was where Jos really learned his craft; it's not difficult to imagine how it became a place of solace away from the conflicts with his father, with Lemmens taking the role of mentor.

Lemmens' all-or-nothing approach to competition, while similar to that of Frans Verstappen, came without the familial conflicts and really resonated with the teenage tearaway, and taught Jos life lessons that would later be put to good use in toughening up young Max. One of Lemmens' former drivers Robert Frijns recalled to Vroomkart.com: 'Paul really only wanted to win, he was really into go-karting and was fascinated about it. He's a very tough one though and he'd let you know if you did something wrong. It was not just about driving, then you go to the hotel and the mechanic takes care of you. It was about keeping your kart clean, having a bond with your mechanic and working for the same goal. It was a tough school, but a good one. In the morning on the way to the track Paul would stop with two or three kilometres to go and say, "You'll run to the paddock from here!" I hated it, but that was his way of teaching young guys to be where we are today. He was always very straight, sometimes scream at you so that you knew you fucked up, but if you won a race, he was always the first one standing there. Everything comes back to the basics. It's a tough world we are competing in, lots of drivers coming and going, but only a few seats available.'

Jos recalled his time with Lemmens at Genk fondly in an interview in 2021, also with Vroomkart.com. 'I still remember the first day they were building the original track in Genk, I was about nine or ten years of age, there was only the track and a lot of orange sand alongside it. Paul was in the basement there working.

'I raced for Paul when I was 13 or 14 years old, he was a very well-known engine tuner and he had a good team. He had lots of engines, also the ones he rented out to customers. The funny thing is that I had to run them in before we went to all the races, but the good thing about that was I selected my own engines, which was good for me!

'When I was 17, I worked for him in the basement rebuilding the engines. On the dyno and helping the people on the track, so I spent a lot of time with Paul. There were lots of good drivers there at the time – Guy de Nies, Jan Heylen, Sophie Kumpen . . .' Sophie Kumpen, as in, his future wife and mother of Max.

Karting was Jos' escape from the everyday and his limited prospects, from a civilian life far too tame to contain him. Lemmens quenched his constant thirst for knowledge about engines and karts, fuelling his competitive fury. It was him that taught Jos how to channel his desire into the formidable work ethic he went on to instil in Max.

It's doubtful whether any driver has immersed himself as fully in the technicalities of karting as Jos Verstappen. The deep knowledge he acquired in not only his own karting career but also as he developed his kart engine-tuning business would all be shovelled into building Max's career. Lemmens was therefore another crucial foundation of the Max Verstappen story, even if it was put in place a generation earlier.

'Paul's character is that he's very emotional and motivated,' continued Jos, 'and I think he may have seen himself in me as well a lot. We are very much the same: I work hard and I was always very motivated to win. I think I learned a lot from Paul – how to build engines and how to tune engines. I had a lot of ideas and would speak to Paul about them, and we'd spend hours on the dyno until three or four o'clock through the night. I had a very good relationship with him and I think he was the basis for me that I really like to build the engines, and it helped me a lot too with Max. There are so many things I remember, working late, running the engines in; it was work, but it was always a pleasure to work there, learning and having a lot of fun.'

Jos went on to recall one wet evening when he and a bunch of other kart racers took the rental karts on to the track and hi-jinks ensued, nudging and spins – until a furious

Lemmens turned up and the fun stopped. Sophie Kumpen was part of this tight-knit social group.

•

It's difficult to imagine Jos and Sophie ever meeting had they not both been karting, such is the contrast in their backgrounds. A couple of years younger than Jos and well-educated, she was from commercial wealth: father Robert ran a major road construction business, was chairman of the JRC Genk soccer team and had dabbled in karting as a hobby when younger. Sophie's uncle Paul – Robert's brother – competed in rallycross. Sophie was in a kart by the age of 10. By 14 she was a serious force, Belgian national champion and subsequently competing in the world championship for five years. But her career was cut short when she became pregnant with Max at the age of 22. That's when her dreams of breaking through into car racing – she was hoping to compete in DTM (German Touring Car Championship) or GT racing – were put on hold, forever as it turned out.

Van der Grint, as Bridgestone's chief karting tyre engineer, was responsible for choosing the squad of drivers who would test the company's products. He wanted only the fastest karters available. 'We only had five or six of those out of over a hundred. They were drivers who were very fast and she was one of them. I don't mean a good driver for a woman – I hate that. No, she was absolutely a top driver. She beat Jos in one of the important races. She won the Andrea Margutti Trophy in '95, beat all the big stars. Sophie is a very lovely person and is the relaxed side of Max. As an example, she'd always bring chocolates, trying to build a team around her. She made it a personal relationship, it was nice. She knew everyone and was very social – and Max also has this.'

'The Margutti Trophy was a big deal,' states Michel Vacirca, boss of the Netherlands CRG karting team. 'It was almost like a world championship. That was a huge result for Sophie.'

A fledgling Jenson Button could also see the potential in Sophie: 'Sophie was my teammate in karts in '95 in Paul Lemmens' GKS team. She was a professional kart racer, there because she was one of the best in the world.'

Christian Horner, who was trying to compete against her in his own fledgling career at the time, believes, 'She was definitely in the top 10 karters in the world at that time. I raced against her back in 1989. There was a European championship in Parma, Italy that then qualified you for the world championship in Zaragoza, Spain, and she was properly quick. And this was the time of Trulli, Fisichella, Jan Magnussen (who won it that year), Dario Franchitti. There was a really strong group of talent coming through and she was amongst it. She wasn't quite as aggressive. But she was a smart racer and I think Max has got the aggression of his dad and the racing head of his mum. She was a formidable racer in her time. You can see a blend of both of them, he has got Jos' fire and that fighting spirit but then Sophie has got a softness to her and is measured, and she is a very personable lady. So he's got a blend of both and you see both of those skills at different moments.'

The premature end of Sophie's career is made all the more poignant by the fact that as a female in a male-dominated world, it took her 'many years to prove myself', as she related to racexpress.nl in 2013. 'I came a long way by working very hard. I don't give up easily and have always come a long way on character.'

Sophie continued in karts even as Jos' career in cars took off. After being together for years, they married in 1996, the year she became pregnant. Jos' graduation to F1 had come in 1994. His winning of the GM Lotus and F3 championships straight out of karting, and his spectacular, all-out-attack style in the car had made him a hot property. He was even hotter after his first try-out of an F1 car, with Arrows in September 1993 at the Estoril circuit in Portugal two days after the grand prix there. Jos created something of a sensation. Within four laps he was doing times that would have got him onto the grid, and by the end of the day he had pretty much equalled the time set in qualifying by the car's regular driver Derek Warwick, a time which would have put him 10th on the grid.

The test had been arranged by Rothengatter, who made sure everyone got to hear about it in the media, and within a few days there were expressions of interest from almost every team on the grid. It looked like the arrival of the most exciting new talent in F1 since Michael Schumacher and Mika Hak-kinen a couple of years earlier. But such is the mine-strewn nature of an F1 career that in fact Jos was more in demand at this moment than he would ever be again.

Ron Dennis' McLaren team offered him the role of con-tracted test driver with the option of possible races in the future. Flavio Briatore's Benetton made him a very similar proposal. There were race seats up for grabs at lesser teams but Rothengatter convinced Jos that getting in at the ground floor with Benetton, a major team, was preferable to being a grid filler, even if that delayed his F1 racing debut. He and Jos decided to accept Briatore's offer.

Despite his aggressive bargaining style, Rothengatter was a little out of his depth at this level of the sport. Without realising it, he had signed Jos up to be part of the Michael Schumacher support network at Benetton, as well as a valu-able business asset for Briatore, one that might be traded down the line. What the pair had not fully understood was that on top of his mercurial talent, Michael Schumacher had a way of operating that engendered complete devotion from everyone around him.

Jos would be Benetton's official third driver behind J.J. Lehto, the experienced Finn who had himself once been seen as the 'next big thing'. The idea was that in doing Schumacher's donkey work in testing, Jos would accumulate lots of mileage in 1994, helping him adapt fully to F1 before making his race debut, possibly the following year. At least that was the plan until Lehto injured his neck in a pre-season testing accident at Silverstone and Jos was brought in as his short-notice replacement for the first two races of the season. A dramatic, roll-over accident on his debut in Brazil, though not his fault, didn't create a great first impression. Lehto would be back for round three, the ill-fated San Marino Grand Prix (in which Ayrton Senna and Roland Ratzenberger were killed).

And here we gather up another thread in the history – scrapyards, Paul Lemmens and Genk, Van Amersfoort, Rothengatter – that was winding its way towards Max Verstappen's destiny, years before he'd even been born. That was the moment Pedro Lamy's Lotus, coming from 22nd on the grid, ploughed almost head-on into the back of Lehto's stationary Benetton, aggravating the fractured vertebra in Lehto's neck sustained at Silverstone from which he would later need time out to recover.

And just like that, Jos was thrust into the glare of an F1 season with a top team way before he was ready. The rocket-propelled momentum that had got Jos to this point immediately began to falter and never properly recovered. That was partly circumstantial and partly down to Jos himself, with his less than full understanding of what was required to succeed at the ultimate level of the sport. The brute force he'd shown in mastering the technicalities of karting needed to be combined with a more delicate touch to understand the art and skill of personal dynamics in something so big and complex as a top F1 team. For someone of Jos' background and personality, it was just too big an ask.

'As a driver, Jos was as good as Max in my opinion,' says Van der Grint. 'But it is not only putting the foot down and turning the steering wheel. There's much more and that's where he educated – from his mistakes – Max. Which is why Max is much more all-round. Max made his car racing debut at 16, in his passport. But mentally he was much older – because of his education from Jos. Whereas when Jos made his debut he was not. He was younger than his years, probably. Neither Rothengatter nor Jos were prepared for F1. What they had in mind was to be test driver with Benetton, but Jos was drafted in as a real novice, a quick driver but the politics and the dynamics are different. So here was this guy used to winning everything, as dominant as Max in karting. Then year one, Opel Lotus and dominated. Year two, German F3 and dominated. Then he arrives at an F1 team built completely around Schumacher. Being technically minded he knew there was a difference in the cars; everything was tricky, with the plank, all these things. It was a difficult start. But what this does to the mentality is crucial. You are used to winning, to getting everything from the tyre men or the chassis men, they are all focused on you. Then suddenly you are the second man. Jos is an emotional guy and speaks his mind without a filter and in this situation, you cannot do that. You cannot talk to a Briatore or a Ross Brawn in that way. No one is able to do that. But Jos did.'

There's a further element to this. Fast though Jos was, he was being compared to Michael Schumacher, one of the greatest racing drivers who has ever lived. Maybe even a fully prepared, fully motivated Jos just wouldn't have been quite as quick as that. That's not so outrageous a possibility, is it? Jos' F1 testing debut was impressive in that he all but equalled old hand Derek Warwick's best lap in the car. But in Schumacher's first taste of an F1 car, in a Jordan at Silverstone, he obliterated any previous times set by the car and proceeded then comfortably to out-qualify experienced old hand Andrea de Cesaris on his debut. He followed that up by instantly out-qualifying three-time world champion Nelson Piquet at Benetton in his second race. It was Jos' misfortune to go up against such a colossus before being more fully established.

Pat Symonds was Benetton's engineering chief at the time, with a close working relationship to Schumacher. His take is as follows: 'There's no doubt Jos was quick but he was up against someone who people were only just realising was more than just that. All the signs were there, but '94 was when Michael had this car that was very much suited to him, tuned around him and that's when he really flowered fully. Jos wasn't as quick as Michael, but who was? Michael was a hard bloke to be up against, as many found since. This was Jos' first F1 drive. Michael was three years in. That makes a hell of a difference. Also, in F1 it's happened before – people look to have the potential in their junior careers, then F1 is a step different.

'He didn't have any specific struggles. The polite way of saying it would be he was a rough diamond. You look at his personal life and he's not someone you'd think you'd want to be friends with and yet everyone did quite like him. He was popular within the team; the guys who worked on his car liked him, he fitted in well. But you cannot but compare him to Michael, not just as a driver, but he was a very, very different person to Michael. For a young guy Michael was extremely refined, knew how to build a team around him. Jos was this rougher character and wouldn't even begin to know how to do that. The work ethic was there but he wasn't as bright as Michael, emotionally or anyway else.

'It did seem an unlikely pairing when they became friends. But that's the funny thing with Jos: people did quite like him and could accept that roughness. Personally, I think that within Benetton he was racing at his level.'

Was Jos as fast as Max is? No, is the verdict of Giancarlo Tinini, proprietor of the CRG kart manufacturer which ran them both. '[Max] adapts better to the track conditions compared to his dad. Jos was also fast and aggressive, but Max, even as Jos himself admitted, is faster than him.'

Jos had reflected that Max, 'Has a better feel for the kart or the car than I did.' On a Dutch talk show in 2021, Jos showed a hindsight level of self-awareness about his F1 career and how Schumacher benchmarked him. 'As a driver, you know exactly how . . . when you come into Formula One you think we are going to win races and we are going to win the championship. But once you meet someone where you think, "fuck, he's fast" and then, if you have done everything you can and you still can't beat him, then you know your role and how good you are. Sure, if we all had a chance again we would try again, but maybe in the back of your mind you know a little bit how far you would come.'

'I always thought it was really amazing and cool that my dad drove in Formula 1,' recalled Max in *Whatever It Takes*. 'Of course, everyone has their own opinions and I think my dad knows it himself that it could have been better. But sometimes things just don't go your way, you make wrong choices and at some point it will be over.'

In that same documentary, Jos himself acknowledges that the die was cast in that first season. 'My worst time in the sport was my first year [in F1]. I made too many mistakes. I think it's difficult when you have a very strong teammate. Everything was set up based on him and you feel that as a driver. I wasn't prepared. I think I could have made more out of it if I had known more, if I'd had someone next to me explaining me things. Someone I could trust. I had to figure out everything myself and when I did it was already too late. I had already made the mistakes.'

That momentum and buzz, once lost, is never recovered in F1. You are perceived differently, the opportunities presented are fewer, the power dynamic is less in the driver's favour and the driver himself doesn't carry that same invincible mentality. In turn he delivers less performance, probably without even realising it. A few years after arriving as F1's next big thing, Jos would be driving the slowest car on the grid and being regularly outpaced by a rookie teammate, Justin Wilson. But by then he was well into running his own karting business, back in a world he had never left, even at the height of his F1 career. And with his five-year-old boy already careering around the track in his upgraded kart whenever his dad would let him, and begging relentlessly to be allowed to race, everything was in alignment for the next part of the story to begin.

3

THE MAKING OF A CHAMPION

'He was such a little boy, with this big helmet, sitting in a baby kart. And you're thinking hopefully nothing goes wrong.'
Sophie Kumpen

In the few weeks between the end of one season and the beginning of another, Max spends time with partner Kelly and her daughter Penelope. But he has also filled his life with another obsession, albeit one closely related to his profession: simulator racing. Four weeks after receiving his 2022 world champion crown at the FIA awards, Verstappen was taking part in the Le Mans Virtual event, an online simulation of the Le Mans 24-Hour race. Sim racing is a huge part of Verstappen's life. In between practice sessions at grands prix, he will be in touch with his teammates at Team Redline, the e-sports team he joined a few years ago to give him greater anonymity than when he was racing online just as himself. He races from his apartment, where he has a space cleared for his 'rig' – custom-made pedals, steering wheel and banks of computer screens. Being part of a team of professional sim racers also gives him good sparring partners as he practises for the next big event, of which there are many, all requiring many hours of preparation to be fully competitive.

But Team Redline appears to have given him more than merely a way to stay sharp and focused away from the track. He takes his role there every bit as seriously as the one at Red Bull. His partner at Team Redline, Atze Kerkhof, a former speed skater who transferred to sim racing and is now a performance coach in real life with the Alfa Romeo F1 team, says, 'He became a very mature personality in the team, to help out behind the scenes as well. Then at some point he became a team leader where he was not driving himself per se but helping others out, explaining set-up, explaining driving styles, explaining attitudes to other drivers. So now I know Max is different to how the world sees him.'

His competitive intensity in this virtual world is every bit a match for that he displays in F1. Watch him and Jos being interviewed by David Coulthard on Channel 4 the day after his 2021 championship win, and Max only becomes really animated when the conversation turns to sim racing. This is his thing, a place where Jos can't follow. Like so many parents of Gen X-ers, Jos cannot comprehend why anyone would want to devote so much time and effort to anything other than the real thing.

But for Max, this is a fascinating challenge, different to actual race driving but requiring exactly the same approach in order to excel. His pursuit of that performance allows us an almost action-replay of the process and mentality that made him so unbelievably good in karts.

'These sim drivers, they are so quick,' he says to Coulthard, 'and it's very interesting to see them drive because they have no real experience of a car, but somehow when you look at how they're braking, how they're steering, using the throttle, it is how it should be, so it's very interesting for me to then compare myself to them because they are naturally quick on the sim and I am naturally quick in real life. For me that's another motivation because I am confident that when I jump in a real car I will be quick. But on the simulator these guys are the benchmark, not me, and I have to push myself to that limit to just test myself and improve and to also learn from them. So in my downtime I am still trying to improve myself which I think also helps me in real life.'

The Le Mans Virtual in January 2023 was an endurance race just like the real thing. Verstappen reckons a 24-hour race requires around 40 hours of practice. It didn't have a happy outcome . . . He and Kerkhof were leading comfortably after over 17 hours of racing when a computer server crashed, possibly through being hacked. This lost them two laps which couldn't be restored, dropping them to the lower places and sending Max into something of a rant about the event organisers before retiring. The footage went viral. 'It's game over,' he said. 'I think I have more chance if I just go to Vegas and the casino . . . I would have more chance to win. I think I'm going to uninstall the game. That's nice . . . frees up a bit of space on the PC anyway. And I really hope everyone uninstalls the game.'

The passion is real. It is easy to see how, having reached the pinnacle of the real-life sport, Max found a new obsession where he could strive for excellence, assimilate afresh the requirements needed to dominate. This gives us perhaps more clarity on just where the urge to race in the first place came from. It wasn't from Jos. There was no rebellion from Max against Jos' dictates because it was Max who was pushing for it and Max who always wanted more. Max soaked up the knowledge and skill like a sponge as fast as Jos could pour it in, until he had surpassed his father.

'It all started when Max was four years old,' Jos told Kartcom in 2014. 'We always talked about competition at home. I was often at races and I remember he insisted often that he wanted to race karts. I've never forced him; rather I yielded to his urgent request!'

Max wasn't actually the first to benefit from Jos' hardcore racing tuition. That was Giedo van der Garde in 2002, who won that year's world Super A championship as a 17-year old and would later go on to a brief F1 career with Caterham and Sauber. He won the karting title with Michel Vacirca's CRG Netherlands team, which was quite an achievement as a semi-factory outfit against the full factory runners. Van der Garde was powered by Jos Verstappen's engines and part of the deal was that Jos would provide support and advice, foreshadowing the role he would later have in his son's karting exploits. Giedo remembers it as the highlight of his whole racing career.

'I had Jos on my side for one wonderful year,' he recalls. 'He didn't have an F1 drive in that year but for 2003 he had an offer to go back to F1 [with Minardi] and took it. Which was a pity for me because I sort of lost the momentum after that.

'Jos was one of the best engine tuners I had ever seen but also as a human being, as a coach, a super lovely guy, straightforward, no bullshit. Also tough sometimes, very hard, if you did not do well he was the one who said, "You are an idiot"; really hard and tough but I had a great season with him.'

Talk of Jos as a 'lovely guy' may sound anomalous given the list of court appearances and convictions against his name. The hair-trigger temper could bring his brand of scrapyard justice to the fore and it's got him into a lot of trouble, not least with former girlfriends and wives. But within the racing world he has always been widely respected as someone who gives absolutely everything of himself and in repose he can be laid-back, friendly and very good company. His devotion to helping Van der Garde was total and sincere and went far beyond being paid for a service.

'Jos was fully committed and fully in,' continues Giedo. 'Every little detail was important and I learned that from him, not only about driving but about the engine, the mechanics, the people who work in the factory, he had so much experience about all of that. His way of teaching was very straightforward; if it is wrong it's wrong, if it is good it's good.

But also the attitude. I remember once, I was doing a series in Finland and had a crash and stopped. When I came back to the pit he was starting to scream and shout, "You idiot, why didn't you push the kart back on, you could try some other things out on track and now you lose time!" And I was like, "Whoa, okay, easy man." But next time I crashed, I pushed the go-kart back on to the track and afterwards I said, "Happy now?" And he said, "This is where you work so never give up."'

Van der Garde became part of the Verstappen family that year: 'They were living in Belgium, I was there nearly every week, I was sleeping in Max's room. It was a great time. [Jos is] a pure racer, he really likes to see go-karts and race karts, the whole family is all about racing. Around the table, they were all talking about racing all the time.

'It was a great year, a lovely family. Sophie was there, Max's young sister Victoria was there. Once in a while I was playing with Max on the PlayStation and if you won he was so angry, throwing away the controller, because he was not winning. You could see that the kid already had something special at a very young age.'

During that 2002 season, Van der Garde experienced the Jos style of schooling in the way Max later would. And already it seemed like an inevitability that Max would be in a kart before too much longer. 'Max would be there in the house, and he sees we've won the championship and if you see that as a young kid you also want to try it out. At that time, it was, "Hey Papa I want to try that." Push, push, push, all the time.

He came to a couple of rounds with Jos and the family. He was always like, "When, when, when? When will you put me in a go-kart?" He was always asking for it.'

Jos was at the Canadian Grand Prix in 2001 when Sophie phoned. '[She] said that he was standing by her side crying because he wanted to drive,' Jos recalled to Dutch TV. 'But I wanted to wait until he was about six, because I thought that was a good age to start.' Max had been particularly outraged to see his friend Stan Pex, son of karting team owner Richard Pex (whose base Jos prepared his engines from), driving on-track at Genk and pointed out that Stan was younger than him. 'He was so insistent,' recalled Jos. 'So I bought him a kart.'

Van der Garde was there at Genk in 2001 as little Max took to the track for the first time in his 'Buffo' mini-kart. 'It was obvious straightaway that he had talent, even at that age, that it came very naturally to him. I remember Jos beaming, thinking it was very cool to see his son driving a kart.' He drove it so fast it soon broke and a couple of days later Jos upgraded it.

'It wasn't all that nerve-wracking,' said Jos later of his first experience of seeing Max out on-track, 'because since the age of two he'd been on a quad bike so he had experience with speed and how to steer. He'd done quite a lot of things before I put him in a go-kart.' In an interview with the BBC's Andrew Benson, Jos went on to recall how, on the quad bike at the age of two, Max 'went on two wheels, had to adjust the steering and went side-on into the wall. Luckily, he was wearing a helmet, which got scratched. But he didn't mind. He was driving all the time. He had a feeling with an engine. Didn't matter whether it was a quad bike, an electric jeep – you know, the small things for children – or whatever. He was always busy with driving. Every day he needed to be on it.'

Easy for Jos to say the run-out in the kart wasn't nerve-wracking. Sophie, even as an ex-racer, was rather more nervous (and still is): 'Max was three and a half,' she recalled in the documentary *Whatever It Takes*. 'He was such a little boy, with this big helmet, sitting in a baby kart. And you're thinking hopefully nothing goes wrong . . . Your heart, it's your own flesh and blood, you can't describe it.'

Jos' mentor Paul Lemmens, who owned the track, was there too. 'It was amazing to see,' he said, 'because his helmet was bigger than him.'

If Jos imagined Max's campaigning would stop when he had a kart to play with, he was mistaken. It only upped the ante. He wanted to be on-track at every opportunity. He was still too young to race but he could drive for fun at the track. He did so in company with some slightly older boys, some of whom were already racing. As soon as Max understood that he was already quicker than most of them, he felt he was being dealt a severe injustice by the regulations which stipulated a minimum racing age of seven.

Jos was not the one who pushed, the impetus came wholly from Max. The manner in which he would race would be entirely dictated by Jos – and, unsurprisingly, it was extreme. But Max was unrelenting in his push.

So great was the pressure on Jos that he roped in Michel Vacirca, his former kart racing contemporary who was now running the CRG Netherlands kart racing enterprise, to get past the strict age-related rules. 'There was a collective test for all the new kids,' he recalled, 'but you needed a racing licence to take part in it. Max didn't have a licence yet because he was too young so I filled in another name so he could at least practice. I put in the name of one of my drivers, and already Max was one of the fastest at the test.

'The problem was that of course if somebody is fast, even if the name is wrong, a lot of people want to know who he is. And then, Mr Luca di Donna from the organisers found that I did actually cheat with the names and he was very angry with me, he told me this is an insurance thing, you cannot do that blah blah blah . . .

'But in the end, he let Max continue. Jos wasn't there actually. Jos is somebody who never goes to the track unless whoever he's running is going to be competitive and there was no reason to think Max would be so fast. But after that day Max went home and told Jos all about it and I spoke with Jos and from that moment Jos was, "Okay, Max is very fast and strong, then we can actually begin with that long journey."'

•

At some point around this time, Jos had the big conversation with his son. The, 'If we are doing this we are doing it seriously. We are not playing,' conversation. How much a seven-year-old can absorb the ramifications of that we cannot know. But he'd quickly find out. Plans were made for Max to race in the local Mini-Junior championships of 2005 with Vacirca's team, all overseen by Jos.

Even before the season began, Max got to experience the Jos brand of preparation. Van der Garde – by this time an F3 driver but still with very close links to the Verstappens and Vacirca – visited the Genk track to find Jos running a little test of his own. 'Jos had Max and two other young kids testing. I spoke to Jos and he said, "We are going to do some testing here, we make some fun out of it, five laps and then we start the race." He was simulating a race between them. It wasn't an official race of course. But they got just five laps practising, enjoying it and then they raced. Because then they have to think much harder. Instead of going around the whole day learning the track, you do five laps then you race 20 laps, but after the 20 laps of the race they were 10 steps ahead of where they would have been just driving around all day.

'Once they'd started with Max, the more years they were going on, the more races he won and started doing really well, then I know Jos was like, "Okay, let's go for it, let's try to reach Formula One and reach the goal of winning the championship". For them it's a dream come true. But they put in so much effort. An unreal amount of effort.'

'We did everything ourselves . . . We were not dependent on anyone,' Max told *GQ* magazine in 2021. 'A lot of drivers, yes, they were great drivers themselves, but they didn't really have a lot of knowledge about how to set up a go-kart or how to make an engine. Their fathers all do their own thing in their own right to try and support their son, and they will always, of course, try to give them their best guidance. But I think our way was way more extreme than others.

'I still played and had a lot of fun,' related Max. 'But I also needed to understand that it was serious, what we were doing, because we were working toward something. Of course, from seven to eleven years old it intensified quite a lot, but he wanted me to be there to see what he was doing. Do you see a crack somewhere? Do you see a problem with the go-kart? I'd see him take everything off the go-kart, then put it back on, so I'd understand the mechanics behind it. All these kinds of things that he was trying to explain to me because he wanted me to understand that it's not a joke, it's not that we're here for fun. Because we are working toward trying to reach the top.'

That was the difference, Max says, between him and his competitors. 'I was just a lot more on it, in terms of just being more professional about it. That definitely came from my dad, because if he wasn't my dad, I would also be running around, playing, having fun. And I need that kind of push.'

Van der Garde agrees: 'Jos was really about the commit-ment, the work ethic, always pushing me and Max: "You have to work hard, sometimes you can have a little bit of fun if you do well but always the work ethic." Jos as a driver sometimes could lose his . . . go over the top, start to get angry and start making mistakes. I rarely saw that with Max. If I had done this with my son, I would also teach him the stuff that I was not good at too because those things you remember. Jos really made Max a very complete driver at a very young age.'

It wasn't just Max who was put hard to work. Vacirca too got to experience a new challenge: Jos Verstappen, karting dad. 'Yeah, sometimes a challenge . . .' he says, with amusing understatement. 'All the dads can be demanding but, for example, with Giedo's father he would be back at his normal job on Monday and I wouldn't hear from him. But with Jos it was full-time; this was his work. So he'd be phoning me Sunday evening on the way home from the track and telling me, 'Okay, we will organise the tyres tomorrow and we should have this, this and that'.

Vacirca experienced Jos' temper first hand when his exacting standards were not met. On one occasion, he was responsible for ordering rain tyres from Vega, the Italian manufacturer, which also had a factory in France. Jos believed the French tyres to be inferior to the Italian ones, but Vacirca, unaware of this, failed to specify that he wanted Italian tyres. When the slicks arrived from France, Jos hit the roof. 'So then there was no excuse, [Jos] immediately started yelling at me, "Fucking hell, the wrong tyres!" It certainly kept you awake, working with Jos.'

Jos had Max working at Vacirca's workshop in between races and would give him instruction in the technicalities. Max has never been as into this as Jos, and to this day is less fascinated by the mechanicals than his father. That would come to be a little bone of contention for Jos, that feeling that Max was a little too relaxed about it all even as he was enjoying great success.

This was not just a weekend pursuit: the work continued after the Sunday meetings, with no day job to take Jos' focus away from Max's karting career.

Vacirca remembers: 'Jos would bring Max into the workshop. The whole day in the shop, they were cleaning and doing jobs on the kart. Of course, he was sometimes a little bit lazy, he was a kid, but then Jos would shout again and then Max would do something again for a couple of minutes. But they were day and night involved in racing.'

'Jos was so good at triggering Max in a certain way,' reflects Van der Garde, 'and was tough sometimes, telling him off if he was doing no good but also if he was doing really well telling him, "I am proud of you."'

It was this imparting of total, rigorous discipline that enabled Max to realise his potential, recalls CRG's owner Giancarlo Tinini. '[Max] had great abilities from all points of view, very important for a driver: track technique, mental strength, determination. He had exceptional control of the vehicle in karting, even in the first laps of the race when tyres were not warm enough and this feeling and naturalness in driving allows him to make the difference in motorsport even nowadays.

'I never saw any resistance or strain from Max to what Jos was teaching. Max always accepted it as a challenge and has always been able to find the solution to get the result his dad was asking for.'

One thing his dad never, ever told him, however, was that he was going to be a champion. 'He was always the opposite,' recalled Max in the *Whatever It Takes* documentary, 'telling me I was going to be a truck driver or a bus driver. In a good way, making me realise that what I was doing at the time was not enough.' He elucidated further on this point: 'He thought I was too lazy and laid back. [He would say] "Goddammit, retarded bastard, stupid pig. You're never going to make it." That's a summary of his reaction when he felt I didn't give it my all. He was really strict. In the end, that's what motivated me to prove him wrong and that I could do it.'

'I think Max had a really tough time,' said Helmut Marko. 'Jos was a really good teacher and instructor. But I think he was more than hard on this young boy.'

'I did everything in my power to teach Max,' said Jos. 'I did everything I could, and I mean everything.'

But even those days when Jos wasn't satisfied with performance, the questions from Max were uninterrupted. This was always a two-way street, not some meek kid just doing as he was told. The questions got deeper and more complex as Max progressed through karting's ranks. By the time they left the local championships behind and committed to the serious European and World Championships – invariably heavily based in Italy where the major karting manufacturers are – in 2010, it had become a very intense experience. An arrangement had been made regarding Max's schooling. His time there was limited, a private tutor was taken on and Max had to pass year-end exams to a required standard to be allowed to continue with the home schooling. He always aced them. 'He has a very high IQ,' says Vacirca. 'The exams didn't seem to pose a problem to him.'

'On Fridays Max was done with school at three and I was waiting at the front of the school in the van,' recalled Jos in *Whatever It Takes*. 'He'd get in and I'd drive full gas to Italy. We'd get there about two or three at night, get into the hotel. On Saturdays, we were testing all day and then preparing everything for Sunday and then on Sunday we'd race till about four or five, load everything into the van then drive home quickly.'

In the van back from the latest meeting there were more questions, always more. Jos had plenty of answers, but sometimes even for him it was too much. 'Sometimes I'd be like "Max, can you please stop talking now,"' related Jos in 2022.

Sometimes Jos' requests weren't quite so polite. Like the infamous time in 2012, when he told 15-year-old Max to get out of the van when Max wanted to talk about the on-track incident that had cost him an easy victory and a world title and had made Jos so furious.

Mum Sophie wasn't far behind, Max had a mobile phone and Jos knew all that – and he later turned around and returned to pick him up. But still, it was pretty extreme. They completed the 11-hour journey in silence and it would be another week before Jos resumed communications with his son.

'Some people probably cannot deal with that kind of behaviour,' said Max in 2021, 'but I needed it. I was that type of character, probably, who needed this kind of treatment.'

The pair hardened themselves to the unforgiving northern European weather as they slogged on in pursuit of those '10,000 hours'. 'Probably two or three times a week we were on the racing circuit, even when it rained,' recalled Jos. 'We didn't care. Even when it was -2 degrees C and we had to test something, we went there. After five laps, he'd come in, his hands were frozen. I said, "Okay, go in the van and warm yourself up." And after five minutes I got him out of the van and he had to drive again. It was not always pleasant for him but I think that created his character as well a little bit. He saw how much effort I put in and he hasn't seen anything different and that's how he is as well. He is very determined and motivated.'

•

Max knew that Jos' lessons were valuable, but as a quite dif-ferent personality he had to find his own way of learning too, and naturally this became more of an issue the older Max got. The petrol station incident that led to him being kicked out of the van might be seen as an example of Max starting to assert himself. For Jos, it was about Max not thinking hard enough for his exacting standards and taking too much for granted. But perhaps it was also about Max's more relaxed persona. He had plenty of the intensity on the track, but he didn't feel the need to take that out of the car. He seemed to be able to switch it on and off as required and maybe that just didn't compute for Jos.

Max didn't get as deep into the nuts and bolts as Jos but seemed to instinctively understand which lessons would be most valuable to him. That together with his mother's influence – whether nature, nurture or both – perhaps con-tributed to Max's more sustainable, equable approach which actually served him far better when it came to fitting into the racing world. Max learned to steer the tricky path between the tempestuous Jos and the requirements of the external world as expertly as threading his car between the walls of a street circuit. That pragmaticism arguably does far more to explain the respective F1 track records of Jos and Max than any difference in innate driving ability.

Jos has this 'make things happen' energy: explosive, sharp, impatient. But Max never sought to emulate that. Even as he was being so intensely tutored, Max had the strength of character to remain himself. He has never at any point tried to be a mini Jos. Sure, the Jos temper is in there at times. But it takes a lot to bring it on and it's invariably justified. The Jos-Max relationship and how that formed Max's career is a complex dynamic, not at all as it might seem on the surface.

Even as a kid, Max was emotionally intelligent enough to understand the sometimes tricky dynamics between Jos and the team. 'Max was like he is still now,' says Vacirca, 'always very cool. At that time to be honest I thought with Jos if you are always shouting at your dog you have to keep shouting your whole life, and . . . maybe Max did play the game. Jos was always shouting; for us it was normal. But if I see now how Max is with other people . . . he never has any nerves, he is like, okay, I will do it another way. That's always been his reaction, so cool, so quiet.

'If you have such a father – and I must say, I like Jos – but sometimes he was not easy and I think the way Max did manage it, stayed calm, didn't go immediately against him, just let him cool down before discussing things, I think that was already very clever. He knows how to keep the team together. He was already a kind of diplomat between Jos and the team, even as a kid. Of course, as a child, in the end he really did listen always to Jos. But still, he did not immediately start shouting or reacting. For his age, he was very clever.'

Max had probably acquired some of this instinct from life at home as Jos and Sophie's marriage broke down over a period of a couple of years before they finally split in 2008. It was a horrible break-up according to those who saw it up close and for sure a 10-year-old kid has to find his own coping mechanisms.

In some respects, even as a kid, *Max* was managing *Jos*. Not the other way around. Jos was giving him what he needed, but also required some careful handling in order for that help to be maximised. Yes, 'Jos the Boss' was still the boss, but Max had his own way of dealing with him from an early age.

When he's racing, Max is entirely devoted to the task at hand. When he's not, he relaxes. It has been his approach since the start – something that would drive his father Jos crazy as it gave the impression Max didn't care. But he always has, and still does.

'I think he just had to get used to my way of doing things,' says Max with a smile. Many years later.

'My dad taught me to live,' Max reflected in 2021. 'How you have to focus on yourself and work with your team. Everything else doesn't matter. After spending a lot of years with my dad, yes it was easy to understand that. He showed me in a lot of different ways; some nice ways, some a bit more angry ways. He made me toughen up, which is good.

'He did that by making me realise that what I was doing at the time was not enough. You can't rely on your talent to be the best. As I went through my karting career I began to understand that and began to work harder for it. I think still for my dad's liking, all the way to F1 I still didn't work hard enough in his eyes. Because I have a bit more of a relaxed personality compared to him in how I approach a weekend, how I deal with setbacks, incidents. But that prepared me very well for criticism or praise – because I just didn't really care. I don't really care if it's negative and don't really care if it's positive. It doesn't bring me anything, being arrogant and thinking I can walk on water. And being negative, I'm just going to be upset. I prefer to be in the middle and forget about both sides. Just focus on what you have to do and what you can control.'

Max may have been choosy about how to incorporate the lessons Jos was teaching him, but he internalised some of his old-school attitudes. This includes something of Jos' machismo, as Max's tale from one of his first tests of a car makes clear. 'I was just getting started in Formula Renault 2-litre testing,' he related in a Dutch TV round table discussion in December 2022, 'and then I got invited for a Formula 3 test and it was a lot tougher, especially because Valencia is an anti-clockwise circuit and normally tracks are clockwise so your neck muscles aren't used to anti-clockwise. After a few runs I could not keep my head up and I needed padding on the side. My dad called it the pussy pad. Since that day, I refuse to use it. In 2020, we arrived at Mugello [also anti-clockwise] and nobody really knew how heavy it was going to be. Some teams had already put the padding in and the team asked me, "Do you want padding as well?" I said,

"Even if my head falls off, I am not using it ever again" and that is what I kept telling them.'

In this can be discerned Jos' disdain for weakness of any kind, for not being able to meet any challenge. That's the unsaid overview and the specifics are all managed within that.

'It's about practice and in general understanding what to do,' explains Max of fully understanding those specifics. 'You can practise it, but you also need to understand *what* you're practising. From a young age, my dad has been working a lot with me to try and understand changes on the kart at the time. Because at the end of the day, the mechanics of an F1 car are pretty similar. It is just more advanced in Formula 1. But going out and actually really feeling what is the difference is what is important.' Though Max might not recognise it as such, this is a perfect explanation of the academics' concept of deliberate practice – the necessary ingredient for achieving elite prowess in any field. And Max could not have done that without Jos.

'It's the same in karts as in F1 now: what do you have to do to try and go faster? And really try to adapt to that as quickly as possible. That's the same if you're driving in the dry and suddenly it starts raining, you have to adapt really quickly or the other way around. So that's things you learned from a young age.'

Ten years, give or take, of lessons and discussion and flogging around deserted wet tracks, adjusting settings when your fingers are numb with cold, hour upon hour in the van driving to every windy kart track on every corner of the continent. This is how the F1 champion was forged. Yes, there was complete intolerance of failure from Jos, intolerance for anything less than total commitment. Yes, he was a moody, ultra-demanding, overshadowing presence.

But it was Max's willingness to keep grafting and learning, year after year after year of his whole young life, that made him the complete driver he is. Repeat and go again.

What Max also assimilated, probably without even being aware of it, was the purity of his love for racing and the disregard for the hype around it. It means he is probably less impressed by the idea of being an F1 driver than almost anyone else in the paddock. Shortly after he'd made his F1 debut in 2015 as a 17-year-old, he was asked if the enormity of it had sunk in. 'No, it's not enormous. It's just like doing a kart race with more spectators.'

That's exactly as it would seem for the boy born and raised in the circus. He's the ultimate insider. When Lewis Hamilton, maybe the ultimate outsider, made his F1 debut in Australia 2007, as he climbed from the car he caught his father's eye and they celebrated. 'We've done it! We've bloody done it!' they said as they hugged and laughed, having pulled off something that had seemed so extraordinarily remote when they started, so impossible. It's not a scene which would probably have much resonated with the Verstappens. Max is a way less complex character than rival Hamilton. But then he's bound to be. He's had a way less complex set of circumstances to grow up in and a far more certain path to achieving his ambitions.

In the midst of his intense fight with Hamilton for the 2021 world championship, there was something significant in Max's response to the question of how he'd feel if he lost out in that battle. 'Well, it helps that I love what I'm doing,' he replied. 'It won't make any big difference really.' Sure, part of that was just deflecting the pressure. But there was also truth in it. He races because that's what he does, that's pretty much all of him. It's the same around the high-gloss venues of the billion-dollar world of F1 as it is around a cold, wet, kart track in the middle of nowhere with no one there to see you but the other teams. A kart race with more spectators is what a grand prix is to him. The scenery around him changes, the motorhomes get bigger, the media time greater, that's all. None of that makes much of a dent on him. Just as reaching the goal of F1 was almost a routine matter; just as winning a grand prix on his debut with Red Bull was too.

'I'm not someone who easily loses sight of reality,' he said in *Whatever It Takes*. 'At the end of the day you just have to be yourself and focus on what you have to do. And that is to drive fast. You can't let yourself get swept up in the fame that comes with it. That's been instilled in me since I was young.'

Jos knew exactly what it would take for his son, even if he was prodigiously successful in karting, to attain the sporting heights that had eluded him. So he brusquely banished any complacent or unrealistic thoughts from Max's young head.

THE MAKING OF A CHAMPION

Despite his F1 pedigree, Jos' world was not rarefied or privileged: it was down to earth, deeply unglamorous, at times punishing. But it wasn't the normal world. Most only visit this place. Max got to live in it every day of his life.

4

DISRUPTING THE HIERARCHY

Richard Pex had seen hundreds of karters race over the years but soon came firmly to believe that Jos would take Max all the way to F1 . . .

Back when Jos was an F1 driver, he'd spend time between grands prix at the kart track or the workshop, preparing engines for his customers, putting into practice what he'd learned at Paul Lemmens' place all those years ago. Jos would even occasionally still race his kart long after his F1 career, taking his last race victory (in the Belgian championship) as late as 2006. But it's not a route Max has followed. He never really did get into the technicalities of karting the way Jos did. A kart track isn't going to pull him away from Kelly and Penelope between grands prix in the way that a sim race might. Besides, Monaco is not a hot-bed of karting, unlike Genk which was always within a short ride of the Verstappens' home.

Max took from Jos what he needed to excel in karts, but it hasn't proven an environment to exert any long-term hold on

him. Instead, sim racing has fulfilled that role of deep immer-
sion, its challenges every bit as enticing for him as karting has
been for Jos.

Even as Max was competing in karts against the other
kids, the goal of F1 was already explicit. There's footage of
him as an 11-year-old being interviewed with Jos on Dutch
TV and when asked whether F1 is the goal, there's not the
slightest ambiguity in Max's response. He was on a path, one
which Jos had defined but which Max had never even had to
think about. Karting was just the means to the end.

Many of those who were instrumental in his karting progress remain deeply immersed in this branch of the sport,
none more so than the Pex family. It was in the corner of a
workshop adjacent to Richard Pex's roofing business that Jos
would prepare Max's engines. This was also where the karts
of Richard and his sons Stan (a few months younger than
Max), Jorrit (four years older) and Yard (seven years older)
were prepared. Although they were ostensibly separate teams
until 2009 (when Max was entered under the Pex banner), the
Pexs and the Verstappens raced together, travelled together.
They were all serious racers, Richard (nine years older than
Jos) winning the Dutch KZ championships in 2002 and 2004,
Jorrit progressing to the heights of winning the KZ (gearbox
category) world karting championship in 2015, Yard the
Belgian KZ champion of 2007 and 2009, and Stan winning
titles from 2010 in the mini category right up to 2020 when
he became WSK Open champion.

Although Stan was Max's contemporary, as Max pro-gressed it was Jorrit who ended up racing him for longer. 'Racing against older guys has been incredibly useful to me throughout my career,' related Max in the *Whatever It Takes* documentary. 'It meant I had to adapt and in motorsport you don't get time to get used to things and to learn. You have to deliver almost immediately. Those years spent with Jorrit Pex brought me a lot. Especially in the latter part of the karting days and my start in F1.'

As we've already seen, there was a lot of preparation even before seven-year-old Max made his mini-kart racing debut at Emmen in the north of Holland. Jos knew he could drive quickly but felt he needed a sterner test – and racing against more experienced racers up to three years older provided that. Jos needn't have worried. Max led from the front, his pace on cold tyres at the start giving him the crucial advan-tage. 'It was tough,' Jos recalled in a BBC interview, 'because the tyres were soft and grippy and at the end of the race you could see he was tired. But that showed his character, the way he was competing. He didn't mind if other people were older or whatever, he wanted to win. You could see that was always inside him.

'The racecraft stood out. When he went out for a race on cold tyres, his first lap was always a second quicker than anybody else. So when he had the lead at Turn 1 after the start, the first time he came over the start/finish line he had a one-second lead and they are running on colder tyres. For me, that's talent. That's feeling and what you also see in the wet where you have very little grip; that's where he is fast.' That comment could stand as a description of, say, his stunning performance in the wet Brazilian Grand Prix of 2016 just as it did of his first kart race as a seven-year-old.

But the memory that stuck with Max the strongest from that first race wasn't what happened on the track. In an interview with the *Guardian* in 2018, Max recalled: 'My dad was far more nervous than me, which was very funny. I saw him next to the fence, holding tight, and you can see from the body language he was really tense and worried. But we got pole and won both races. It was perfect – but I spoke to my dad after the first race. I said: "I saw you were very nervous." He said: "Of course. It's your first race." But I was just enjoying it and driving as fast as I could.'

This was in the mini junior category, for drivers aged between seven and nine. Max didn't win the provincial championship, simply because he didn't contest the entire 2005 season. But he did win every single race he took part in. Jos' old mentor Paul Lemmens watched as the next generation of Verstappens began his story. 'You could see from his first race that he had an extreme talent. The other competitors, when they started here and they knew Max was here, they knew they were going for second place.'

So no one was surprised when Max won the Belgian championship for the category the following year in dominant fashion. And it was much the same story for the next four years as he made his way into the faster Rotax MiniMax series as age permitted. Basically, his record over those five years of Belgian and Dutch regional racing can be summarised as 'if he finished, he won'.

·

Max's style on track was quite Jos-like in its full-out attack from cold tyres to finishing flag; in the bold overtakes, the fighting spirit and the aggressive racecraft. But the driving style, as opposed to the racing style, was already more elegant, as Jos acknowledged. 'I was wilder,' is how he summarised it later. That elegance is derived from feel, of anticipating the kart's behaviour rather than reacting to it. It becomes increasingly important the further up the racing ladder you go, especially in car racing, where the vehicle is much heavier than a kart and pressed into the ground by aerodynamic downforce through tyres not designed to perform at the sort of big slip angles which are routine in karting.

Courtesy of YouTube, it is possible to go on-board with 12-year-old Max for a MiniMax race in 2009, at Ostricourt in France, where a retirement from one of the heats saw him starting the final from the back of the grid.

His recovery drive to victory is a beautiful demonstration of how he can decouple, in an instant, his natural 'elegant' driving style from the competitive necessities of the moment when overtaking sometimes demands a more brutal approach. Some of his out-brakes of rivals are far from elegant, but still require incredibly finely-honed skills to be made to work. It's not only his super-precise sense of where the last possible braking point is (which is very different to the best braking point in terms of the ultimate lap time), but also the subsequent control which invariably rescues the wild moments his manoeuvres have given him. So he can drive with all the flamboyance and apparent wildness in the world when he needs to, but the default is the elegance which enables him to extract the ultimate lap time from a kart or car. And even at 12 years old – and almost certainly from well before then – he can effortlessly, unthinkingly, switch between the two at will.

Fast-forward six years to the 2015 Chinese Grand Prix, Max's third F1 race, where he shows the exact same ability to ambush other drivers from so far back they had no idea he was about to come through. Witness the already total mastery, keeping the car straight as he begins the move, knowing he doesn't need to get to the apex at the optimum angle but just get alongside on the inside, blocking the rival and somehow scrabbling through the remainder of the corner. To pull off moves like these without locking the brakes or running so wide on the exit that the other car can simply repass requires that same pinpoint precision. Max's incredible feel for the available grip gives him total confidence that his car control can cash the cheque his boldness has issued.

Many great karters fail to make the leap into car racing purely because of the adaptations to driving style that are required once suspension enters the equation. 'There are basically two ways to be quick in a kart,' according to the late John Surtees, the only man to win world championships in both bikes and F1, who ran his son Henry in karting decades after his own retirement, 'the "rock-ape" way, which looks more spectacular, and the more sensitive way. Only one of those driving styles transfers to cars where your inputs are going through suspension.'

Max clearly had that sublimely sensitive feel almost from the start, incredibly attuned to the messages the car and tyres were giving him in a way that few have ever matched. He didn't know as much about the technicalities of karts as Jos and never sought to. All he needed to do was translate that feel into descriptions of what the kart was doing and artic-ulate what changes to its behaviour would allow him to lap yet faster. Jos would know what to do to achieve that. It was a formidable combination.

There was the odd lapse in Max's years of domination. In 2008, at the Eindhoven track, he spun while leading, having arrived at a corner to find it much wetter than on the lap before. He collided with another kart as he rejoined and finished well down the field, with damage. It was only the second time in his first 69 races that he hadn't won, the other having been a mechanical failure. By Jos' exacting standards this was unacceptable, coming just as Max was close to seal-ing another championship. So when he got wind that the Horensbergdam track on which Max would next be racing had been resurfaced, they took the kart down there to test, leaving nothing to chance. Thus prepared, Max won on race day, sealing the BNL MiniMax series in addition to the Belgian cadet title (for 8- to 13-year-olds) he'd already won.

Between races, Jos would be at Richard Pex's workshop preparing Max's engines or at Michel Vacirca's CRG Team Netherlands base. 'The great thing about having Max in the kart,' recalls Vacirca, 'was that when he went on the track he needed two or three laps maximum and then he knew what things were not good or whether a change had made it better or whatever. Mostly drivers need seven or eight laps, so it is difficult to be sure, to find something better with the set-up.

'Also, Jos has no patience so after three laps he would want to know how it is so maybe it pushed Max a little bit to get on with it. There was no time for warming up, or let's see how the seat is sitting or my pedals are wrong. No, just go and then okay, this is wrong, this is right . . . Jos did keep the pressure on.'

That ability would come to win him many races.

Despite Max's domination of the results, however, Jos would always be pushing him to find more performance. In testing he would send Max out among the traffic to practise overtaking, something he didn't get much experience of in the races. 'There is a bad way to overtake which loses you lap time and a good way which doesn't,' explained Jos.

Richard Pex had seen hundreds of karters race over the years but soon came firmly to believe that Jos would take

Max all the way to F1 and that Max had the talent to become world champion.

As well as racing together, the families holidayed together too, and Pex recalled to journalist Ivo Op den Camp in a 2014 interview how even a beach break in Italy ended up at a local track. The break from racing karts ended up being . . . driving some more karts! 'Oh, sometimes we went to the beach,' he recalled, 'but Jos and I . . . looked at each other, picked up the towels, went back to the campsite with the boys, packed the van and drove to a go-kart track.'

If this paints a picture of a carefree time, father and son following their shared passion, punctuating their victories at the track with social time spent with other karting people, in reality it was intense, even at this regional level. There were financial concerns too. 'I paid for everything myself,' recalled Jos in *Whatever It Takes*, 'and never asked about the price. I would buy it and see in hindsight how we would solve that financially.'

'There was a moment when there was no more money left for Jos,' recalls Vacirca today, 'and for us it was difficult to spend too much money on Max's racing because the costs were very high compared to what we gained.

'So I called CRG [the kart manufacturer] in Italy. They allowed me to borrow a kart from them; that is a little bit how it started with Max and the factory. Then there was a moment when I even could not go to all of Max's races because I also had to do national races, so he had my mechanic and with my mechanic combined with all the stuff from CRG, they were able to continue. We would organise together how to get to the track and CRG took care of the material.'

•

By 2009, thanks to his rapid progression through karting's ranks, Max was marking time, obliged to remain in his class by dint of his age even though he was more than ready to step up to take on the older boys. It was set to be this way again in 2010, with Max obliged to remain in the restricted KF5 category.

Jos worried that it was coming too easy, so total had been his son's domination of these regional series for five seasons. He was concerned that when the time came to step up to international karting, the standard of competition might come as a shock. 'My dad always told me you need to push yourself to the edge,' Max recalled to Andrew McCutchen of *Time+Tide Watches*. 'You shouldn't need anyone else to push you to the limit. You should always push yourself and ask yourself how can I be better, how can I do better?'

Jos was probing whether it might be feasible to at least race further afield, perhaps in the Italian championships which were the heartland of international karting and where the factories were invariably based. To that end, he whisked Max off to a pre-season test in Muro Leccese, south-east Italy, where he whipped off the engine restrictor plate that had rendered Max's CRG kart compliant with the KF5 category in which he looked set to be racing in that season. Without the restrictor, Max drove the more powerful KF3 kart, even though at 12 he was still too young to race in the higher category.

CRG boss Giancarlo Tinini, watching the test, was keen to know who the little kid was – so much smaller than the other KF3 runners – who was immediately cornering faster than the rest. He recalls: 'At the time, the reference driver in the KF3 category was Nyck de Vries, who was racing with our Zanardi team, and Max was immediately able to match his lap times on a track which was unknown to him and with very little experience in that international category. He impressed me in a crazy way. He was very confident and seemed like a little professional of the steering wheel. This from someone of his small height, it impressed me a lot. I watched two practice sessions and he was the fastest in both of them.

'So I followed Max as he was walking out of the track, not knowing who he was, and then I saw Jos walking towards him. That's when I understood. I realised it was Max. I had seen him as a much younger child with the friendship we had with Jos and Sophie and I had heard so much about him from Michel Vacirca in the Netherlands and we had been support- ing him there. Now it all made sense!

'At that point, I walked up to Jos, asking him if we could have Max in our team for [2011]. The fact that, every session, he had the best lap in his group even though he wasn't old enough, made it very clear that there was a huge talent in that small driver.'

Maybe that had been part of Jos' plan all along. If so, it was an inspired move. The offer of a factory drive took away the financial uncertainty for that season at least, even if 2010 was still up in the air. But even better was to come. Before the 2010 season was underway the sport's governing body, the FIA, lowered the minimum age for the KF3 class to 12. Max was eligible to take up Tinini's offer a year early. Tinini says now that Jos was initially reluctant, feeling that Max was still too young for such a level of competition against older, more experienced racers. But if he really was, the financial imperative perhaps took precedence. Driving for a factory team – as Jos himself had done all those years ago – eased that burden immensely.

Jos would continue to prepare the engines at Pex's workshop and his coaching intensified as Max now had to step up to international level – and as a factory driver. 'We provided all the equipment and the mechanic,' explains Tinini. 'Although Jos was there as Max's coach, Max was run by our team manager at the time, like all the other drivers. Max always had a great relationship with all his teammates and various team members.'

•

Before the 2010 European KF3 championship began in earnest, there was a prestigious one-off event to begin the season, the South Garda Winter Cup at the Lonato track. This would be Verstappen's first KF3 race, his international debut. Some

120 karts entered, many full factory teams in addition to the CRG squad of which Max was now a member, mostly piloted by drivers older and more experienced than him. Tinini was expecting a composed debut from Max. What he got was a whole lot more. 'I knew that he couldn't have won at the first race,' he recalled. 'But he almost did! He raced brilliantly, fought for the win and finished second by an incredibly small margin.' The winner was 15-year-old Egor Orudzhev in his third season in the category, driving for the factory Intrepid team. Finishing fourth was another experienced driver in an Intrepid, Alex Albon, already established as the category's top driver. In seventh was another driver who Max would soon become very familiar with, Esteban Ocon in his second season of KF3. Pierre Gasly and Charles Leclerc also figured in the results. All future F1 stars.

Max's 2010 campaign, his first at international level, was a victorious one as he won the WSK Euroseries ahead of Albon in the KF3 class. Albon won the CIK-FIA World Cup event in what was to be his final season of KF3. For 2011, he would move up to the KF2 class for boys 14–16 years, with Max obliged to do another season at KF3 level. He won the Euroseries for a second time, with Ocon and Leclerc his closest rivals and a rookie George Russell coming on very strongly. Max again suffered bad luck in the FIA World Cup event, retiring from third place while battling with eventual winner Leclerc.

'The first time I raced with Max Verstappen was in 2010,'

recalls Esteban Ocon, a tough French kid from a working-class background who moved from French regional kart racing to the international level at the same time Max was graduating from the Benelux scene. 'It was a tough year for me transitioning into international racing. Karting is very tough anyway. I was alone with my dad pretty much, fighting the big teams. Max and I were always quite close on-track and sometimes it came too close! In 2011, we were fighting for the world series championship and he won in the end. I remember a race in Italy I came out on top, but me and him were a long way ahead of the rest. It was a rivalry which started then, and it soon became even bigger.'

Intrepid team owner Mirko Sguerzoni convinced Jos to switch Max to the Intrepid team for his move into the KF2 class in 2012. Sguerzoni made a big deal of his track record of assisting Intrepid drivers in getting to F1, beginning with Sebastien Buemi and Jaime Alguersuari, both of whom had begun their F1 careers with Toro Rosso. Jos had been around the block enough times not to be unduly swayed by that claim, but the financial part of the equation was better than CRG's and Intrepid had, after all, been providing competitive equipment to the likes of Albon and Leclerc as Max had raced against them. The financial strain on Jos of keeping Max racing probably played a part in him switching.

Away from the kart tracks and workshops, Jos' life continued to be incident-filled. In January of 2012 he was arrested for attempted murder, following claims that he drove a car into his then ex-girlfriend in the Dutch city of Roermond. The charge was withdrawn and Jos was later awarded a reported 41,500 Euros by the police in compensation for wrongful prosecution. But his two-week detention in the cells cost him vital time in the preparations for Max's first KF2 season.

The 2012 season began well enough as he reeled off victories in the South Garda Winter Cup and the six-round Master Series with Intrepid, though the latter was a relatively low-status series without all the top names. Nonetheless, it was good preparation. Next came the more prestigious four-race KF2 European championship, held over two weekends at Wackersdorf, Germany and Brandon in Britain's Lincolnshire. Max was leading the series at the end of the German races, after close fights with Charles Leclerc. He'd been leading the wet first race when he spun 360-degrees after touching a kerb and though he recovered to second, Leclerc took the victory. Max won the second race, on slick tyres on a damp track with Leclerc only eighth after a chassis problem. Two weeks later in Brandon, there was controversy after Max was penalised for a collision with British driver Ben Barnicoat (Leclerc's teammate in the ART team) and although Max won the first of the two races, the final outcome was decided in the British RAC appeal courts and fell in favour of Barnicoat, who thereby took what would otherwise have been Max's title.

In the later KF2 Euroseries – won by Leclerc – Max was sixth. It was in the second round of this series, at the Val de Argenton track in France, that they had a coming together which would foreshadow their collision in the 2019 Austrian Grand Prix. Both were disqualified, Max for deliberately forcing Leclerc off the track in retaliation for earlier contact when Leclerc had relieved Max of the lead. Leclerc's disqualification was for driving Max off the track after the end of the race in a fit of pique.

Max and Intrepid lasted only half a season together. Though they had actually been a very competitive combination, which might easily have won the European championship, Jos became impatient when results fell short of the achievements established with the KF3 titles in the previous two years. However, some of that was down to Max himself. He'd spun away a win in that first Wackersdorf race, an error he himself called 'amateur', then had the unnecessary run-in with Barnicoat in the UK, both incidents which cost him the championship. He spun away another likely victory in the rain in the first round of the Euroseries, at Sarno, handing victory to Leclerc.

Jos would certainly not have been impressed with those errors and he'd have let Max know about it. A much bigger bust-up was to come. But before then, Jos pulled Max out of Intrepid with half a season still to go, despite Intrepid's constant promises of a clear path to the top. 'Yeah, Jos doesn't care if somebody talks F1 blah, blah, blah,' believes Michel Vacirca. 'He just needs the material to go racing and after half a year of things being a little late, patchy results but saying to Jos not to worry, we will help you get Max to F1, I can imagine how Jos would have reacted. They argued. I talked with Jos at this time and very slowly I tried to convince CRG to give Max a second chance and return. In the end, they did so without my direct involvement, but it wasn't an easy thing.'

Whatever the political and financial challenges, Jos was pushing against an open door, so big a Max fan was CRG boss Tinini. 'Every race with Max was a bet,' he says today. 'The euphoria that he put in the whole team gave you a passion to go watch his races. Every race, his grit gave us a different emotion. And this put all eyes on him.'

When asked what made him special, Tinini immediately cites Max's ability on cold tyres. 'In this way, he reminds me of the great Danilo Rossi, who did not win five karting world championships by chance. Another distinctive trait is the aggressive full-on racing style, certainly inherited by the paternal DNA, as Jos was the typical "bad dog" that nobody would like to have as an opponent. Max has the same determination but faster. Max was so fast. Sometimes you could see at the end of the race that he had a flat tyre, but you didn't see that in the lap times. Because of his aggression, you never saw that he was in trouble. That was impressive. You were already 90 per cent sure that Max was going to be world champion. Also, he has the same competitive instinct as another of our old drivers, Lewis Hamilton, someone who had to be first in everything, even if it was going down the stairs or drinking a hot chocolate!

'To have a dad like Jos has surely been an added value, not only because he too has been a Formula 1 racer, but also because Jos is a person who lives the racing environment always in a genuine manner, without having any problems in getting his hands dirty with grease like any of the mechanics. The only danger, at the time, seemed to be that the guide could become a harness which, while preventing too many falls, also risks limiting the movements only in one direction. Jos' personality has always been strong, and the boundary between advice and order can become very subtle to decipher, especially for a son. Today, we know the advice was wise, and the kart racing son has grown up to become a great champion.

'Max has important qualities that very few have, like spontaneity. He still has fun; he has always been playful and funny with the guys in the team. I have seen guys with half of the championships won by Max being way too cocky. His spontaneity gets to people and he does not criticise.'

Max returned to the CRG fold (entered under Michel Vacirca's CRG Netherlands banner to ease the political difficulties within the factory team) for the second half of the 2012 season. In addition to his KF2 campaign he was also racing in the gearbox class, as he was eligible for the first time as a 15-year-old. This category – labelled KZ2 – isn't usually for those on the ladder to car racing but a more senior class, with bigger, faster karts for professional kart racers, many of whom compete there for years. Many of those Max was racing against here had competed against Jos first time around. But it was more experience, more skills to acquire, more lessons to be learned as Jos sought the ultimate fast-track to their F1 ambitions.

Heavier, more powerful, with brakes on the front as well as the rear and a six-speed gearbox, these karts demanded quite a different driving style, but that seemed to present no drama to Max. 'With a KZ kart you drive angular,' observed Jos at the time, 'and with a KF, which has no gears, a bit rounder. But Max now drives that smoothly with a KZ and therefore takes a lot of speed out of the corners, which is not normal. Max is doing amazingly well . . . his way of driving is just insane. I can't say anything else.'

So well that he was all set to win the KZ World Cup at his first attempt as they prepared for the final at Sarno. This was the infamous occasion of Max's second-lap misjudgement, with Jos' resultant fury getting Max kicked out of the van at the petrol station.

He'd won the pre-final quite comfortably, despite having started from 10th after a clutch problem in one of the heats. He was up to second at the end of the opening lap and leading by the second. His win there put him on pole for the 33-kart final alongside Daniel Bray, a Kiwi racer 10 years older. They were wheel-to-wheel for the first few corners but Max prevailed and at the end of the opening lap the pair were already pulling clear of the pack. Bray was providing a stern challenge though, pushing and probing, forcing Max to be quite defensive. On the second lap Bray managed to slipstream Max down the back straight, enabling him to slip up the inside at the following right-hander to take the lead. This was a 26-lap race, though, and it wasn't so unusual for the lead to change multiple times. It was a situation Max had been in many times before and Jos would not have been too concerned at this stage. Max would surely figure out the high-speed puzzle and know where and when he needed to place himself.

Once in the lead, without the aid of the slipstream, Bray's pace wasn't as hot as it had been and in the next few corners the pair were being caught by 20-year-old British driver Jordon Lennox-Lamb. Perhaps feeling that he didn't want to be caught in a multi-kart dice and that he needed to repass Bray and pull out a margin, Max dived down Bray's inside into a fast right-hander, a pretty risky passing place. It was almost a forerunner of the Verstappen/Hamilton crash at Silverstone 2021, but with Max in the role of Hamilton and Bray in the role of 2021 Verstappen. Bray began to turn into the corner leaving Verstappen out of options, his front wheels on full right-hand lock as he desperately tried to avoid contact. His front-left wheel connected with Bray's right-rear, the leader's kart reared up into the air and Verstappen slid straight on. His kart fatally damaged, he climbed out, paving the way for the race and the World Cup to be won by Lennox-Lamb.

'It was dumb,' admitted Max many years later. 'There were 26 laps and for sure I could have passed him later.'

The Pex family saw the familial fall-out and it wasn't pretty. 'Jos demanded a lot from Max,' said Richard Pex in *Whatever It Takes*. 'The bar was high and when Max didn't meet it Jos could go berserk. But that was his way to push Max.'

All that effort, the hundreds of thousands of miles in the van, the hours spent on the engine dyno, the grind of test days, not to mention the financial strain of it all: these were likely foremost in Jos' mind in his reaction to the simple on-track error. The moment was re-lived by the Verstappen and Pex families in *Whatever It Takes*.

'It was such a stupid move,' recalled Jos, who had only just finished installing a new clutch on the kart after Max had burned the original one out in the heats. 'I had done so much for that race. Time and energy. And I was so mad. I tore down the tent and threw everything in the back of the van. I was so depressed. Max was crying.'

Richard Pex: 'It was heartbreaking to see Max that disappointed and we know Jos didn't like it when we consoled Max so we had to be careful.'

When Max asked for help bringing his damaged kart back to the van, Jos snapped back: 'Bring it yourself.' Stan Pex helped him carry it. 'Max wanted to come home with us,' he recalled, 'but he wasn't allowed. He had to deal with his angry dad for 1,800 km. It's scary when Jos gets that furious. At least we were scared.'

'I've never seen my dad like that,' recalled Max. 'He literally grabbed the go-kart and just threw it into the van. Of course, when we sat in the van, I wanted to talk to my dad about the incident. My dad said, "Stop talking, I don't want to hear anything, just sit in the back, I don't want to hear anything about it."'

After Max insisted on continuing to talk, they stopped at the service station and Jos left him there. Max: 'I called my mum and she was behind us on the motorway. Five minutes later, she arrived. We were about to drive off and then my dad returned with the van and was like: "Get in, but I do not want to hear a word." Because my dad was with his at-the-time girlfriend, for sure she talked to him and said, "You cannot do that."

'At the time, I wished I was able to throw him on the floor. But I wasn't strong enough. But inside I had this anger towards him. I was desperate to show him how good I was.

'I was working with my dad to try and get the best out of it. At the time, I thought: "Should I really be like this? Should it be the way I am working?" But I am really happy we did that.'

Jos is insistent that the 2012 Sarno incident and the subsequent fall-out were absolutely key in making Max the full package, someone who finally properly understood at a deep level the lessons he had been trying to instill in him all these years. 'Losing has to hurt,' said Jos. 'I think he finally understood after this.'

Probably he did, once he got over the anger and shock. As he told *GQ* in 2021: 'Even before then, Dad had said, "It's going great, but you will lose. It's not gonna be great forever.' It helps a lot later on – like now, in Formula 1. You learn to lose, to give it its place. Because you have to accept that you cannot win every race.

'I really started to understand the importance of being patient in the race. I think I needed a hard reset at the end of that year to be better the year after.'

There was only one more 2012 event after the KFZ debacle: September's KF2 World Cup in Zuera, Spain where Max was a photo-finish second behind 21-year-old Felice Tiene.

And then in 2013, Max's final year of karting, he won pretty much everything – and there has really been no turning back ever since. Though desperate to show his father how good he was, the Verstappen stubbornness would ensure he did it in his own way. The fists that Jos reportedly used to challenge his own father in such situations, Max would keep down at his side. He had the nous to know that none of it would happen without Jos. Nevertheless, Jos was not going to dominate him. Not even after that extreme display in Sarno. *Especially* not after that. It was such a fine line Max was treading, internalising the toughness without assimilating the anger. And that's perhaps the most remarkable thing about him, the trait which, allied to his stunning raw ability, has made him the phenomenon he is.

'The driver must have the talent,' says his one-time Toro Rosso team boss Franz Tost, 'and Max has the skills but it's like a diamond; to bring him really to the highest level you must work on him and Jos did a fantastic job, one of the best jobs I've ever seen from a father. Other fathers are there, they give the money, but they don't understand it like Jos did.'

Max came back better the following season to win the prestigious 2013 titles in both the direct drive KF (European champion) and the gearbox category KZ championships (European and World Champion). The KZ world championship was a single event. 'The equipment worked fine,' he said after the race. 'The start went well, I took the lead on lap five and I gradually got away, leaving my rivals to fight behind me. A perfect race! The fact that it was my father who prepared my KZ engines enhanced the satisfaction of winning the world title. I can now move to cars with the certainty of having a successful and outstanding last season in karting.'

The only one which got away was the KF world title, held over two meetings at Brandon, UK and Sakhir, Bahrain, the latter around the kart track within the grounds of the F1 circuit. Verstappen won comfortably in Britain but his kart didn't seem to be at its best in Bahrain and victory there – and the crown – went to British driver Tom Joyner, five years Verstappen's senior. But even Joyner acknowledged he'd only taken the lead of the race 'when I saw Verstappen in trouble.'

The FIA, as the sport's governing body, summarised its 2013 karting season as follows: 'A leader of the younger generation, disrupting the hierarchy, Max Verstappen imposed his immense talent on the face of the world. He managed the feat of winning the CIK-FIA European KZ and KF Championships just a few weeks apart, ahead of the top specialists, before being crowned world-wide in KZ. Although the CIK-FIA World KF Championship narrowly escaped him at the closing meeting in Bahrain, he was undeniably the #1 driver of 2013, rich in high level clashes.

'The 15-year-old Dutch prodigy Max Verstappen (CRG) won the CIK-FIA European KZ Championship in two Competitions. After two victories, he took the lead on renowned professionals like Marco Ardigo (Tony Kart) and Anthony Abbasse (Sodi).'

'Disrupting the hierarchy', an arresting phrase within such a dry journal of record, captured the mood perfectly. That is, after all, what Max had always done up to that point. And it is what he would continue to do, until there was nowhere higher to fly.

5

MAN AND MACHINE

'You can talk to him on the radio when he is in a 300 kilometre-per-hour corner and it's like he's sitting down having a cup of tea.'
Helmut Marko

There was a time, around the age when he first began karting, that Max was also into soccer. He loved playing but it wasn't an enthusiasm shared by Jos, so it never really developed into anything. It seems unlikely that he would have excelled at that game as he did in racing. But who knows? A retired fellow player once asked soccer legend George Best to stand still so he could look at him. George asked why and the other player replied, 'Because I only ever saw the back of you.' It was as if Best had more 'frames per second' than other players, could process the movements and positions of players more quickly and read the ball so instinctively that he would dance through gaps rivals had not yet seen, leaving them uncomprehending.

Max Verstappen's skill in a racing car is of a similar order, although of course it's a very different skill. So what makes one driver faster than another? It's not a well-researched subject, maybe because it's so much less visible than a soccer or tennis player's skill. But a British defence company that sponsored the Williams F1 team for a time once shared some of the data it used to select physiologically suitable candidates to train as fighter pilots. It found that sensitivity to yaw and rotation were the crucial skills in that endeavour, and it's quite feasible that these are equally important in determining the 'natural' speed of racing drivers. The researchers suggested that this sensitivity originated in the lower spine, from where nerves relay messages unconsciously – and therefore without any reaction delay – to the middle ear. There is significant variation between individuals in the efficacy of this neural pathway, and this could go some way towards explaining differences in natural ability.

It's commonly assumed that fast reactions – the time it takes for your central and peripheral nervous systems to receive a stimulus, process it and create the correct response – are what the best racing drivers have in common. But this is almost certainly a myth. Michael Schumacher, one of the sport's very greatest, had his reaction times measured when he was at Ferrari and they were found to be distinctly average – 'about the same as mine,' as team boss at the time Ross Brawn put it.

Dr Riccardo Ceccarelli, whose Formula Medicine concern has trained and monitored a high proportion of F1 drivers over the last couple of decades, has also conducted this test and found no significant correlation between reaction times and performance. 'The range is completely normal from fast to slow reactions within a group of racing drivers, no different from that of any control group,' he reveals. 'My secretary actually had one of the best scores.'

Faster reactions are probably better than slower in rescuing any emergency situations in the car. But they don't seem to play any significant part in guiding a car around a circuit faster than the next guy. Understanding what the car is doing through physical sensations in the feet and lower back, being sensitive to the messages it is delivering, filtering out which are irrelevant and which critically important, is the key.

That filtering process, as David Epstein explains in his book *The Sports Gene: Talent, Practice and the Truth About Success*, is common to all elite performers from chess grandmasters to NFL quarterbacks, but it is not genetic, he concludes. 'No one is born with the anticipatory skills required of an elite athlete,' he believes. Instead, they are honed by years and years of dedicated practice.

What the research shows is that intensive training enables top performers to develop sophisticated cognitive models, a vast database of mental templates that allows this filtering process to take place incredibly efficiently and without conscious effort. As Epstein explains: 'Where a novice is overwhelmed by new information and randomness, the master sees familiar order and structure that allows him to home in on information that is critical for the decision at hand.'

Epstein explains that research tracking sportspeople's eye movement has shown that: 'Experts swiftly move their attention away from irrelevant input and cut to the data that is most important to determining their next move. Perceiving order allows them to extract critical information from the arrangement of opponents or from subtle changes in movements in order to make unconscious predictions about what will happen next.'

All his rivals have done the hours on the kart tracks, but Max really did them and had them scrutinised mercilessly by Jos. He may have developed better mental models than the rest, perhaps since strengthened by his endless hours of sim practice, allowing him to start responding to his opponents' moves before they have made them.

But what lies at the core of the basic raw speed, there right from the start? Max always downplays it by saying, 'It's just two pedals and a steering wheel.' It's probably something he never dwells upon; why deconstruct the magic if it's working perfectly well?

It is worth drilling down a little further. Which of his inputs give him the biggest advantage on lap time? What does his sensitivity allow him to do in the car to increase that performance gap? Once you get past the low hanging fruit – taking the optimum line through a corner (the racing line), hard braking up to the turn – what is Max doing that the car is responding to?

The car's limits under braking and through a corner are

defined by the grip of its tyres on the track surface. The part of the tyre in contact with the track at any given moment is called the contact patch. Those four small patches of rubber are all that is connecting the driver to the asphalt. The feedback from them to the pedals, the steering wheel and, literally, 'the seat of the pants' gives the driver the sensations on which, in addition to the visual cues, their inputs are based. Through the left foot, they will sense the available grip of the track as they brake, and from this they will decide how much speed to take into the corner.

In an F1 car, as much as 3,000 kg of aerodynamic down-force forcing it into the ground through the tyres further complicates that braking phase. Because downforce squares with speed, there is a lot more downforce as the driver begins to brake than when the car has slowed. In mathematical terms, the downforce reduces at a rate of the square root of the speed – in other words very, very fast. So drivers stand as hard as they can on the brake pedal initially, but must then modulate that pressure, as the downforce plummets, to stop the tyres from locking up. The better the driver can feel the reduction in downforce through their braking foot, the more accurately they can match that with pedal pressure so that the tyre is always just on the right side of locking up. Push too hard and you lock the tyres and ruin the lap, not hard enough and you are surrendering lap time. Meanwhile, what is too hard or not hard enough is constantly changing.

Through their bum (probably via those sensors in the lower spine and their direct pathway to the inner ear), the driver will feel the 'rotation' of the car as they turn into the corner and triangulate that with what they are seeing. The word rotation is used a lot in driver coaching and vehicle dynamics: it means the transition from straight ahead to the angle of the corner. This cannot happen instantaneously; the tyres need time to build up their grip. How quickly and predictably the car rotates determines the driver's approach and speed into the corner. Up to a point, the sooner it rotates, i.e., the quicker its response from straight-ahead to the desired angle, the faster you can be.

In the transient state between getting the car to begin turning, and the point where it is pointed straight at the apex of the corner with the steering lock removed, the car is in 'yaw'. Yaw is the difference between the direction of travel and the angle of the car. The shallower the angle of the car's nose to the direction of travel, the more the front is trying to run wide in a state of understeer. The greater the yaw, i.e., the deeper the angle of the car to the direction of travel, the greater the oversteer (where the car turns more than the driver is commanding it to with the steering wheel).

The quicker the driver achieves that transition through the yaw to where the car no longer needs to be steered to maintain its angle, the earlier they can get back on the gas pedal. Steering, dragging the front wheels across the track, bleeds lap time. You need to get that over with as quickly as possible, preferably well before the apex.

But if the car rotates too quickly for the rear tyres to keep up, it can induce a time-consuming slide as they skid across the surface.

The driver can set up the car's suspension and aerodynamics to give what for them is the optimum amount of rotation. The more agile the car upon corner entry – i.e. the quicker it rotates – the faster it should be through the corner. But the driver has to be confident they can retain control of that rotation with their pedal and steering inputs so as not to spin or slide. Where and how they apply the brakes doesn't just influence how the car slows down, it also determines how quickly they steer through that yaw phase in the corner.

Finding and extracting all the grip available between the beginning of braking and getting the car to the apex of the corner is where the magic lies for F1 drivers. It requires them to use the brakes and steering to instinctively manipulate the weight of the car between its four contact patches as it goes through that transition. Under braking, the weight moves towards the front, under cornering towards the outside, under acceleration towards the rear and that determines how each tyre behaves. How the driver determines where that weight goes is a very dynamic process, typically blending the braking and cornering phases together. It's invisible from outside the car, but in that brief-blink moment resides most of the difference between a fast and a very fast driver. It's where

Max Verstappen becomes a shaman of speed, doing things most other drivers cannot.

'I like a pointy car but with a rear that is *just* stable enough to have a controlled balance,' he explained in an interview with *Autocar*. 'I like a strong front end, I don't really like understeer, it's just killing the whole feel of the car. But yes, a strong front end with a rear that is just on the edge. But of course, you still need that rear to rely on.'

The point at which a car's rotation can no longer be controlled by braking and steering inputs – the rear stability limitation – is different for each driver. The less rear stability the driver can live with, the faster the car can be made to go. A more benign car with lots of rear stability will be slower to rotate and therefore easier to drive. But for the same level of total grip and power, its lap time potential will be slower. The optimum balancing point of stability will be largely deter- mined by the driver's feel and sensitivity, the fidelity of the sensations they are experiencing and the inputs they make in response.

'Max has a total self-confidence and ability to deal with a car that is a little bit loose at the rear,' says Christian Horner, 'and an ability to use that on entry into a corner. So, where the big difference between him and his teammates has been, it's never really been in the high-speed stuff – Pierre Gasly, for example, in a high-speed corner would be as quick if not quicker than Max. But it is that whole braking phase into the corner. Look at Turn 3 in Austria, for instance, which is always a standout corner for him. If the rear of the car isn't completely planted, because of his sensitivity and feel – almost like a motorcycle rider – [he can] effectively be right on the edge of adhesion on corner entry and if the rear is moving around, it doesn't bother him. What he wants is a really positive front and he will deal with the rear.'

Michel Vacirca, who ran Max in karting for all those years, an ex-racer himself and someone who has worked with hundreds of drivers, observes: 'Somebody who wants to drive like Max, you have to brake late and then feel that pressure from your feet to the brake. I have people here who are asking, "How many bar of pressure should my son brake on the pedal?" And I say, "Yeah well, I can tell you easily, but in the end, you also must *feel* how the grip is on the track."

'Max's responses are so fast, the moment when he feels that the car is going away, it is like he's already making the response. Mostly drivers, they don't do it wrong but the response is too late and that is why the kart will spin. But they don't want to admit they feel it too late. They always have an excuse. You get a lot of theory and data . . . sure. But that is the crucial difference.'

It can look like faster reactions, but it's not. He's just feeling what the car is doing earlier through those neural pathways, which go direct to the brain, enabling him to respond earlier with the necessary inputs.

Max intuitively understands the dynamics and how to make the car go faster, even if not always the technical reasons behind that, something which Frits van Amersfoort observed in his F3 season running Max. 'The best thing about Max in F3 was he always knew where to find time, he didn't need to see the data. He just felt it. And that's something you don't see that much. An average race driver, normally gets better where he was always good, but forgets where he was weak. And it was the opposite for Max. He knew where he was weak and what he had to work on, and that's the talent, that's something you can't teach. Charles [Leclerc] was exactly the same; from day one they knew what to do.'

Atze Kerkhof, Max's partner in the sim racing team Redline and a driver coach in real-life F1, has the advantage of being able to see Max's simulator input data. Many real-world racers – particularly those of a previous generation – just cannot perform on a simulator and so give up as it doesn't interest them.

Similarly, there has so far been no super-successful transition from sim to real-world racing. If you are to succeed in real-world racing, the hours need to be put in, in the real world. The sim cannot be a substitute for that because those hours on the sim are not teaching the brain all the same things.

Max applies the inputs he has learned from the real world to the simulated medium, whereas sim racers generally learn those skills from copied data from actual racing – as that is how the software has been set up. But it's the same data and such is the sophistication of the simulators that the same inputs are rewarded in the same way. Making those inputs doesn't feel the same, however: there is no accurate representation of the sustained g-forces and the feedback loops so these have to be learned. In sim racing it is all visual. In the real world, it's feel and vision. For Max to apply what he has learned in the real world to the sim requires hours of training.

But now that Max has mastered sim racing and can apply his natural style there, his inputs are representative of what he's doing in the real car – and this gives Kerkhof a very good understanding of his skill.

His summary – on Verstappen's YouTube channel – is very similar to Vacirca's, just expressed slightly differently, from the digital age rather than the karting tracks. 'Someone just slamming on the brakes as late as possible and hitting the throttle would be whole seconds off the pace. You need to be very dynamic in your driving to be quick and Max is incredibly dynamic. He can drive an impossible car and still send it over the limit just on the edge of optimal performance better than anyone.

'When the Red Bull was a bit of a lazy car [at the beginning of 2022] it was very easy to drive leaning towards understeer. Understeer is a very boring way to drive a car because whatever you do with the brake pedal, at a certain point the car just doesn't rotate more. A pointy car wants to rotate more than you want and what Max does very well is he can balance the car that is too pointy for everyone else because for them it starts sliding. Max can make that car perfectly smooth and make use of that extra rotation and he can cancel it with his inputs on the points where he doesn't need it.

'You can extract more from a car if you can handle that kind of balance. With a textbook driving style – aggressive on the brake and very smooth coming off, turning at the right time, you can get within five-tenths [over a lap]. But that last five-tenths is dancing on a very thin line, balancing the car and stepping away from that textbook braking style – it's still there in the basics but it needs to be adjusted intermittently in millimetres to have a positive effect on the balance. And that's what he and Charles Leclerc can do better than others. Also, getting to 101 per cent straightaway. The sooner you reach the limit the more accurate your feedback can be to the engineers because the time on track is so limited.'

Kerkhof then goes on to recall Max's pole-setting qualifying lap in the Bathurst 12 Hours simulation, around the mountain course where the walls are close. 'The difference was he was always able to take a bit of a deeper line in because he was able to rotate the car just a bit better [than anyone else].'

The lap time value of Verstappen's sensitivity to yaw and rotation will vary according to the traits of the car and the demands of the corner. The way he can so exquisitely trade-off braking and cornering forces can enable him to either turn in later for a more geometrically perfect line and maximum apex speed, or earlier for a faster approach but a lower apex speed. The first might be more effective on a slow corner leading on to a straight, where the higher exit speed will continue to reap rewards all the way down the straight. The latter may be optimum where there's time to be gained on corner entry and the exit speed isn't so important. In this case, he will be turning in earlier, with a shallower angle which will require more turning to be done at the last moment, from inside the ideal line. In this case, he will overlap the brakes with the cornering to create more rear yaw, enabling him to scrabble through the corner and lose less on the exit than he's gained on the entry.

Both approaches require strong front-end grip from the car. For the aerodynamicists, the ideal F1 car, the one with the theoretically fastest lap time, will have more downforce at the front, where it is less costly in drag than at the rear. Hence the push to bring the downforce balance on the two axles as far forward as possible. But that means at high speed, as the downforce squares with speed (it's squaring on both axles but the increase will be more on the heavier-loaded axle), the car will naturally want to oversteer. At low speeds, even with the forward balance, it will tend towards understeer as the bigger, more powerful rear tyres push the car on with less opposing aerodynamic force. The more comfortable a driver is with high-speed oversteer, the less understeer they will have to contend with in the slow corners.

His teammate of 2019 and 2020 and former karting rival Alex Albon observes of Max: 'As well as a very good understanding of the limit, he also seems to not feel things in certain ways which can make a driver feel uncomfortable when they're driving. For instance, with the wind or instability in the car he seems to be able to switch off his brain when it comes to that side of racing. If you speak to any of his teammates, including myself, they'll say he seems to be able to drive a very difficult car.'

The closer a driver's set-up can be to that aerodynamic ideal, the more potential lap performance there will be. 'What Max is brilliant at,' says Jenson Button, 'is getting the best from a car with an aerodynamic balance which the wind tunnel says is the best. Most drivers find that balance horrible and adjust the car away from that to give them the confidence they need to commit to corners. But he can just drive it like that.

'Lewis [Hamilton] can drive with pretty much any balance, it doesn't seem to matter. He can seem to be struggling but when the moment comes he can just pull the big lap out of the bag regardless of the balance. But Max does seem to be at his absolute fastest with a very unstable car. I think he can get even more from such a car than Lewis. But maybe Lewis' spread is wider, I don't know. It's very close.'

•

The 2022 Red Bull initially had a weight problem, an excess of 25 kg over the minimum permitted by the regulations. Just in terms of power-to-weight ratio, that would cost around 0.7 seconds of lap time. But for Max it was worse even than that. The weight distribution was too far forwards, which made the front tyres prone to lock up under braking, creating the sort of understeer which places a false ceiling on Max's potential. With development through the season, the team was able to take more weight off the front than the rear, freeing Max up to use those dynamic, weight-shifting skills to blinding effect.

'Developing a quicker car definitely means having a stronger front for Max,' says Horner. 'You saw that with Mercedes as well, as they developed their car, that gap diminished between Lewis and George [Russell]. I think some of it was a characteristic of the new [for 2022] regulations; as teams start to learn about the tyres and the set-up and you start to optimise the car, you inevitably start to create a car that has a stronger front, and that then started to play more to Max's strengths.'

Ironically, a couple of years earlier, Max's ability to wrestle a very pointy car so consummately had led Red Bull to go too far in that direction, as we'll see later, masking a problem with a car and sending the team down a blind alley of technical development.

Red Bull's Helmut Marko describes how Max's race engineer 'GP' (Gianpiero Lambiase) will say, '"Look after the temperature of the front tyre." He does but eventually the tyre wears and the temperature starts to drop – but the lap time stays the same! He keeps the same speed, makes a different balance from the engine controls or drives a different line and just finds another way to do it, straight away.'

That same ability is what saw Max extract enormous performance from the improvements to the 2022 car. This was never more apparent than at Spa for the Belgian Grand Prix when he showed a staggering level of superiority through the demanding high-speed corners in a car with visibly oversteery balance. Meanwhile the car was incredibly fast into and through the slow corners, as the usual understeer there was banished. On seeing this in qualifying, the race engineer of Sergio Perez in the other Red Bull advised his driver over the radio that the only way to close the lap time deficit to Verstappen would be to increase the front wing angle – which would reduce the slow-speed understeer but bring a less secure feeling in the high-speed corners. There was a pause before Perez replied: 'I cannot carry any more front wing.' Taking grid penalties for power unit replacements, Max started the race from 14th place but was leading by one-third distance and pulling away. It was the most resounding of all his victories so far.

The only driver that Helmut Marko has seen that he thinks comparable is Ayrton Senna. 'Similar. But Senna was more structured. With Max, it's more natural. You watch the early laps on a wet track, he's three seconds faster than anyone. Or a dusty new track – it takes three or four laps for the others to begin to close the gap. You can talk to him on the radio when he is in a 300 kilometre-per-hour corner and it's like he's sitting down having a cup of tea.'

'Look at Brazil 2016 in the wet,' says Marko. 'He can even make a spin 360-degrees and it hardly costs him any time and he is flat out again immediately, not even looking for a gear or anything. He has like a 360-degree gyroscope or something in his head!'

That spare cognitive capacity even when driving a car close to the limit is one trait all the great drivers seem to share. Dr Riccardo Ceccarelli has spent decades monitoring driver performance as part of his Formula Medicine driver training business.

One of his early areas of research was heartbeat and its relation to performance. Once a driver is up to the necessary physical condition, all variations in heartbeat are stress-related, he explains. Typically, when a driver is asked to extend himself – at around the pit stops, say – his heartbeat will increase by around 20 bpm and the lap time improves. Why, Ceccarelli asked himself, could a driver not maintain that level of performance throughout? Where that question led was to research on brain activity during driving.

The correlation between performance and heartbeat tracked uncannily closely in every race he monitored where a driver was wired up. Back at base, studies on drivers' brain activity while on simulators – which parts of the brain were being used and how much bloodflow (and therefore energy) was going to them – showed a very high correlation between brain energy usage and heartbeat.

Driving an F1 car on the limit is mentally exhausting and just stepping back slightly from that limit reduces the stress disproportionately. But rather than lose performance to give the brain a rest, Ceccarelli's training concentrates on making the brain more economical, using up less energy, thereby reducing the stress upon it which in turn makes it possible to drive closer to the limit for longer.

His studies show that repetition and familiarity with the task increase the brain's economy during the performing of those tasks. The more energy-efficient the brain, the less taxing it is to drive.

'Also, without the adrenaline, driving the car, working and mixing with many people, being without those things can have a bad effect on the mental clarity and sharpness,' Ceccarelli says.

'So it's important that you set targets for each day. A monkey needs to be fed with bananas. A racing driver needs to be fed with competition. Every day. So it can be that instead of just riding the bike on the rolling road, either they set a target time to beat, or they use the software that allows them to compete with others.

'A simulator is great but don't just go on the simulator; set targets, compete against yourself, try always to be better, then analyse the data. This is all necessary in keeping the brain working efficiently.'

Clearly, Max takes his sim racing very seriously and competes at the highest level, spending many hours preparing for each event. Does this give him an edge? Ceccarelli's research would suggest so.

'Picking a line, defending or attacking, finding the limit on the braking,' lists Kerkhof. 'There's a lot to it and it can only be done fully if you drive with the subconscious mind where everything is natural and in a flow and you can survive when you send it [out-braking a rival] without locking up. If you cover that with hours of practice on every corner of every track and understand where you're strong and where you're weak you become a much smarter driver.'

As Horner says, 'I think Lewis started racing online because he thought that it was giving Max an edge. Whether it gives him anything I don't know, only he can judge that one, but he just loves that adrenaline rush of racing.'

Ceccarelli doesn't claim to be able to make everyone into Max Verstappen. 'I don't think I can transform the last driver to the best,' he says, 'but I can make each driver as good as he can possibly be. The brain is a muscle. If you have a weak area, it doesn't mean you are psychologically unsuited, it can just be you are not using your brain at 100 per cent because the muscle is not developed.'

One small detail Max revealed to David Coulthard may sound insignificant but suggests just how relaxed and confident Max is in his own ability, how well his inner gyroscopes work and perhaps also how relatively little of his brain capacity he needs to perform – and therefore how he could be achieving that 'brain economy' that Ceccarelli seeks to instil.

'He told me he doesn't wear his seat belts very tight,' reveals Coulthard, winner of 13 grands prix. 'The fact that he has the confidence to be free in the car I find quite remarkable. I wanted to be bolted to the car, didn't want to move. The fact that he is able to feel relaxed with a looser physical connection to the car is, I think, very interesting.'

Ceccarelli cannot talk about specific drivers and their performance but if we are looking for what might be the link between talent and training, in the case of Max Verstappen we can appreciate he has benefited from enormous amounts of both.

Combine all that with the psychological make-up of Max as someone so intensely competitive and convinced in his own mind that he can prevail over anyone and you begin to get some idea of just how near-impossible it might be for anyone to prove that wrong. As Kerkhof believes, 'Max is as good as he is right now because of a brilliant natural gift and millions of hours of training. He's only got better. The rough edges have gone and now he's like a machine. You cannot beat him.'

6

FAST TRACK TO FORMULA 3

*'We could put Max in an F1 car tomorrow.
After one day. That's the truth.'*
Frits van Amersfoort

It is not normal to do only one season of car racing between karting and F1. Kimi Raikkonen did it in 2000 as a 20-year-old, and the next person after that was 16-year-old Max Verstappen in 2014.

It was during Max's final season of kart racing in 2013, when he was only 15 years old, that he tried a race car – a Formula Renault 2.0 – for the first time at a secret test in Pembrey, in the middle of rural Wales. Formula Renault 2-litre was a good entry point into cars from karts, with slick tyres and downforce-producing wings but relatively low-powered engines. It was the category in which both Kimi Raikkonen and Lewis Hamilton had won their first championships in cars. It was Jos' initial choice for the next phase of the project to get Max to F1.

The car was run by the Anglo-Dutch MP Motorsport team and had been arranged with the help of Dutch TV commentator and former racer Allard Kalff. 'That whole period up to F1 was very well thought out. Even the move into cars,' recalls Kalff. 'Jos would always phone lots of people, taking their readings, getting different opinions and I think that's something that Huub [Rothengatter] didn't do in Jos' career. Jos realised that had probably been a mistake.

'He phoned one day and said, "Find me a team to do a Formula Renault test, but it has to be in secret." Hence Pembrey, well away from anywhere. But they did many follow-up tests with other teams at other tracks and after listening to Max's feedback about the cars, Jos decided to miss out Formula Renault.'

MP Motorsport was run by Tony Shaw and his engineer wife Sarah for the Dutch co-owner Sander Dorsman. Dorsman was more than aware of the sensation of Max Verstappen in karting and after being contacted by Kalff offered Jos the test for free. Back in 2000 when he was an employee of Manor Racing, Tony Shaw had run Raikkonen in his Formula Renault title-winning season. He oversaw Hamilton's first test in cars the following year. Thirteen years later he was about to encounter another phenomenon.

'Max was a lovely lad, very grounded and sociable. In the car, he was just incredibly rapid straightaway. Not really much more to say. It was a two-day test and it was wet the first day, eventually dried out on the second. We brought our driver from that year, Oliver Rowland, along but really Max didn't need any coaching either from Oliver or the engineers, he was just totally on-point straightaway. On his out-lap in the wet he was so committed we were a bit disbelieving that this could really be his first time in a car. But Jos said seriously, it's the first time. He never put a foot wrong and was so deft with the controls. That calibre of driver makes the others look a bit wooden.'

'He was making Jos nervous,' Kalff remembers. 'When he first came in Jos said, "Can you just take it easy and get yourself keyed-in first," and Max said, "Dad, I am taking it easy." On that wet first day he did a 360-degree spin on to the pit straight out of the final corner and just carried on as if nothing had happened, lapping just as fast next time through.'

Hamilton had been only a few months older than Max was now when Shaw had overseen his first outing in a car, in 2001, also in a Formula Renault. But Shaw is keen to clarify that it's impossible to make a direct comparison. 'It was a different situation. First of all, Lewis did half a day in the car at Mallory Park which is a bit trickier than Pembrey, especially on a cold October day and on a general test day with lots of other cars flying around. Whereas Max's test was very structured and over two days of exclusive track use. Secondly, the car back then was less sophisticated than the one Max drove. It was more of a handful back in 2001 than in 2013. It had a stick-operated shift, sequential but still requiring you to match it carefully with the braking, smaller tyres, less grip.

Lewis just eventually lost it over the bump going into Gerard's when he was really going for it. It didn't faze him; he was absolutely on it again when we put a corner back on the car. But he just took the thing by the scruff of the neck in a very limited amount of time. He didn't mess around, Lewis. He just went hell-for-leather straightaway. Whereas the test with Max, it felt a lot calmer. That day with Lewis you got a sense that we might have a bit of work to do later on – accurately as it turned out – but we didn't feel that with Max's test.

'What they had in common as young teenagers is that they were both bloody quick and totally unfazed to be in a racing car. With both of them you just knew they were going to be incredible. With Kimi, it was slightly different again, because he stayed in karting until he was 20, because they didn't have the money to move up. So he was a much more experienced racer by the time he first sat in a car and as a 20-year-old, probably rather than a 15 to16-year-old, he was closer to his real potential. But he too was incredible.'

Without a shadow of doubt, then, Max's explosive skill in karting was going to translate into cars. But exactly which car it would be, with which team and, perhaps most importantly of all, how it would be paid for was not at all clear at this stage.

'There was no Dutch backing at all at that stage – no sponsor wanted to help,' says Kees van der Grint. 'I was there when Max had won the World Karting Championship at Fiemme in France. Max was the last champion on Bridgestones when it was still a free tyre competition rather than control tyres. I have a picture from that day of me with Max, Charles Leclerc who was second and Jordon Lennox-Lamb who was third. Jos was there, Huub Rothengatter and Raymond Vermeulen. Together with me and Max, that makes a total of five Dutch people who were there. No one else. No one was interested.'

But even without the finance in place, Jos pressed on with the test programme once the karting season was over. There were more Formula Renault tests all over Europe as Jos and Max completed their due diligence. MP Motorsport had him in the car again at Zandvoort, Hockenheim and Jerez. Sarah Shaw recalls: 'I had a driver who had already done two years in the category and who went on to win races in 2014, so he was no slouch. But in the tests Max was so advanced that I went to him for feedback on the car and circuit in order to help my driver.'

'As an Anglo-Dutch team we really wanted him in the car,' recalls Tony. 'At every track we tested with him, he was either on the pace or he was the pace. We'd have run him for free; would have just put him in the car, told him to win some races and earn us some money from future custom. That's how certain we were about him.'

But from Jos' side, there was no reason to commit to anything just yet. The next move had to be right. Max also drove with Team Koiranen – the Finnish outfit with which Valtteri Bottas, Daniil Kvyat and Carlos Sainz Jr had all won Formula Renault titles – in Alcarras, Spain. Then with Team KTR at

Hockenheim and at the official Formula Renault rookie test in Barcelona. He was fastest of all the Formula Renaults while testing for Tech 1 at Budapest's Hungaroring, just ahead of his former karting rival Alex Albon. Then he got his first taste of the formidable Spa where, driving for the Kaufmann team, he was again fastest. Now creating a stir, the German Motopark team invited him to try out its Formula 3 car in a test at Valencia. He went fastest of all the F3s there.

•

A Formula 3 car is a much more sophisticated piece of kit than a Formula Renault 2.0, with considerably more downforce and power. Usually, a driver would step up to it after a season or two in the Renaults. Yet Max adapted to it instantly. In fact, he much preferred it.

'The F3 is a bit heavier but it's an absolute joy to drive,' he reported to *Autosport*'s Marcus Simmons. 'I was able to adapt rather quickly to the car so I felt confident to push, but I honestly did not expect to be fastest. Working together with my engineer and the whole team was a great experience. It's all very professional and a step up from FR2.0, there's a lot more data and attention to detail needed.'

'I think it was Huub who had arranged that F3 test,' recalls Kees van der Grint. 'At the time Huub was saying, "This guy is so good we [should] go immediately to F3". But Jos was saying 'No, no, no, we must do it a step at a time and do Formula Renault". So they had big arguments about this.'

As well as being faster, Formula 3 was also a lot more expensive than Formula Renault, which was something of a dilemma for Jos.

Then came a left-field call: the Ferrari Driver Academy was going to run a short winter series in Florida for F3-like cars (Formula Abarths), organised by Lawrence Stroll whose kart-racer son Lance was a Ferrari junior driver at the time. It would give Ferrari a chance to benchmark the latest emerging talent against their Academy drivers Raffaele Marciello (who was racing in F3) and Antonio Fuoco (from Formula Renault). Max was invited to take part. The catch was he'd have to pay almost 100,000 Euros for the privilege. Rothengatter took care of that.

In addition to the Ferrari juniors, Max would be racing against F3 racers Nicholas Latifi, Tatiana Calderon, Dennis van der Laar and Ed Jones, Alex Bosak from Formula Renault and karters Vasily Ramanov and Takashi Kasa. There would also be a media guest car shared between Will Buxton, Ben Anderson and Oliver Marriage to maximise exposure for the series, held over four venues.

Everyone's telemetry would be available to everyone else. Max – the youngest driver in the series – established himself as the quickest, with three poles and two wins. But it was his telemetry traces which made the biggest impact on his rivals. Despite lacking any car racing experience, he was often able to take more speed into slow corners than anyone else. It put him very much on Ferrari's radar.

But Florida wasn't an entirely happy experience for the Verstappens. 'There were arguments between Jos and the organisers, because he thought the electronics were not consistent between cars and Max was at a disadvantage,' recalls Van der Grint.

While Jos was no stranger to a bit of competitive paranoia, there is always that element of doubt with a control formula – where the engines are provided by the organiser of the championship rather than by independent companies, as in F3 – that someone might be getting an unseen advantage. Whether the feeling was justified or not, it played a part in Jos' decision to forget Formula Renault and do as Huub had suggested by going straight to F3.

'Jos hadn't been convinced about F3 but in the Florida series there had been races where Jos was absolutely furious, you know, telling them the engine was shit. So whether it was not true or true, for me that was a good sign,' says Frits van Amersfoort.

On the other hand, Renault, with a ladder of categories and an F1 involvement (even if only as an engine supplier at that time) looked on the surface to be a useful link to F1. But as we saw in previous chapters, Jos was determined to retain full control of Max's career and was absolutely opposed to him being part of anyone's junior driver squad. Van der Grint recalls how Jos had knocked back what he saw as an insulting offer from Renault when Max was still in karting: 'He came to me and said, "Read this", and it was a ridiculous proposal where

Renault would have him under contract and he'd get support and be a test driver in the future – but they were required to pay Renault. Jos knew what they had in Max and said, "No way". Renault should regret that whole episode, it was ridiculous.'

So slowly, Jos began to come around to Huub's way of thinking, especially after Max had proved so rapid in his F3 Valencia test. 'Jos had thought about it very carefully, weighed it all up,' says Allard Kalff. 'I recall him phoning me and telling me they were now thinking F3 because Max had been so at ease in the F3 car, much more than the Formula Renault. I was baffled – and said, "Are you sure? If you win Formula Renault, Renault will help you." He said, "There's a bigger chance we won't win in that category than we will win. But if we go F3 it's our first year so if we don't win the championship, it's no big deal and we can do another year." Also, it was a change of regulations for F3 going into 2014 so it was a good time to go in because everyone starts the same.'

Rothengatter was keeping his friend and F3 team owner Van Amersfoort up to speed with these discussions. 'Everybody could see that he was going to be a special driver,' says Van Amersfoort, 'because he was fastest in nearly every test they did. I spoke lots of times with Huub about that in those days.

'When they returned [from Florida], Huub came by and said the plan was looking more like Formula 3 now. Obviously, I was keen to get him in the team somehow. I didn't know how, but . . .'

It's true that Van Amersfoort's team was not the obvious destination on paper. The team hadn't exactly covered itself in glory in European F3 the year before. It had been their first year in that championship and they had not been competitive. Van Amersfoort is the first to admit the season had been 'a bit of a mess'. European F3 was a big step up from German F3 and his days running Jos and other Dutch drivers in the GM Lotus category (where he had gone on to further success with Vincent Radermecker and Tom Coronel).

'Although we were no fools, we were not completely sure if [2014] would be a great year or not, because it was a big step for Max and our record wasn't great. So I said if Max drives for me and it's not super-successful, you can always say, yeah the team were shit, they're an amateur team, they're new in F3.'

Also working in Van Amersfoort's favour was the fact that Prema, perceived as the category's top team, had a direct affiliation with Ferrari – which was a problem for Jos who had a pathological aversion to ceding control over Max's future. And after all, Van Amersfoort Racing hadn't won all those championships in the lower categories by chance and the team had been Jos' foundation to success all those years ago. So now Frits' close relationship to Rothengatter brought another Verstappen to his doorstep.

But Jos had his doubts, as he explained at the time to Dutch journalist Linda Vermeeren. 'We didn't know how fast they were. I know team boss Frits Van Amersfoort very well. He's great and I immediately had faith in engineer Rik Vernooij, but I still had my doubts. But since it's a learning year for Max, it's great to start on familiar territory. The better he performs, the more distance I will take. But I'll keep an eye on things. After all, Max is only 16 and still has a lot to learn.'

'When they said, "Let's do it", we still had no car and no engine,' Van Amersfoort relates. 'I had a good relationship with Volkswagen from our German F3 times through [VW Motorsport boss] Kris Nissen, but he had gone by now and in his place was Jost Capito. He organised a works Volkswagen engine. But at that moment I didn't have the finance to buy the 2014 Dallara. They were trying to find sponsors but no one was interested. They had some friends, I called them, and everybody said no. We phoned all the rich people of Holland, the [Korean chemical company] Youngbo guys and the [Dutch digital company] Trust guys and everybody said no.

'Today, the director of Trust says, "Oh, it was the biggest mistake of my life not backing Max" but back then there was nothing coming, it was already February and we didn't even have a bloody car.'

Jos' colourful back story was causing some resistance even among potential Dutch backers. 'Jos has always been good for a drama, let's say,' says Van Amersfoort, 'and that's why people love him; you know, it's not the fine, polished article. But it's also sometimes why people were reluctant to align themselves.

'That's when Huub said, "Fuck it, then I'll do it." In the beginning he didn't want to, because you know Huub is famous for trying to drive a bargain. But in the end, he realised, now we have to switch to first gear, we need the car.

'Jos didn't want to invest in the car, Raymond didn't want to invest in the car. I can't judge whether they had the money or not, but you know, putting a new Dallara on the road was nearly 200,000 Euros. So Huub really started the career of Max financially.

'Huub organised the finance, Huub also organised the first instalment of the championship. We made the deal and it was all decided within two hours. We started working on it immediately. We worked hard to get the car together; you bought the car from Dallara, the electronics from Bosch, you put it together, you bought a clutch, you bought shock absorbers, the wheels, the whole thing. So it was pretty tight!'

So tight that the car wasn't ready in time for the first official pre-season test in Most, Czech Republic; Van Amersfoort borrowed a chassis and built up a car around it. But they had their own car ready in time for the next, in Budapest. There, Max was quickest, ahead of all the more fancied teams, and Van Amersfoort dared to think about readjusting his horizons.

'That's a Verstappen!' he gushed in a BBC interview. 'They keep amazing you. Any Verstappen, whether it's Jos or Max, they will always astonish you with what they can do. Their drive to be fast is so phenomenal, so intense. It sounds a bit weird, but after one day inside the team, we said to each other: "We could put Max in an F1 car tomorrow." After one day. That's the truth.'

•

For all the hyperbole, Van Amersfoort's words were more prophetic than even he could have bargained for. The whirlwind season ahead of them, 33 races over just 11 weekends, was supposed to be the dress rehearsal for a more serious assault on the title the following year. But that plan was dust almost from the moment Max took to the track in anger. By June 2014, he would become the hottest of F1 properties.

Though they didn't know it, 16-year-old Max's speed in testing and practice for the opening round of the European F3 championship on the April weekend of the Silverstone 6 Hours immediately put him on the F1 radar. Red Bull team principal Christian Horner monitors the junior racing ranks closely and even though he was at the Chinese Grand Prix that weekend, he found time to catch up with the F3 practice times. Verstappen had been third in the first session, (within a few hundredths of the Prema drivers Ocon and Fuoco) and fastest of all in the second session.

'He was in a team that wasn't expected to be near the front,' recalls Horner. 'For a guy that had just literally stepped out of karting, he was *hugely* competitive. So there was a bit of hype around him, and I was impressed for someone so young to make that step, knowing how big the void is between karting and F3. And I was very impressed how quickly he managed to adapt to get up to speed. I think Helmut [Marko] then obviously started to take notice of him.' More notice, perhaps. Marko had been in touch with the Verstappens on and off since 2010 about the idea of Max joining the Red Bull junior driver roster. True to his covenant of not allowing Max's destiny to be controlled by anyone else, Jos had always resisted.

While that opening Silverstone weekend went downhill for Max, with a clutch problem in the first race and a poor start in the second which limited him to fifth, there was a promising third race in which he chased down and passed Esteban Ocon and finished second to Fuoco.

But there was a very significant breakthrough at the season's second meeting, in Hockenheim, Germany, as recounted here by Linda Vermeeren, who was there keeping a close eye on Holland's racing prodigy.

'It was intense. Both Max's parents were there. There was drama, there were crashes, Jos got mad, his mom Sophie emotional. And Max, he was so young. It must have been so difficult at 16-years-old to deal with all this. Having to deal with yourself at that age is hard enough, let alone dealing with the pressure of his parents and the expectations of the media and the entire motorsport community.

'I remember him standing in the garage, slightly dazed, picking at the carbon fibre nose of his F3 car. He'd broken that nose in a crash during the weekend's first race. He'd had contact with Nicholas Latifi, after which the team told him to stop. You could read the disappointment on his face and at 16 the resemblance to Jos was uncanny, both just as frantic. But you could tell he was intelligent – great feedback, driven, focused and a nice, humble character.

'He'd got a decent start from fourth position, unlike [Antonio] Giovinazzi who blocked him, causing him to lose two positions. Eager as he was, he wanted to make up those places almost immediately. He tried to out-brake Giovinazzi on the inside of the Spitzkehre but misjudged the situation after which the collision with Latifi was inevitable. "I braked too late," was his short explanation. The damage was manageable: bent wishbones and tie rod and a dent in the nose. While Jos frantically helped fix the car with an angry expression on his face, Sophie was there to comfort her son. "I saw the tears in his eyes," she said. "I would have loved to have given him a hug, but on track that's not done of course," she said with a smile. A couple of hours later I found Max still sulking. "I should have known better," he said sadly.

'This is only his second race weekend. He'd been immediately on the pace at Silverstone, a sign that had justified the bold choice of the Verstappens to skip Formula Renault. But as we all know, Jos isn't one to beat about the bush. He's always straightforward and gets angry when necessary. Of course, Max is allowed to make mistakes, but this crash was just stupid and I told him that. I always speak my mind. I've always done that and I'm not going to stop now. Max knew it wasn't a smart move. So I explained to him what he could have done better and hopefully he learns from it.

'However, disaster struck again as soon as Max left the pit lane. The car refused to shift gear. In the end the team managed to get the car out the pit lane in time but Max never reached the grid due to a gearbox problem. As a precaution for the final race all the electronics were replaced, only for the team to discover another issue 20 minutes before the start of race three. They changed the ECU with just enough time for Max to reach the grid. The tension was palpable. But Max got away well, leading and opening out a gap over Ocon. The team and parents seemed relieved.

'Then a safety car and a period of consolidation but Sophie was agitated, much to the amusement of Jos. He laughed at her nerves but he had been chewing on a plastic tie-wrap for over half an hour himself. When Max won, his first victory in cars, at just 16, everyone was overwhelmed in ecstasy.

'Although Max was overjoyed, he was also remarkably calm about it. "Actually, in F3 it's easier to get ahead than in karting because you know the competition can't get too close anyway because they lose downforce. So to be honest it was quite a relaxed race for me," he said without batting an eyelid. But he admitted that he didn't actually expect to be able to win races in his first F3 season. "But I feel comfortable in the car. So now I want to win as many races and finish as high in the championship as possible," he said. You could sense the determination behind those words, determination that was previously there but now re-directed at a higher target.'

There were a couple of barren meetings between that first win and Max really hitting his stride. Around the streets of Pau, he was not on the pace of the dominant Ocon, his karting rival from three years earlier. After spinning out of the wet second race there, Max had a first-corner collision with Ocon at the start of race three, ruining both their races. Ocon was a tough competitor, never one to back down, and extra formidable now he was in the crack Prema F3 squad after a two-year grounding in Formula Renault. He would become Max's big title rival in this season and there was little love lost between them.

In Hungary, a clutch problem and another driving error left Max a long way behind double winner Ocon in the points table. 'That difficult race at the Hungaroring, when Max ended eighth was the one time the relationship with Max and the engineer was starting to crack,' recalls Van Amersfoort. 'Max was already very demanding and the engineer was standing his ground. Raymond can sometimes be the mediator, so we survived that. And of course, afterwards came these fantastic three races in a row.

'But you know the funny thing is, from the side of the race team, working with such a kid, it's so easy. You don't need to do anything to get him fast. He was always fast. Always . . . the only thing is, they want to be on top of the list every, every day, no time to relax.

'These guys are incredible in terms of how they live their racing, sometimes even maybe a bit too much from the human side. I don't want to judge that but I receive a lot of emails from young drivers, and especially fathers, who don't realise what Jos did with Max, to raise him in a way that from the human side they would find unthinkable. But I think many top sportspeople were raised in a special way.

'Anyway, we felt we needed to gain something again from the car and from Max, and we planned a test not specifically but by coincidence exactly the period that Jos got married somewhere in the Caribbean. And the test went really fantastic. But I remember that Max, each time he got out of the car, he was phoning with Jos, telling him exactly what was happening.'

Max bounced back from that tricky Hungary weekend in the best possible way at Spa, technically his 'home' circuit as he was born in Belgium to a Belgian mother, even though he's always maintained he feels more Dutch. The mix of super-fast turns through the Ardennes valley, punctuated by three key tight corners along its four miles and the long slipstreaming straights make for a formidable challenge. On Max's first visit pre-season, he'd been quickest in the Formula Renault. Now it was for real and he dominated the whole weekend, emerging victorious in all three of the races, the last of them particularly impressive in the way he soaked up enormous race-long pressure from Ocon.

•

A week later the F3 circus decamped to the Norisring, Germany. Victory in the first of the three races came after fighting his way to the front from third on the grid with dramatic out-braking moves, notably on Ocon for the lead. He led the second race from pole on an initially damp track which became wetter and despite several safety car restarts, he was in commanding form. The more slippery the track, the bigger was his advantage. It was only the safety car that limited his winning margin to nine seconds.

Although he didn't know it, this weekend would shape the rest of Max Verstappen's life. Watching the live coverage on line very carefully, monitoring the lap times, was Red Bull's driver 'guru' Helmut Marko who had been intrigued by Max ever since that first Silverstone race and had made contact with Jos shortly afterwards.

'It would rain, begin to dry, then rain again,' Marko recalls of the second Norisring race, 'so very changeable conditions, the corners different every time and Max was in a class of his own. There were times where the others were braking and he was still accelerating and changing up. He was up to two seconds faster than the others at times. In the rain, he's in a class of his own, looking for where the grip is, and immediately he has a feeling of the limit. Nearly everyone else has to find it, he is immediately on it. He had a few moments, but in controlling them he always gained. No other guys do this.'

The final race was similarly changeable and was eventually red-flagged short of its allocated distance but Verstappen's win was never in doubt. Ocon followed five seconds behind. He'd now won six races in succession and was hot on Ocon's tail in the championship.

Marko says: 'Max was educated by watching with his father and by the internet. That helps if you can use your intellectual capacities in racing. The way he overtakes, he has that concept in his head of all the variables and the spatial awareness that even many successful drivers don't really have.'

Marko had been speaking to Jos about the idea of Max joining the Red Bull squad since the Monaco Grand Prix in May and this is where Jos' careful playing off of Red Bull and Mercedes really began. Although Mercedes did not have a fully structured junior programme at the time and its F1 seats were occupied by Lewis Hamilton and Nico Rosberg, both Toto Wolff and Niki Lauda had spoken with Jos about the possibility of Mercedes backing for Max to move into GP2, the next step on the ladder to F1. Ferrari too was maintaining contact.

Given how the speed of his own rise had been part of his downfall, Jos may have been anxious about how fast things developed in 2014. But he had made sure Max was far better prepared than he himself had been. There was also a financial impetus to grab the passing opportunity created by Max's stunning form – it was still not certain how a second F3 or first GP2 season could be funded. Max's on-track momentum had got them this far, but motor racing is an extremely fickle business. Big chances rarely come around twice.

Marko had followed up on that Monaco discussion by way of a sit-down with Max in Austria, and the teenager impressed him with his interviewing skills. 'Max and I had the longest discussion of any driver,' he relates. 'He has a supermarket sponsor. I asked him about them and he knew how many people it employed, where its headquarters were, how many outlets it had. I had an advantage because I'd researched it before. By contrast, once we signed an American driver and when he told me he was going from Graz to Munich I said he should stop at Salzburg. 'Salzburg? What is Salzburg?' Mozart, I said. 'Mozart? What is this?' Unbelievable . . . If I was going to Red Bull to talk about a contract, I'd make sure I knew all about the place. Max arrived very well informed.'

After the weekend at the Norisring, Marko resolved to strike while the iron was hot. He was on the phone to Jos early the next morning. "Jos, forget about all the other stuff. We want to take Max straight to F1."' There was silence at the other end of the phone. 'I said, "Jos, Jos, are you okay? Talk."'

Just four months had passed since Jos, Frits, Raymond and Huub had been discussing how to fund Max's F3 season. Now he was going to F1. Jos and Raymond would negotiate the terms but essentially it was agreed.

'Jos did exactly the right thing with Helmut,' says Van Amersfoort, 'by keeping them at bay for as long as possible, and then at a certain point, "Now it's time, we will talk", and then he had his F1 contract. But these characters fit together. Helmut likes the risk, likes the adventure. You need balls to say no to Helmut. But that's Jos. And I don't think he even thought long about this. He just thought in the early days, Max is not ready for Red Bull, we keep Red Bull at bay, and funnily enough Helmut also said, "Okay, I'll wait." And I don't think Helmut will do that ever again. It's fantastic to see how that materialised, the whole deal.'

Meantime there was an F3 season to complete. Although the next round of the championship would be in Moscow, before then there was a non-championship event which Max just couldn't miss: the Zandvoort Masters race. This traditionally brought together the front-runners from all the national F3 championships and had been won in the past by Jos. The advent of the European championship had probably reduced its status since its heyday in the 1990s but the chance for Max to perform in front of his rapidly growing Dutch fanbase was just too good to miss. But it was for older-spec engines than the European championship and with Van Amersfoort committed to the logistics of getting from Norisring to Moscow, Max arranged a drive with the F3 team for which he'd tested pre-season, Motopark. In front of full grandstands, despite the rain and the wind, he blitzed the race from pole to take his consecutive victory tally to seven.

That run, however, would come to an end in Moscow where Ocon emulated the triple that Max had achieved in each of the previous two rounds. Max fought Ocon hard for victory in race three after a mechanical retirement in race two and a third place in the first race. Not ideal, but it still left the championship wide open with four rounds to go.

The Red Bull Ring, perhaps because it was the home track of the team that had agreed in principle to recruit Max, seemed to upset his equilibrium. Maybe he was too keen to impress. He got involved in incidents with Ocon and Fuoco for which he received grid penalties. The only saving grace was that Ocon went winless too.

It was shortly after this race that Max's recruitment by Red Bull and his 2015 F1 drive with Toro Rosso was made official. A 16-year-old had just been announced as an F1 driver. For the next F3 race, at the Nürburgring, Germany, Max's car would be in Red Bull livery. In the meantime, he drove some publicity laps in a Red Bull-liveried Formula Renault 3.5 at the Red Bull Ring.

Van Amersfoort still doesn't know exactly what went wrong with Max's car at the Nürburgring. He'd just won the first race and was leading the second when the engine lost oil pressure and the conrod went through the side of the block. It dealt his championship prospects a body blow because the regulations insisted that any engine change would mean 10-place grid penalties for the following three races – effectively giving Ocon a clear run to the title.

'The Spiess family running the Volkswagen engines, they're as much in my heart as F3 is,' says Van Amersfoort. 'They are lovely people and care passionately about racing. They were building these Volkswagen F3 engines and there was the new 2014 engine, with a 28 mm restrictor, and in the beginning, it was not so reliable. Basically, after each test the engine had to go back to Spiess and we got them back on the Thursday before the race and had to build them in again. A couple of times, the gears on the front, the bolt sheared. We were managing that problem early in the season but they worked very hard and came up with a fix, so at a certain point they became really reliable and fast. But why it blew at the Nürburgring we don't know.'

Max wasn't giving up without a fight. At Imola race two, he made a brilliant charge up through the field (having qualified fastest, his engine penalty had him starting from 11th). He made it up to second, only narrowly losing out to Tom Blomqvist. With the grid position for race three determined by the finishing position in race two, and Max's penalties now having been served, he started the last race from the front row and duly converted that to victory. But it wasn't enough to prevent Ocon from sealing the championship.

It was back to Hockenheim for the championship finale. He won the first race from pole but on the following day the pace mysteriously disappeared, with Max 0.8 seconds slower than he'd been for the first qualifying. Starting ninth, he could do no better than fifth in race two and sixth in race three. It meant Max was jumped for runner-up in the championship by Blomqvist. In career terms, with an F1 contract already in his pocket, it didn't really matter. But still, there was a sense of the season petering out in a very un-Verstappen way – a low-key end to a truly spectacular campaign. No doubt that would have caused major ructions within the team, with Jos at the heart of it, if the playing field had not already changed.

'We never did get to the bottom of that,' says Van Amersfoort. 'I think it was engine-related and we had some discussions with Spiess but it was not resolved. I remember that Jos was very pissed off.'

All that was left now was the traditional F3 season-ending non-championship race around the streets of Macau, the single most prestigious F3 race of them all, won in the past by Ayrton Senna and Michael Schumacher. Max wasn't destined to add his name to that particular list, but was in typically attacking style throughout the weekend. Jos came to oversee things.

'The funny thing was, Jos had never done Macau in his day,' recalled Van Amersfoort. 'He was due to do it but Huub pulled him out to do the F1 test at Estoril. But we had been there, we had experience of the track. Max was out there in qualifying and it wasn't going very well and Jos wanted us to bring him in and make changes to the wing angle but we knew it was just a matter of Max getting knowledge of the place and we wanted to keep him out. A big row developed on the pit wall between Jos and my engineer Rik. "Get him in!" Jos was shouting, "No, fuck off, we're not doing it!" said Rik and as they were arguing Max crossed the line to go third-fastest. I thought it was very funny.'

That determined his starting slot for the qualifying race, the finishing order of which would determine grid position for the main race the following day. Desperate to be on pole for the main event, Max crashed out trying to take the lead of the qualifying race on the fourth lap. That put him a disastrous 24th on the grid for the main race. From there he finished seventh. But there was a story behind that result.

'There was a pile-up in the feature race,' recalls Van Amersfoort, 'like usual in Macau, and Max's car was badly damaged. The only way to continue was to get back to the starting grid, but all the marshals told him to get out because they wanted to tow it away.

'He refused to get out. He stayed in the car and there he was, hanging from a crane as they lifted it free of the crash! As soon as they put him back on the track, he drove back on three wheels to the grid and we were able to repair the car. He ended up finishing seventh from the back.

'This incredible drive, this incredible will to win, I haven't seen anything like that before, and I've seen a lot of race drivers.' And with that, Van Amersfoort's thrilling ride with his second Verstappen came to an end.

'It was fantastic working with these guys,' he says. 'They were two copies in the car, going full throttle all the time, no limits, always bang straightaway.

'They are not programmed to lose. But at this level you have to be prepared, because it becomes unbearable for the team otherwise. Max was able to do this better than Jos. He didn't like losing, of course, but he was able to deal with it better. In some ways, he was already more advanced than Jos.

'Even in the garage Jos was sometimes unreasonably demanding. I could understand where it came from but I could also see when it was too much. Sometimes the team suffered from having him there because of the pressure he was putting on us. But you know, so what? Because he is also the kind of guy who, when there was a problem with the gearbox once in practice, Jos just stepped into his Audi, went full gas to Dallara a thousand miles away to pick up the new gearbox and was back the next morning. That is also Jos. He can be a pain in the ass but also works really, really hard and gave everything for Max, the full 100 per cent. Just like Max gave us in the car. It was a privilege.'

7

FROM ROOKIE TO RECORD BREAKER

'Max Verstappen, you are a race winner. Fantastic.'
Christian Horner

'I take my hat off to Max . . . He is a talent of the century . . .'
Niki Lauda

Max Verstappen's F1 experience began while he was still in the midst of his F3 season. It was mid-August 2014 when Red Bull announced on Austrian TV that it had recruited a guy who was still 16 to race in F1 for Toro Rosso the following season. This was just days after it had confirmed Verstappen would be joining the Red Bull junior driver roster. Some had assumed a Red Bull-backed GP2 drive would follow, not realising that Jos had only allowed Max to join the squad on the basis of a rock-solid F1 contract, one which even included a few practice outings at three of the remaining 2014 grands prix.

After the shock of Marko's post-Norisring phone call to Jos, Max had raced his F3 cars at Zandvoort and Moscow with the F1 promise still to be hammered out and signed. On a weekend off from the F3 schedule, Jos and Max went as Red Bull guests to the German Grand Prix where they discussed things further with Marko. But still they didn't sign. Maybe that pressured anticipation, with nothing yet down on paper, contributed to Max's erratic performance at the Red Bull Ring the following weekend. But it wasn't going to deter Marko. A few days later Max, Jos and Raymond Vermeulen travelled to Marko's hometown of Graz. The deal was done.

Once it had been announced, Max revealed there had been interest from other teams. 'Yeah, we got some phone calls when we started winning in F3,' he replied. 'But we'd been already talking with Red Bull since 2010. It was the feeling which made the decision.'

Allard Kalff, the F1 commentator, breathed a sigh of relief: he could finally step down from his role as a go-between. 'I'd had three or four F1 team bosses telling me they wanted to talk to Jos about Max,' he recalls. 'So I'd pass the message on. And Jos would say, "Yep, but I'm not going to sign." I asked why and he said, "The longer I can keep it open, the more control of the situation I have." That was very clear thinking.

'They never thought they were going to do F1 when they did. [Jos] was talking to Toto and to Helmut and thinking, who is going to give me the best deal long-term? There was no hidden agenda. They each knew he was talking to the other. One day he phoned me and told me the options,

Mercedes has offered us this, this and this. But basically, with Red Bull we can do F1 next year. I said, "Repeat that!" I thought I'd misheard. Then I thought about it and told Jos if he thought Max was good enough, why not. "Just make sure you sign for three years, get a commitment."'

Jos was pretty sure – but not as sure as Max himself: 'Even my dad was saying, "Are you sure? Are you sure you want to make the jump straight to F1?"' he recalled to Channel 4's David Coulthard. 'And I said yes, because even if I make mistakes there, I'm in.'

In an earlier interview with F1i he had expanded upon the emotions behind it. 'As soon as I heard, I was jumping up. I was like, "I'm ready for it, I want to go for it," because after a season and a few races of F3 I felt, "Okay I think I can make the jump now." As a driver you always think you can make the jump. When you get that opportunity, you don't say no, you go for it.'

No amount of inner certainty and confidence, however, could insulate him from the visceral sensation of watching an F1 car on the track. On that visit to the German Grand Prix, his initial reaction was: 'Oh my god, how am I going to drive those cars?!' as he related to Chris Medland of F1i. But he knew, really, that he would be just fine.

'It has to come from yourself,' he said in the wake of the announcement. 'Even if your dad is pushing you, for five or six years it might be alright but in the end, you wouldn't enjoy it any more. Luckily it wasn't like that. Dad knew what went wrong in his career and we're trying not to make the same mistakes. He's trying to make Verstappen 2.0!'

They were missing out GP2 – the traditional bridge between F3 and F1 – just as they had missed out the Formula Renault step between karting and F3. Only Max's incredible ability had made such short cuts feasible at such a young age.

The normal rules just didn't apply. Red Bull, specifically Helmut Marko, felt they needed to act decisively to secure what he believed was a phenomenon, a once-in-a-generation talent. But it still seemed quite a leap of faith.

That was certainly the view of quite a few within the F1 establishment. Mika Hakkinen, world champion of 1998 and 1999: 'It's too young because in F1, the risk is high that you damage your reputation if you are not ready.'

Jacques Villeneuve, 1997 world champion: 'It's the worst thing ever for F1. It's like getting all the presents without deserving anything. You need to pay dues; you need to deserve it because that is only how you will become a man.'

'I hope he hasn't been accelerated up to that level too quickly,' said Damon Hill, 1996 world champion, 'because that can set you back for a very long time if you're not careful.'

There was a suspicion, too, in some quarters that setting a new record for the youngest-ever F1 driver was just another attention-grabbing marketing move by Red Bull. But while it's true that the hire was a good fit with the we-do-things-differently Red Bull brand, the impetus was purely a racing one for Marko.

For the Verstappens, F1 was just another racing car and they were used to confounding everyone. Disrupt the hierarchy: it's what Max had done in every new category he'd ever taken part in.

'I knew what the reaction would be,' said 17-year-old Max in *The Next Generation* documentary. '[They would say] too young, not good for F1 . . . they just think I'm a 17-year-old guy [who] jumps in an F1 car. But we already had so much work before to have even the chance of getting in an F1 car.'

Marko had seen enough to know Max was a special case. And that belief quickly spread through the rest of the Red Bull organisation.

'He was five years ahead of his age mentally,' says Marko today. 'I could see the maturity and the commitment and how his programme had been with Jos. He wasn't a kid when you met him. He was a very seriously committed racing driver who had shown fantastic ability already.

'I said at the time that I thought the only guy I could compare him with was Senna and I got a lot of criticism for that, even from my good friend Gerhard Berger. But now Gerhard says I was right, that the comparison is valid.'

There may have been a certain schadenfreude for Max's detractors when, on his first appearance in an F1 car, in a publicity event where he drove an old Toro Rosso over the bridge in the port of Rotterdam, he snagged the front wing against a barrier as he was making a spin turn. 'Yeah, we got all the "teenager in an F1 car" barbs from that,' laughs

Christian Horner. But in reality, it was simply that he had not experienced an F1 anti-stall system before. 'I was trying to turn the car,' he explained. 'The anti-stall kicked in and it pushes you forward again. I was too late to take the clutch.'

From there, Max was off to the Toro Rosso factory in Faenza, Italy, where he would be shown around by his new team boss Franz Tost. Another Austrian, Tost had started out as a driver in Formula Ford in the 1980s (he won the Austrian championship in 1983) but made his career in team management. He came to F1 via Ralf Schumacher as BMW's track operations manager and was recruited by Dietrich Mateschitz to run the Toro Rosso team after he bought it in 2005.

Tost is fanatically hard-working and characteristically Austrian in his eccentricity, unbending in his views. As F1 was discussing how sustainable a 24-race calendar might be, Tost replied in all seriousness: 'The year has 52 weeks in it. I don't see why we can't have a 52-race calendar.' He has no time for under-performance.

Marko's role in relation to the team principals was un-usual. Even though his only official role in the company was as head of driver development, as a long-time close friend of Mateschitz – a genial, low-profile presence at the top – his roving role carried a lot more weight in reality than on paper.

Mateschitz didn't get involved in the actual running of either the Red Bull or Toro Rosso teams, leaving that

respectively to Horner and Tost. He'd make the big investment calls, ensuring they had everything they needed within
the budget they had been allocated. But Marko did not answer
to them, indeed he had never answered to anyone in his life.

From a family of lawyers, he'd been something of a teenage
tearaway in the early 1960s, along with his local friend Jochen
Rindt (who would go on to be the tragically posthumous F1
world champion of 1970). Among many shenanigans in the
snowy Austrian winters would be sneaking out of their homes
in the dead of night for some automotive duels. Marko would
'borrow' his parents' powerful big Chevrolet and Rindt would
turn up with his own VW Beetle. In the darkness, they'd race
through the mountain roads. The Chevrolet wasn't allowed
to pass on the straights because of its power advantage and
in trying to out-manoeuvre Rindt's Beetle one night, Marko
plunged into a ditch. Rindt stopped to check his friend was
okay, but once that was established, he simply laughed and
left him there. That was the spirit of their adventures; if you
got into trouble, it was your mess to sort out: 'No risk, no fun,'
as Marko put it later.

Their local school could no more handle them than their
families (Rindt had been orphaned in the war and was raised
by an uncle and aunt) and they were sent to boarding school.
The same one. Hence their escapades continued, their fierce
independence only intensified. At the end of the year, rather
than go home to hand their bad reports over to the grown-
ups, they travelled down in Rindt's Beetle to watch practice

for the 1961 German Grand Prix. That's when Rindt decided he was going to be a racing driver.

For Marko, without the inheritance Rindt enjoyed, that seemed an impossibility. Upon leaving school, he studied law and qualified with a doctorate in the subject. By the time he too took up motorsport – buying and selling cars to fund his exploits – he was a few years behind his friend. But he was good and in the late 1960s was established as the man to beat in European Formula Vee. A young upstart called Niki Lauda came along to provide some competition in 1969 and at the Nürburgring, Marko had to resort to some fairly brutal defensive moves to keep him behind. So began their adversarial relationship.

Marko was competing in a hill climb when a young fan called Dietrich Mateschitz introduced himself. He'd been inspired into following the sport by the exploits of Rindt who by this time was established as F1's fastest and most exciting driver. Marko and Mateschitz became firm friends.

Marko's career continued in the ascendancy even after Rindt was killed in practice for the 1970 Italian Grand Prix. Together with Dutch driver Gijs van Lennep, Marko won the prestigious Le Mans 24 Hours of 1971, driving for Porsche.

Later that year he made his debut at his home grand prix (as did Lauda) around the track then known as the Osterreichring (but which in later years would become the Red Bull Ring), a track that had only come into existence because of Rindt's successes.

And so we see the cross-pollination of the Red Bull, Marko and Rindt stories, a vital chunk of F1 history that has played a direct part in Max Verstappen's success. (Rindt, incidentally, had been managed by a young entrepreneur called Bernie Ecclestone who, after Rindt's death, moved into F1 team ownership.)

Marko's F1 career continued into 1972 with the BRM team and when not racing there he continued to compete in the sports car world championship. An amazing performance in that year's Targa Florio for Alfa Romeo so impressed Ferrari that he was invited to stand-in for the injured Clay Regazzoni there at his home sports car race, the Zeltweg 1,000 km (at the Osterreichring). He led for a time before mechanical problems. His reputation hot, when he arrived at Clermont Ferrand in July for the French Grand Prix, he had in his briefcase a 1973 contract offer from Ferrari for a combined F1 and sports car programme.

He'd qualified his BRM on the third row and was racing Ronnie Peterson around the mountainous circuit when a stone thrown up by his rival's car pierced Marko's visor and lodged in his left eye. He managed to pull the BRM off to the side of the track before falling unconscious with the pain. Safety provisions were awful in those days and it took hours before a doctor could be found to operate. He lost the eye and with it his F1 career. Lauda took over the BRM drive the following year and subsequently the Ferrari drive Marko had been offered.

Marko invested in hotels in his home town of Graz and in the 1980s returned to racing as a team owner in the junior categories. He established a reputation not just for the quality of his team but also as someone who understood the psychology of his drivers and could coach them to be better. Gerhard Berger and Juan Pablo Montoya were among those who raced for him in F3 and F3000 respectively. Montoya recalls: 'He invited me to his house for lunch once. He offered me vegetables, which I didn't eat in those days. I had the meat. He then made me run to his office and back. It was about an hour of running. I was pretty miffed at the time. But he was doing it to move me forwards . . . He had me living in Graz, I hardly had any money but he took good care of me.' Tough love. Does that sound familiar?

Marko's team came to be sponsored by the soft drinks company of his old friend Mateschitz: Red Bull was also sponsoring the Sauber team from 1995. But by the late-1990s, Marko was looking to ease off and set about selling the assets of his F3000 team. They were bought by a very young Christian Horner, who had hung up his helmet after a moment of realisation when he'd witnessed Montoya doing something in the car he couldn't dream of.

Marko suggested to Mateschitz that he could continue his F3000 sponsorship with Horner's new team with Marko taking on the driver development role. Horner's Arden International team won its first F3000 race, in the Italian championship with Warren Hughes at Imola in 2000. It went on to success in the European championship with Vitantonio Liuzzi and Bjorn Wirdheim in the following years. By the time Bernie Ecclestone had convinced Mateschitz to purchase the Jaguar and Minardi teams in 2005, Horner's dynamite record in F3000 made him the obvious candidate for team principal of the rebranded Jaguar team, Red Bull Racing.

Red Bull became one of the most important sponsors in F1's history, finding and backing young talent, not only in motorsport but in almost any high-risk adventurous activity. 'No risk, no fun,' was a phrase Mateschitz and Marko would come to repeat to each other.

It was also a phrase Marko used when asked whether signing a 17-year-old to F1 was not a risk. There was definitely an element of Marko cocking a snook to the prevailing racing wisdom. He'd already helped Sebastian Vettel become the youngest ever world champion. Now he'd try to better that record and in Max he thought he saw everything he needed to do that. Not only the talent but the attitude, the commitment, the appetite for risk, the straight talking. This was a very personal thing for him. It's tempting to imagine Max awakened the spirit of the rebellious young Marko. The Verstappens were the beneficiaries of his enthusiastic crusade, probably way more than they had anticipated. It made Max's position far stronger than it would have been at, say, Mercedes or Ferrari. He was much more than just another driver in the Red Bull programme. He was Marko's pet project. This would come to have an influence on the dynamics of the team in 2015.

Jos had driven for the Minardi team in 2003, his final season of F1. This was two years before Mateschitz bought it as his junior team and rebranded it Toro Rosso. So, as Tost took Max on his factory tour there in 2014, there were people being introduced to him who had worked with his father 12 years earlier. Some of them even remembered Max as the small kid Jos had brought with him a few times. Now he was their driver.

He would be replacing Jean-Eric Vergne, the Frenchman who had been given his F1 chance there in 2012 but who Marko had decided had not shown the stuff of a future world champion, having been generally out-performed by Daniel Ricciardo in his first two seasons and by rookie Daniil Kvyat in 2014. He was a good hard racer, more than worth his place on the F1 grid, but Marko needed to create a space for this new phenomenon. Vergne was the casualty of that imperative. But there was the possibility of a career lifeline later in the year when Red Bull's multiple champion Sebastian Vettel informed the team in late October that he would be leaving to join Ferrari in 2015.

Kvyat was instantly promoted to the senior team as Vettel's replacement, leaving a vacancy at Toro Rosso. Vergne therefore had hopes he might be retained, after all. But Marko, keener to try new talent than persevere with a guy who he felt had been given his chance and not measured up, was already in serious talks with Carlos Sainz, the legendary multiple rallying world champion of the 1990s, about his 20-year-old son Carlos Jr. He had been in the Red Bull junior driver roster for the last four years and had won the European Formula Renault 2.0 championship in 2011 and the faster Formula Renault 3.5 title in 2014. Red Bull had given him a test run at Silverstone in Vettel's car in 2013 and he'd impressed enormously by lapping faster than the then three-time world champion. His sealing of the Renault 3.5 title just underlined his serious F1 credentials. His rise had not been as rapid as Max's, he didn't mark himself out so early as an obvious F1 driver, but he'd become steadily more impressive as he progressed through the ranks and although he'd join Verstappen at Toro Rosso as a fellow F1 rookie, he had five seasons of car racing behind him to Verstappen's one.

Verstappen was ear-marked for FP1 Friday sessions at the 2014 Japanese, United States and Brazilian grands prix. The first of these would come in between his Nürburgring and Imola F3 races. By this time, Sainz had been confirmed as his 2015 teammate and he would handle the car at the post-season Abu Dhabi tests.

But before Verstappen could take part in an official F1 practice session he needed to be issued with a super licence. To acquire this, he needed to complete a 300 km test without problems. This would be at Toro Rosso's local track, Aida. There, the 16-year-old took the wheel of the 2014 Toro Rosso

STR 09, its hybrid Renault V6 turbo power unit delivering well in excess of 900 horsepower – around four times that of the F3 car he was still racing. 'The first few laps your eyes cannot keep up and your stomach is like it's in a rollercoaster,' he reported.

This was when Max first worked with the guy who'd be his race engineer throughout his time at Toro Rosso, Xevi Pujolar, who had previously worked at the Williams team where he'd engineered Ralf Schumacher, Juan Pablo Montoya and Mark Webber among others. It didn't take long for him to realise he was working with something a little bit special in Max.

'For someone just coming in, he's the best I've seen so far,' Pujolar told GPUpdate.net. 'You can see the potential is there. You can see he's going up. Friends told me how extremely talented Max was. So that I knew already. But then, it's still a matter of time to see how someone will cope in a Formula 1 car. His skills as a driver are of a very high level. Because he is so talented, he grasps everything very quickly. Everything with Max comes naturally.

'Aida is a low-speed track not really suited to F1 cars. But Max really showed he has a very advanced car control and made no mistakes.'

Team boss Tost was also an instant believer. 'In Aida you could immediately see that Max didn't have any problems with the speed and the brakes. This is a very decisive factor because normally the young driver coming to F1 has big problems at the beginning with the speed and the brakes. It takes them a couple of test days to get used to how hard and late you can brake. The acceleration and the deceleration is completely on a different level to anything they've ever driven before. With Max, he immediately got used to it and therefore I didn't see any risk to race him the next year and I didn't see any risk to start doing FP1s with him.'

An eager Marko was waiting at the end of the phone to hear Tost's report at the end of the day and it's tempting to imagine he was almost purring as he listened to the details.

After tests at the Red Bull athlete fitness centre in Spielberg and a visit to the simulator in Milton Keynes, Max travelled to Suzuka, Japan for his first participation in an F1 weekend. He would drive the Toro Rosso in the first practice session of the Japanese Grand Prix, having turned 17 just three days earlier. This was just one of many records he was destined to set.

Suzuka is not the sort of track where a rookie would normally be given a try out. It's old-school, very fast and with little margin for error. Solid banks lie in wait very close to the track, which climbs and dives furiously, following the contours of the undulating terrain. It was created in the 1960s as a test track by Honda, which still owns it. The initial plan had been to construct a circuit on flat grounds nearby but when company founder Sochiro Honda heard of this, he was furious: 'What do you think you are doing?' he is reported to have said. 'Destroying the rice fields to build a racing track!' Food production had to be the respected priority and so the track was built in the hills. There is a surreal atmosphere about the place, a very Japanese combination of misty landscape and bright fairground lights, with perhaps the world's greatest racetrack threading its way through it all.

Max had been there as a child back in 2003. 'Yeah, the paddock was like a playground for me then,' he said. 'Coming back 10 years later and you think whoa, I used to play around here for fun.'

In 2014, I watched the Japanese Grand Prix's first practice from the outside of the Esses, a demanding interconnected series of fast uphill sweeps, for my first sight of Max Verstappen in action. It was overcast but dry and as usual, the two silver Mercedes of Nico Rosberg and Lewis Hamilton were setting the pace, their grip visibly superior. The most remarkable thing about Verstappen's passage was perhaps that it didn't look any different to any of the others. It looked like he'd been doing this for years, fully confident with his entry speeds, very controlled and composed. The left-handed Turn 3 is approached faster than the very closely following, tighter, right-handed Turn 4. So picking out the best balance between a) good speed through 3 but compromising the line into 4 or b) compromising 3 to get a better run at 4, is not straightforward. Max tried the fast approach into 3 first, confidently catching the Toro Rosso's slides on the exit, then tempered that down and quickly settled into the regular groove of prioritising 4. It took him no more than three laps to work it out.

You can watch the in-car footage still of that session, as he makes his attack lap near the end on soft tyres. What stands out is the nervous balance of the car, with the rear doing most of the 'rotation' into corners and Max just going with it, like it's nothing. Even through the faster corners, he's often correcting before the apex and he's certainly not surrendering much lap time to understeer at any point. He'd been flat in top gear through the formidable 130R corner pretty much immediately – just as if he was doing it on the sim – and this had initially made Franz Tost nervous. Until he saw him repeat it lap after lap.

The car's engine broke on his in-lap, smoke and fire trailing as he brought it in with a suitably dramatic flourish. It was something of an omen for his fortunes with Renault engines over the next few years. He finished the session 12th fastest of the 22 cars, just over 0.4 seconds shy of teammate Kvyat who had been in the car all season. Max was dismissive of that afterwards. 'I wasn't anywhere near the limit,' he said. 'I was just concentrating on getting the track time and making sense of the car. The worst thing to do would have been to damage it because then you lose all that track time and it doesn't make a good impression.' Maybe that was just bravado on the day, because a few years later he recounted: 'The sensation of power was so great I was thinking "Whoa, how do I keep this car on the circuit?"'

Today, Tost recounts that day with the hindsight of the Max Verstappen who came to be, rather than with the trepidation he felt at the time. 'There was a lot of criticism of us in the media putting a 17-year-old in an F1 car at Suzuka in the most difficult track blah, blah, blah. If a driver has the ability and talent to drive in F1, it doesn't matter which race track you do it. In his first free practice everything went smooth, no problem, nothing. He continued doing FP1 and in Brazil you could really see his car control because the car oversteered through Turns 6 to 7 very heavily and he really controlled it in a very professional way.'

The moment he is referring to was one of the most remarkable pieces of raw car control anyone is ever likely to see. The car was at one point virtually at 90-degrees to the direction of travel. If you saw a still of that moment it would seem impossible that the car could be rescued from spinning – it looks already mid-spin. But he rescued it. The cameras shot to the pit wall where Jean-Eric Vergne, the car's usual driver, was open-mouthed. He shot a look to Tost on his left who was just shaking his head and smiling. This is not a skill that can be deployed in setting a fast lap time – the car had scrubbed so much speed off by the time Max rescued it, he had to change down a gear – but it illustrates the margins he has in reserve to keep control of a car past the apparent point of no return. It makes possible for him manoeuvres that would be out of bounds to others. He would give a similar demonstration at the same track at the top of the hill in the rain of 2016. But it was in FP1 at Brazil in 2014 that the world of F1 got to see for the first time the extent of those remarkable skills.

In between the Suzuka and Brazil appearances he practised also at Austin. He was asked there if he considered Lewis Hamilton – on the verge of sealing his third world championship – the best driver in F1 and replied, 'I don't know. Give me his car and I will tell you.'

Max was sixth fastest in the Brazil session and within 0.1 seconds of Kvyat. So ended his F1 appearances for 2014. The following week he signed off for good from F3 at incident-filled Macau. From now, he would be a full-time F1 driver.

•

Over the 2014–15 winter, the Toro Rosso STR10-Renault that would be raced by Verstappen and Sainz was given its shakedown run in Misano, Italy, before the team decamped to Spain for the official F1 tests with all the teams present. One of these would be at Jerez, with two following in Barcelona. Mercedes set the pace and the Mercedes-powered Williams was generally the next fastest. The Toro Rossos seemed to be somewhere in the midfield and technical director James Key professed himself satisfied with the progress of his drivers, saying at the end of the final test, 'We arrived in Jerez exactly a month ago with two rookies and we leave Barcelona tonight with two young drivers who are ready to make their Formula 1 debut. They have definitely grown as drivers in a very short time, showing a good learning curve as well as growing in confidence as the days have gone by.'

Verstappen and Sainz between them had covered around

5,000 km over 10 days as they arrived in Melbourne for the opening round of the F1 world championship. When Max took up his grid position on the Sunday at Albert Park he became the youngest ever driver to take part in a grand prix, at 17 years 166 days, comfortably beating the previous record held by Jaime Alguersuari (another Red Bull driver) at 19 years 125 days. He had just short of five years if he was to beat the youngest world champion record of Sebastian Vettel (yet another Red Bull driver) at 23 years 134 days. It was a record Marko very much wanted Max to achieve and in which he had full belief.

But it wouldn't be with this car. The 2015 Toro Rosso STR10 had its good points – it was very competitive through fast corners, for example – but its Renault hybrid engine (shared with the senior Red Bull team) was well down on the power of the Mercedes and Ferrari units and the car's slow-corner performance was somewhat limited by its mechanical aspects. It was a mid-grid car, but in the hands of Verstappen and Sainz it would get a good workout over the season. For the first time in Max's career, he would be driving uncompetitive machinery. But that was just the way of it in F1. It was rare indeed for a rookie to get straight into a competitive car, as Lewis Hamilton had eight years earlier when, with McLaren, he'd come close to taking the world championship at his first attempt.

Max's goal this coming season was clear: produce the sort of performances that would bring that fast car to him sooner rather than later. It was a task he was relishing. 'This guy fears nobody,' says Giedo van der Garde, his old family friend. 'He doesn't give a shit about who he is, what his ranking is, who he is as a driver, he just comes in, wants to show to everyone that he is the best and he is very confident when he does something. I think that also helps when you come in as a young teenager that has no fear and just wants to show how good he is.'

Van der Garde himself – having competed in F1 the previous season with Caterham – had been hoping he might be able to share the track with the kid who had so wanted to emulate him all those years ago. He was one of three drivers signed by Sauber and there was space for only two of them. He'd essentially been gazumped by a driver with a bigger budget and it became a legal matter. In order to prove he was there and available to race, Van der Garde had turned up in the Melbourne paddock, got changed into his race suit and walked – with a bevvy of photographers in front of him – down to the Sauber garage to present himself. But he never got to drive and his F1 career was essentially over, just as Max's was beginning. 'It is a really big pity,' he reflects. 'If we could have raced together, that would have been really nice. From sleeping in his house when he was four years old as I was winning the karting championship, playing PlayStation with him and then 14 years later to be racing together in Formula 1. That would have been a really big dream.'

There was a lot for Max to get used to in F1. The first had struck him when Tost had taken him around the factory: there were *so* many people involved just to prepare two racing cars. Hundreds of them. All essential. Xevi Pujolar as his race engineer would be his closest colleague and guide. But the other big difference was Jos. He could no longer be so directly involved. He'd be there in the garage of course, observing, and around for Max to confer with and they'd still arrive and leave the track together. He'd be there talking in the ear of Marko too and so had influence. But no control.

Given that Carlos Sainz Jr was on the other side of the same garage and that Carlos Sr, the multiple rally champion, was there watching his son make his F1 debut too, it was a strained dynamic at times and would remain so throughout the year as the two rookies proved very closely matched.

Max went fourth-quickest in the Q1 part of qualifying, but that was slightly flattering as the top guns had done only what was necessary to get through to Q2. Max fell at the Q3 hurdle, getting out of shape at Turn 4 on his crucial final Q2 lap, but Sainz got through. Under the regulations of the time, this obliged Sainz to start on the less durable soft-compound tyres in which he'd set his Q2 time but for Max, qualifying outside the top 10, the tyre choice was free and he chose the tougher medium tyres on which to start.

'When the lights come on and you roll up to the start you're a bit nervous,' he related of his first ever grand prix start, 'but only because the procedures are new. As soon as you are into the race, you're not nervous any more. It's only a quick heart-rate increase and then it's fine.'

Which of two Toro Rosso tyre strategies would have turned out better is impossible to say, as both drivers suffered problems. Sainz's car suffered an electrical glitch at his pit stop which delayed him, although he got to the end to score ninth place points. Verstappen's engine broke down on the out-lap from his own pit stop eight laps later. Without their respective problems, they would have been on course to fight for seventh place, but the fact that Sainz had started ahead and ran ahead in the first stint of the race gave the impression that he had the upper hand.

Jos, as an experienced racer, having observed how the timing of Max's runs and tyre choices compromised his qualifying, had an input and wasn't shy of expressing it. Sainz's strong performance aggravated the situation and Jos went about using the implicit power of their position within Red Bull to ensure there was no repeat.

Things changed in the Toro Rosso camp after that and it's difficult not to detect the hand of Jos fighting his son's corner. Whatever was said, Marko subsequently gave Max and his engineers carte blanche to make their own timing and tyre choices – even against any choices made by Tost, if necessary. The team was already beginning to split into two camps.

Tost, who knew nothing of this arrangement, tried to keep a lid on the building tensions and the mild mutiny within. For such a veteran of the sport it was no big deal, just the normal competitive jostling among two drivers new to F1 and looking to make an impression.

'Carlos had much more car racing experience,' he recalls, 'and was very quick. Both drivers were skilled but maybe Carlos was closer than Max expected because of the advantage of his experience. But they respected each other and the atmosphere was okay. The fathers? They made their politics, as usual. I think otherwise it would be boring for them being at the track! It did feel like that. We knew all these games but there was nothing surprising. I think it was clear to Jos that Max's future was with Red Bull but maybe Carlos' father didn't feel that about Carlos.' So any campaigning within the Toro Rosso camp tended to come directly from Carlos Sr. Jos' was done away from the junior team garages and directly with Marko. It's easy to imagine the paranoia.

It wasn't serious – yet – and it never was between Max and Carlos Jr personally. But if the Sainzs couldn't escape the feeling that they were not there on the same terms as the Verstappens, they would have been right. As recalled, Sainz had fought his way through the multi-driver Red Bull junior squad over several years, needing to win to retain the backing to move up each rung of the ladder. Max's precocious talent and the buzz it created had made him a Marko 'asset' and it gave Max a different relationship with him. Marko didn't need any convincing that he was a future world champion. He'd thought so before he even stepped into an F1 car.

So Max drove that rookie season with the calm assurance that he'd just do his stuff in the car and everything would fall into place. Carlos drove with the tenacious determination of someone needing to show the world that there was more than one future top driver in the team. The perceived gap between them was bigger than the one measured across the timing beams for the rest of their time together.

Two weeks later in Malaysia, qualifying was wet and Max starred, punching way above the Toro Rosso's weight to place sixth. Sainz – having been fourth in Q1 – had made what he described as a 'rookie error' in Q2, pushing hard and running wide near the end of his lap. He would line up only 15th. Max had lapped only very slightly slower than the second Red Bull of Kvyat.

In the dry of race day, things were rather more fraught. Max was bundled down to 10th in the space of a few corners, while Sainz made up four places on the opening lap, to be sitting right behind his teammate. They were put on to diverging strategies: Max on a three-stop, Sainz on a two. After all their stops, Sainz was ahead but Max was tracking him down on fresher tyres. On the approach to Turn 4, Max came from a long way back, braked super-late, seemed almost caught by surprise at how early Sainz had braked and jinked instantly for the inside. Allowing the Toro Rosso to slide beautifully into the apex, the place was his. That was how he became F1's youngest-ever points scorer, with a seventh-place finish. Along the way, he had overtaken the Red Bull of Daniel

Ricciardo with a particularly finely judged move around the outside of Turn 1.

Max's attacking style and amazing overtaking skills were on even fuller display at the next round, in Shanghai. After hurling his car down the inside of Kvyat's Red Bull on the opening lap, he followed up with an ambush move on Marcus Ericsson's Sauber into the hairpin from a long way back, taking the Swede completely by surprise. He repeated the manoeuvre at the same spot on the other Sauber of Felipe Nasr a few laps later. Each time he would aim his car straight, keeping the load equalised between all four wheels, ready to accept the maximum braking force, getting himself fully alongside on the inside, blocking the other car, taking them both past the normal turning-in point. It would slow both of them up, but the position would be Max's. The rookie, in just his second season of car racing, was showing F1 veterans how it was done. He did the move for a third time on Sergio Perez's Force India, but it was all to no avail as his engine expired without warning near the end.

Toro Rosso technical director James Key, for one, was enjoying the ride. 'You could immediately see that he had it, [he was] incredibly fast and, to match that, [he had] immense determination to win and to get ahead of people. His race-craft in those very early days was exactly the same: regardless of who it was in front of him he wanted to beat them – just this huge inbuilt determination. So it was obviously all there and imprinted right from the outset.

'Carlos was very quick and competitive too. I think Max was a bit more aggressive with the car; certainly, his aggressive approach to races was very strong from the outset. Carlos pushed hard, but in the races I'd say he took less risk, and didn't want to stick his car in the wall. So I suppose in their early days their racecraft was slightly different. Also, in their interaction with the team, Carlos was quite technically minded whereas Max was able to relate very clearly to what he was feeling. He wouldn't necessarily know what particular phenomenon was going on, but his description of exactly what he was feeling was very, very clear.'

'He motivates everyone in the team,' Xevi Pujolar told *De Telegraaf.* 'Everyone sees his talent. But also his way of racing. Max is an attacker and that is something that captivates your mind. Especially in an Italian team, where the people in the factory really have a passion for true racing. And Max is a true racer.' Pujolar's description of the emotions Max's style creates for those in the team is remarkably similar to that expressed earlier by Giancarlo Tinini, the Italian CRG karting boss.

The rest of that Toro Rosso season was a mixed bag. In terms of results, the highlights were the two fourth places Max scored in Budapest and Austin. The latter was arguably more impressive, as in Hungary a heavy rate of attrition in front of him flattered the result, but in America he really had to fight and was there fully on merit. There were flashes of brilliance, a hint of what was to come, elsewhere too: like that astounding first practice session on his first visit to

Monaco – second-fastest, just 0.2 seconds slower than Lewis Hamilton's Mercedes.

In his race day accident at Monaco, he simply misjudged things in his eagerness to pass the older-tyred Grosjean. Max claimed at the time he'd been caught out by how early Grosjean had braked. For those interested enough to check, Lotus made available Grosjean's telemetry which showed he'd actually braked five metres later for Sainte Devote than on the previous lap. But Max's comments when reflecting upon the accident later were interesting. 'It gave me more confidence. Because I had a big crash and hit the wall . . . But [I'm fine]. You're always a bit scared to crash or touch a wall, whatever, but now I had a big crash and it gets a bit more relaxed, I think.'

Later in the year, there was his pass on Felipe Nasr around the outside of the flat-in-top Blanchimont corner at Spa during the Belgian Grand Prix, which was subsequently voted the move of the season by F1 fans. It was a quite astoundingly committed manoeuvre, around a flat-out corner which convention dictated was absolutely not a passing place: the full width of the corner is needed for a single car, such are the lateral loads at around 190 mph. But Max had never been overly concerned with others defining for him the realms of the possible. Plus, he had an engine-penalty compromised grid slot of 15th to recover from. Getting a slipstreaming run on the Sauber as they flew along the valley floor like a couple of dicing fighter jets, it was plain from how Max continued to close that he was going for the move. Nasr did the conventional thing at this point, which was to place his car on the inside, essentially obliging Max to go the unfeasible long way round if he wished to pass. Normally, that blocking manoeuvre would resolve the duel into that particular corner and the challenger would have to wait for an opportunity elsewhere. So there were sharp intakes of breath all round when Max refused to back out of the challenge, staying absolutely flat-out around the outside and trusting that Nasr a) had seen him and b) would not himself be forced to run out wide. The prospect of interlocking wheels at that speed was quite appalling. But still Max came and they went through there side-by-side, Max's outer wheels using some of the painted kerb and kicking up the dust. They made it through, Nasr still marginally ahead but on the outside for the following right-handed entry into the Bus Stop chicane, making it a simple matter for Max to use the inside line to out-brake him and take the place.

There are very occasional totemic moments in F1, very special moves by a new force of nature, demanding respect from everyone. Fernando Alonso had made a similar move on Michael Schumacher's Ferrari at the 2005 Japanese Grand Prix at 130R corner. Max's Spa move, further down the field and against a lowly Sauber rather than the world champion's Ferrari, did not carry quite the same symbolic significance but in terms of the degree of difficulty, skill and commitment it was every bit its equal.

For all his inexperience in F1, it was Max's assiduous 'homework' between races that gave him the confidence to make such an audacious move, to start to push at the boundaries of what was accepted as possible on the track. As recounted by his sim racing partner Atze Kerkhof on his You-Tube channel, 'In the week before Spa we linked the sims up and we found it was possible to overtake at Blanchimont. We practised it many times and many times it didn't work. So you replay certain scenarios and practise that specific scenario again and again, try different permutations, you stay wide, or you stay on the inside. At some point [if you're the car ahead], you start to defend the inside so the only way around is the outside.' That was the scenario Max and Kerkhof practised over and over again so that when Max was presented with the opportunity in real life, there were no second-thoughts.

Arguably Max's best drive of the season, however, came on his first visit to Singapore. He'd qualified well, eighth-fastest on the island's long, bumpy, arduous street track in highly humid conditions. He'd attacked the place with huge commitment right from the off, keeping it out of the walls throughout. His kart-like technique of generating oversteer well before the apex, then straightening out early was really working for him. But all that great work counted for nothing as the Toro Rosso's power unit cut out while he sat on the grid. The car had to be wheeled into the pit lane where the engine was brought back to life, obliging him to join the race at the back after the pack had swept by. As the various pit stops and safety cars (one for a drunk man who had wandered on to the track) played out, Max and Sainz were nose-to-tail overtaking cars in formation – Nasr's Sauber, the Lotus of Maldonado and Grosjean – and now were closing down on Sergio Perez. But as they edged closer to the Force India, the early grip of their new tyres was wearing off and with a bit of defensive driving Perez was able to contain Max's attacks. Sensing opportunity, Sainz – on slightly fresher tyres than Max – radioed that he was sure he still had the grip to pass Perez, if they would move Max aside for him.

It is a fairly common scenario in F1: the team will request one of its drivers to move aside for the other so as to attack the car ahead of them and if they fail, they hand the place back before the end. This request was relayed to Max who replied with a furious 'No!', to which Pujolar said, 'Max, just do it.' Max again point-blank refused. After a few laps, Sainz too was running out of tyre grip and they remained in formation to the end, in eighth and ninth.

Dutch journalist Linda Vermeeren went straight down to Toro Rosso in the paddock post-race and found Jos there. 'He still had steam coming out of his ears,' she recalls. 'Full of adrenaline, he fired his words at me and my Dutch journalist colleagues – "I would have kicked him in the balls if he had let Sainz past" – and I could see in his eyes that he meant it. "Max is a competitive driver," Jos continued, "he doesn't let anyone pass him. If the title was on the line, I could under-stand a request like this, but now?" Just then Max walked past and Jos said, "Daddy is proud of you." Later, when we spoke to Max, he was much calmer than Jos had been. He said it was his best race of the season and that, "When Xevi asked me that, I thought that's not going to happen. I don't think it's the right thing to ask when both drivers are on the same strategy and there are only limited laps to go."'

'I'd quoted Jos' comment about kicking Max in the balls in a tweet,' continues Vermeeren. 'It became the third most popular tweet in Holland on that day. Hilarious, but also a sign of how much F1 was coming alive again in Holland.'

Team principal Franz Tost later acknowledged that in hindsight, Max had been 'totally right to say no' and that issuing the instruction had been a misjudgement of the situation.

After the Japanese Grand Prix in which Max beat Sainz to ninth place, Max put in a terrific drive to fourth in Texas, again flexing his increasingly muscular style. He incurred the wrath of Kimi Raikkonen when defending his place, foreshadowing events of the following season: 'This guy keeps pushing me off on the exit,' he radioed. 'If that's legal I will do the same.' As Giedo van der Garde observed, reputations meant nothing to Max.

As they headed for the season's final round in Abu Dhabi, the internal contest between Verstappen and Sainz was still to be fully resolved. Although Max had scored many more championship points, this didn't fully reflect the competitive state of play between them, Carlos Jr having suffered worse reliability. Their qualifying score ran at 9–9, so whichever of them qualified ahead in Abu Dhabi would at least have seasonal bragging rights on that front. It went to Sainz by a few hundredths of a second as they qualified their Toro Rossos 10th and 11th in Q2. That seemed to trigger Max into one of his occasional OTT performances.

An attempt at passing Kvyat's Red Bull on the first lap was firmly rebuffed by the Russian driver, losing Max a further place as he was bundled out over the kerbs. Shortly afterwards, he was particularly brutal in his defence of his place against Vettel, leading the Ferrari driver to complain over the radio that Max was moving in the braking area, very much an accepted no-no among the drivers, but not something Max had bought into. After the pit stops he was running directly behind Sainz but on faster tyres and just ahead of them was Kvyat. In a reverse of the situation in Singapore, Max insisted he could pass Kvyat if Toro Rosso moved Sainz aside. Sainz reluctantly agreed, but almost immediately Max locked up in trying again to overtake Kvyat. With flat-spotted tyres he was forced to pit for replacements, ruining his strategy.

Given the middling competitiveness of the 2015 Toro Rosso, there'd been some very strong highlights in Max's rookie season and he remained very much on the trajectory of a future star. But the flourishes of brilliance and the attacking style helped disguise the fact that on average over the season, Sainz was pretty much as quick. Few could now doubt that grabbing the opportunity of F1 at 17 years old after only a single season of car racing – a move that would have surely sunk a lesser talent – was absolutely the right move for the Verstappens. But that lack of dominance over a more experienced quick teammate – and the occasional unremarkable weekend – did illustrate that it had been a bit of a stretch, even for one of Max's phenomenal gifts. When Lewis Hamilton had fought for the world championship in his rookie season of 2007 and gone head-to-head with the great Fernando Alonso as teammate, he had done so as a 22-year-old with five seasons of junior car racing behind him. Verstappen arrived in the top category much greener, more of a raw talent. Which was why the relative obscurity of a mid-grid Toro Rosso was much better for him at this early stage.

All that mattered was that Toro Rosso and Red Bull's Helmut Marko remained completely wowed by him, while in terms of driver talent the situation at Red Bull remained somewhat fluid and was perhaps starting to align in Max's favour. Daniil Kvyat, who at 21 had been promoted to Red Bull in 2015 as Sebastian Vettel's replacement after just a single year as a Toro Rosso rookie, had had a pretty tough season. Towards the end, he had rolled his car in qualifying for the Japanese Grand Prix – a straightforward driving error, just getting his wheels on the grass approaching the fast kink before Suzuka's hairpin, and it did not please Marko at all. There had likely been an element of pressure behind that rookie mistake: in the lead-up to this race, Marko had told Kvyat that he had not yet made the Red Bull drive his own, that they were looking for more from him.

Measured against Daniel Ricciardo in the sister car, Kvyat had averaged around 0.2 seconds slower and was 10–4 down. He'd garnered slightly more points but that was just a reflection of the appalling reliability of Ricciardo's car in the second half of the season when it was more competitive. It was a respectable showing for Kvyat given his rapid promotion and in any other team in any other season, without a Max Verstappen waiting in the wings, it would have been more than satisfactory. But Marko, with Jos on his case and a contract which might let Max escape in a year or two, was becoming more demanding than ever. Kvyat would retain the Red Bull drive into 2016, but he was on borrowed time.

•

The Toro Rosso line-up of Max and Sainz would be unchanged into 2016 and they would each be driving the new STR11. Politics between Red Bull and engine supplier Renault meant the junior team would no longer be using the French engines and instead would be powered by 2015-spec Ferrari power units. They would be reasonably competitive at the start of 2016 but, with their development frozen, they would fall further behind through the season as the other engines continued to be improved. It looked increasingly unlikely that the cars would be moving up the grid anytime soon.

Keeping the intensely competitive Verstappen and Sainz pairing for a second season had done nothing to reduce the internal team tensions. This would only intensify in the first race of 2016, in Melbourne, for the one-year anniversary of their debuts. Max gave himself a great grid position with the fifth-fastest time in Q3, albeit slightly slower than Sainz had managed in Q2. Sainz's Q3 time put him seventh.

A bad start by pole-sitter Lewis Hamilton saw him down to fifth place by the first corner, with Max running fourth and defending perfectly against the faster Mercedes. Sainz was running just behind Valtteri Bottas' Williams, still in seventh. Though the Toro Rossos soon began to lose front-tyre performance, still Max was able to prevent Hamilton from coming through and still Sainz was able to keep the pressure on Bottas. Eventually, Toro Rosso brought Sainz in for an early first stop so as to undercut him past the Williams. Max was urging his crew to do the same as his tyres continued to deteriorate but they resisted as there wasn't a suitable gap in the traffic to drop him into. He eventually took matters into his own hands.

Five laps after Sainz's stop, a despairing Max simply told the team he was coming in. This caught them by surprise and his new tyres were not quite ready as he arrived, delaying him by a few seconds. He rejoined still in front of Sainz, but only just. The race was suspended under a red flag after Fernando Alonso suffered a heavy crash in his McLaren, with Verstappen and Sainz running fourth and fifth. When a race is suspended, everyone is permitted to change tyres. There were 39 laps still to go and Toro Rosso fitted both cars with new soft-compound tyres, believing these would be durable enough to go to the end. They weren't – and that created yet more conflict within the team.

Max ran the early laps of the restart tight behind Ricciardo's Red Bull. The turbulent wake increased his tyre degradation and after a few laps he was already struggling to maintain pace. Sainz, feeling he was being held up, asked the team to move Max aside – that chestnut again! The team radioed Max but he refused to comply. Then Sainz's tyres also began to suffer. Both drivers were asking to be brought in for fresh rubber, both were being denied, the team feeling they could hang on to better positions by staying out rather than pitting and having to catch up. But then Sainz locked up his worn front tyres and flat-spotted them, making it absolutely necessary to replace them immediately. Max was furious as he saw in his mirrors Sainz disappearing into the pit lane to do what he had been denied. So for a second time in the race, he announced he was coming in. Again, this caused a delay at his stop – enough this time to bring him out behind Sainz, which triggered a rant of expletives from Max, who believed Sainz had sneaked himself ahead. Determined to get back ahead and trying to get himself on to the tail of the other car, he made light contact with its rear wheel and spun, leaving Sainz to finish a relieved ninth and Verstappen an angry 10th.

Understandably, Franz Tost was not happy that Max had twice gone freelance with his strategy calls. This was beyond merely assertive, it verged on mutinous. It was for Marko to try and smooth the waters.

In Bahrain two weeks later, they qualified 10th and 11th, Max marginally faster, but, as in Australia, his grid-setting time was not as fast as Sainz had managed in the previous session. It illustrated once again that the margins between them were tiny. Perhaps in an attempt to keep them out of each other's way in the race, Toro Rosso split their tyre strategies, starting Max on the super-soft and Sainz on the soft. As it happened, Sainz's race was ruined by Perez crashing into him and Max drove a strong race to sixth. In China, Sainz qualified ahead but Max turned that around in the race.

Next stop, Sochi, Russia. Max outqualified Sainz but – though Max didn't know it – Sainz was no longer his competition. Moves were afoot at Red Bull senior management level and it was Kvyat whose performances were being put under the microscope. Although he had taken a third place in China after incurring Vettel's wrath for an aggressive first corner, it was a result heavily aided by attrition. Scrutinising the underlying performance, the team could see that the pace deficit to Ricciardo seemed to have grown. His performances were heading in the wrong direction.

'I thought Kvyat did pretty well in 2015 actually,' says Christian Horner. 'He had actually scored more podiums than Riccardo in the drivers' championship and then going into '16 we changed brake supplier and it seemed to completely have over Daniil who from pre-season testing just wasn't able to adapt.'

As discussed earlier, that initial grip reading of the track a driver takes from the brake pedal is crucial to his performance. Different brake materials bring different sensations through the pedal – and this can often completely change a driver's performance. It was very unfortunate timing for Kvyat that this should happen just as Marko was looking for an opportunity to promote Max. Aside from the long-term contractual implications, swapping Max for Kvyat would make life easier at Toro Rosso, where internal tensions again flared up in qualifying at Sochi.

In Q2 Max came out of the garage sooner than Sainz, against the plan Tost had outlined. True to their arrangement with Marko, Verstappen's engineering team was merely doing what it considered best for its driver even if this went against the overall team plan. And it worked – it was crucial in Max making it through to Q3 and Sainz being baulked by traffic on his final lap and stranded in Q2. But Franz Tost was angered by the apparent insubordination and this led to Xevi Pujolar and two of his engineering colleagues ceasing to work for the team subsequently. 'For some time there had been some miscommunications, misunderstandings and discussions between some engineers and the team,' says Tost, 'which made it difficult to co-operate properly, so it was decided we part, as normally happens when these frictions arise.' In the race – his final one at Toro Rosso as it turned out – Max would retire from sixth place with engine failure.

Kvyat further sealed his own fate with a chaotic first lap in which he twice hit Vettel's Ferrari, spinning it hard into the barriers on the second occasion. A furious Vettel – who already held Kvyat responsible for having ruined his race in China – remonstrated with his old boss Christian Horner on the pit wall, telling him he needed to control his driver. Not that he was going to be Horner's driver for much longer, as it happened.

'Ricciardo had got a puncture when leading in China,' recalls Horner, 'and while Kvyat managed to get a podium there, it wasn't based on pace. There was a big offset between the two drivers that was being highlighted and there was an opportunity within Max's agreement to say, "Okay, well look, we need to do something about this, we are in a privileged position where we have got two teams." It's unorthodox but with two teams under common ownership, why shouldn't you move them up and down within your A and B team to put your best foot forward? So after the disastrous Russian Grand Prix, the decision was made to do it, to switch them around.'

This was all still top-secret, however. While a throwaway Marko comment had led Jos to believe something might be afoot, even he wasn't sure. Max was even less so. In the *Becoming Max Verstappen* documentary he recalls, 'The first few races I had that season were good. It was all going quite well. We were getting some good results. I got a call from my dad first at home in Monaco and he said, "Max I think there's a chance you're driving for Red Bull the next race," and I said, "Don't talk crazy, what you talking about?" I didn't believe him. Then at some point Helmut – I think it was on the Tuesday – called and said, "You have to come to Graz". So we went for lunch, the hour went by, nothing was said and I was thinking, why are we here, there was nothing coming out. Then suddenly Helmut said, "Oh, by the way, next week you're driving for Red Bull at Barcelona so get ready."'

•

Just five races into his second season of F1, his third season of car racing, 18-year-old Max Verstappen would be racing for one of F1's absolute top teams. Kvyat recalls how he was given the news he'd be going in the opposite direction back to Toro Rosso.

'I was in Moscow, lying on the sofa, watching a TV series and then the phone call came. It was Dr Marko, "Hello, well, we have some news for you" and there was a 20-minute talk about . . . There was no real explanation to be honest. I think if the bosses want something to happen, they just make it happen. Simple as that . . . The people who made the decision can give a better answer to the reason. It's a question for them.

'We finished the talk and I went back to finish my TV series.' The show? *Game of Thrones* – a series about the machinations of power.

Attending to Kvyat's car at Toro Rosso would be a new race engineering group, as Tost had indeed fired Max's team for their actions in Sochi. Pujolar had been caught between two conflicting sets of demands and had gone with Marko's rather than Tost's. Marko was then instrumental in getting Pujolar a new job at Sauber.

Race-engineering Max at Red Bull would be Kvyat's old engineer Gianpiero Lambiase, or 'GP' as he's known in the team. He'd arrived there two years before, recruited by Horner from Force India with the intention of putting him on Sebastian Vettel's car as a replacement for his long-time engineer Guillaume Rocquelin (aka 'Rocky') who was moving up to become head of the Red Bull junior driver academy. 'Seb had actually interviewed GP for the job,' recalls Horner. 'Because it was going to be for him. In GP I saw a great race engineer who was very practical and after I interviewed him he was grilled by a four-time world champion and responded impressively well. He's a tough character, but calm. Sebastian buggered off to Ferrari and GP ended up with Daniil, then Max stepped into the role.

'Max can be very demanding and very sharp when emotions are running high. He's a thoroughbred, very strong-willed and there's many an engineer who will wilt under that pressure because Max's expectation is incredibly high. GP is able to handle that and they each can give as good as they get, so much so that sometimes you forget which is the driver and which the engineer.

'It's a quite different relationship to that between Rocky and Seb. Rocky really got into the mind management of how to get Sebastian in the right mental frame whether it was writing things on his balaclava, naming his car, all these little things. It's a lot less touchy-feely with Max and GP. They are just brutally honest with each other, no holds barred, and in that respect, I think it's a very pure, very honest, relationship.'

But before that relationship developed, Max had to get himself comfortable in the car. He did a seat fitting at the Milton Keynes factory but had not even driven the RB12 on the sim before he drove it for real in the first practice session of the Spanish Grand Prix.

'I'm very happy with the chance they have given me,' he said at the FIA press conference at the start of the weekend. 'I'm racing for a top team now and that was always the plan, what I wanted to do. As for it being a risk [to be in a top team so early], to be honest I think it was a bigger risk to be so young in Formula 1 but I've handled it pretty well. From now on it's just getting used to a new car, which is not easy in the season, but already with the things I've done in the factory they've given me a lot of confidence.'

It was prior to this weekend that Sophie began a ritual she has maintained ever since, as told to WagsF1: 'I go to the little church here in town and I burn a little candle and make a prayer. Then I send the picture to Max.'

Watching him in that first practice session from the outside of Turn 7, the left-hander at the bottom of a hill with a tricky, slightly downhill braking zone, I could see that his muscle memory was still attuned to the less grippy Toro Rosso. He'd begin turning earlier than the fully familiar Ricciardo and the car would respond instantly, too early. He had to learn he no longer needed to slide this car up to the apex with understeer but could turn in late and hard – and it would respond. He was doing it like that after a few laps. But that's how new this all was.

Verstappen had a high bar in Ricciardo who had arrived at the Red Bull senior team a year too late to take advantage of its title-winning competitiveness. In 2014, the first year of the hybrid formula, Renault's power unit was uncompetitive but Ricciardo's reputation soared regardless as he out-performed the incumbent Vettel and won three grands prix. The 2015 Red Bull had been out-gunned not only by the dominant Mercedes but by Ferrari too, and Ricciardo hadn't been able to add to his win tally. The 2016 car was much better and though still no Mercedes, it was fully competitive with Ferrari.

'There were very few people quicker than Daniel Ricciardo over a lap at that time,' recalls Horner, 'and in Spain Max came in, having never been in the car before that weekend, went quicker than him in Q1, edged him out in Q2 and only lost out to him in Q3 because he didn't want to change the wing angle and ended up picking up a bit of understeer.

'That switch had put Max under *enormous* pressure. But he just got in and delivered against effectively our lead driver, he was hugely impressive. It was a "wow" moment definitely.'

But that was just the start of it. In fact, qualifying behind Ricciardo may actually have won him the race.

To understand how Max Verstappen won first time out for Red Bull, becoming at 18 years, 228 days the youngest-ever grand prix winner (beating Sebastian Vettel's previous record of 21 years, 73 days) you have to know three key facts. First, Mercedes drivers Lewis Hamilton and Nico Rosberg crashed into each other on the opening lap, beaching their damaged cars in the gravel four corners into the race. Second, the race then became a strategy contest between Red Bull and Ferrari, with both teams opting to split strategies between each of their drivers. Third, finding himself – like Ferrari's Kimi Raikkonen – on the better strategy, Max soaked up enormous pressure from the Finnish former world champion without the hint of an error, to capitalise on points one and two.

In the first part of the race, as Raikkonen made a poor, wheel-spinning start dropping three places, Max ran second to new teammate Ricciardo, having gone wheel-to-wheel with Vettel's Ferrari at the first corner and prevailed. This put in place a choreography that saw Vettel run over the astroturf at Turn 3 and lose position to the Toro Rosso of Sainz. It would take Vettel a few laps to find a way back ahead of the slower car but once he'd done so, his pace alerted Red Bull to the possibility that he may be three-stopping – which presented a strategic conundrum for them on the pit wall.

Horner: 'Once it was clear Vettel was three-stopping we had to take a tactical decision at that point to say, "Do we try and cover Vettel with one of our cars?" The car we believed had the best chance of winning the race was the lead car [Ricciardo] and so we elected to go for the three-stop with him.'

This decision turned out to be disastrous for Ricciardo – and not great for Vettel either. With the tyre degradation not as great as Red Bull had feared, the two-stop worked better. It meant after they'd all made their stops, Max was leading from Raikkonen with Vettel and Ricciardo in third and fourth going faster on their fresher tyres, but not by enough to make up for the time lost to the extra pit stop. All that remained for Max to do now was to look after his tyres for another 32 laps while keeping the Ferrari filling his mirrors behind. He had to work out how best to deploy his battery charge only to defend, not to try to pull away – as that would have left him a sitting duck after the battery had emptied itself a few laps later. And he had to do all this in a new car for a new team.

'It was like driving on ice for the last 10 to 15 laps,' he recalled on Red Bull's YouTube channel, 'and we were not sure if we were gonna make it to the end.

'The tyres were gone but I could see Kimi behind me was also struggling. I knew if I locked up or missed the apex I was sure he was going to get me.'

Leading races was a familiar feeling for him – it's what he used to do all the time before his rookie F1 season the previous year. As he'd said then, a grand prix was just like a kart race with more spectators, after all. But towards the end of what must have felt an endless 32 laps, he admitted that the momentousness of what he was about to achieve did get to him a little. 'With five laps to go I started cramping a bit because of the excitement and the focus. I was literally counting the laps down. There was a lot of pressure. My dad got so excited towards the end that his nose started bleeding. I can't even imagine how it was for him sitting in my driver room, seeing the final few laps unfold.'

As he took the flag, Horner came on to the radio: 'Max Verstappen you are a race winner. Fantastic. What a great debut.'

'His mental resilience is the strongest I've ever seen,' says Horner. 'His ability under pressure is phenomenal. And the more pressure you put on, the better he delivers.'

While that innate quality brought F1 victory to the 18-year-old at the very first available opportunity, he wasn't yet in a position to do it on a regular basis. In fact, he would have to endure another five seasons of less than title-calibre cars, five years of treading water. There were times when that strained Max's loyalty to the team, when Jos and Raymond made no secret of their concern about Red Bull's ability to provide a car with which he could fight for championships and fulfil his potential. But that mental resilience, that toughness, allowed him to hang on until he finally had a Red Bull good enough to allow him to fight – really fight – for a world title.

Watching that first victory unfold was Marko's old adversary Niki Lauda, fresh from a 45-minute post-mortem in the Mercedes motorhome with his errant drivers Rosberg and Hamilton. He made a point of going over to congratulate Jos who was clearly holding back tears of joy. 'I take my hat off to Max,' said Lauda. 'He is a talent of the century . . . Normally I am against fathers telling drivers what to do because they cannot be an emancipated personality. But he couldn't emancipate Max because he was so young. What Jos did, he did everything right. To make him safe, to make him comfortable so he can race with Kimi Raikkonen right behind him for so long and not make a single mistake. I have to say it: Marko made the right call. He is the master of the Verstappens.'

Jos was lost for words. It's one thing to plan and train for this moment for a decade, but quite another to witness it actually happening. 'He's only 18 and the way he raced, it was unbelievable. I don't know what to say.'

'If I have to name the three proudest moments of my life,' Marko said some years later, 'one would be winning Le Mans as a driver, another would be Sebastian Vettel's first world championship, and the third would be Max's victory in Barcelona 2016. Because I had taken so much shit about signing a guy too young for F1.' This one was very personal for the tough old bear.

There was lots of celebrating that evening. Max's life had just changed fundamentally. This success would also come to change the lives of Jos, Sophie and Victoria. There was a long road stretching out ahead of all of them. Where it would lead couldn't be known. But it was going to be an exciting journey.

8

TENSIONS RUNNING HIGH

'You can't say that my grandson has to go to a psychiatric institution. You're the loser who should go instead.'
Frans Verstappen

For all that winning the 2016 Spanish Grand Prix on his first race for Red Bull was a monumental achievement, it perhaps raised expectations a little too high among the growing army of Verstappen fans. Max and Red Bull continued their journey together, but with only occasional opportunistic glory providing punctuation in an essay of Mercedes dominance.

There were times during the first couple of years of that relationship when Max's inexperience showed. The thrills were accompanied by occasional spills. It turned out the driver who'd proved so totally at ease running at the front in Barcelona was less well-suited to scrapping for crumbs. There were times when competitive desire overrode focused assessment. With his penchant for rewriting the rules of etiquette in battle, he didn't make many friends among the establishment either.

It didn't seem to matter to his Dutch fans, however. At that year's Belgian Grand Prix – the nearest they had to a home race until the Dutch Grand Prix was rebooted in 2021 – the orange-clad hordes filled the place to squeezing point, creating a whole new carnival atmosphere. Getting about in the surrounding towns became something of an expedition amid raucous celebrations. Two decades earlier, 'Jos the Boss' had inspired a similarly energetic following but this was already larger, more visually identifiable – and spreading around Europe. Orange threatened to usurp Ferrari-red as the dominant colour of the crowd scenes, in Hungary and Germany and without any question in Belgium. (Max was, after all, Belgium-born to a Belgian mother.)

They cheered him regardless of the result, but in the next few years he was only able to offer the odd flash of hope. He had just such an opportunity in the very next race after Barcelona: Monaco. Around this track, the Red Bull even looked to have the edge on Mercedes and Ferrari. The tight street circuit was relatively kind to the Renault engine's power deficit and allowed the car's responsive handling traits to be exploited to the full. Daniel Ricciardo – with a new, more powerful version of the Renault engine than Verstappen – was fastest in second practice.

That things might not go so smoothly for Max became apparent in Saturday's FP3 session, when he lightly brushed the barrier at Massenet, taking off his front wing. Worse was to come in Q1, when he crashed heavily. Just as in Barcelona, his muscle memory still seemed to have some Toro Rosso in it, as he could still occasionally pitch the Red Bull fractionally too early for its grippy front end. It was like that as he turned hard right to exit the swimming pool section of track and the car turned exactly where he'd pointed it – which was just to the inside of the barrier, hitting it rather than shaving it, a difference of no more than a centimetre. A broken track rod and a broken dream. One Red Bull, Ricciardo's, would start from pole position. The other, Max's rebuilt one, would start from the pit lane. His progress from there on an initially wet track was thrilling – he gathered up a huge oversteer moment through the kink of the tunnel at one point – but doomed. Shortly after changing to slick tyres on the still damp track, he crashed into the same Massenet barriers he'd glanced on Saturday. Ricciardo had been all set for victory when a mix up in the pit garages meant his tyres weren't ready as he pitted, losing him the race to Hamilton's Mercedes.

Max's race accident likely wouldn't have happened had he not crashed in qualifying. That would stand as his season's biggest blunder, losing him the chance of winning his first two races with Red Bull. Such chances were going to be sparsely spread over the next couple of seasons.

The remainder of his 2016 races ranged from ill-judged (Spa) to incredible (Brazil) but were never fought with anything other than full commitment and passion. He was a tenacious fourth in Canada, as much as the car deserved, and an attrition-aided second in Austria where he'd made a lap-two pass on Ricciardo into the Rindt Kurve from outrageously far back. At Silverstone, he got the chance to showcase his rain skills, tracking down and passing Nico Rosberg's second-place Mercedes in the wet only to lose out to it once the track dried (though Rosberg was later penalised, giving the official second place to Max).

In Hungary, he upset Raikkonen again, just as he had at Austin the previous year. His late-race battle for fifth place saw him make more than one defensive swoop in the braking area. Max would wait in the middle of the track for Raikkonen to choose a side before moving that way to block him. Then, when Raikkonen swapped sides, so too would Max. It was very much outside racing etiquette but not covered in the rules of the time. 'If he does it again, I hit him,' warned Raikkonen, but he never got close enough.

Max's actions may well have been influenced by his anger at having been held up by teammate Ricciardo in the first stint of the race as the Red Bulls ran third and fourth. 'I'm driving like a grandma,' he complained. He believed his teammate had deliberately forced a slow pace on him so he'd be caught and undercut by the following Ferraris, which is indeed what happened, though Ricciardo insisted – with plausible deniability – that all he'd been doing was taking care of his tyres. Max was later able to get back ahead of Raikkonen, but not Vettel. His savage defence against Raikkonen might be seen in this light.

There was some tension in the Red Bull camp between its two drivers at this time. While the race team endeavoured to give them equal opportunities, Ricciardo got the feeling that the Verstappens had a better line of communication than him with Helmut Marko. That sort of competitive paranoia, with the wily Marko at its centre, wasn't a new thing. It had been there between Sebastian Vettel and Mark Webber some years earlier, culminating in their collision while fighting for the lead of the 2010 Turkish Grand Prix. In an emergency meeting, Webber had laid it all out to Marko, saying that the Doctor's obvious preference for Vettel put Webber under extra pressure. Marko replied that he hadn't realised Webber was so sensitive and would take on board what he'd said, before adding, 'But it won't matter much at the next race in Valencia, because you're always useless there!'

Marko's brand of macho, old-school toughness was perfect for the Verstappens. It is easy to imagine how it might have been difficult for others to muscle in on that – though Marko actually had immense respect for Ricciardo too, as he expressed when I interviewed him in 2017. 'They are a fantastic pair,' he said. 'Max jumps in the car and is immediately quick, no matter what, new circuit or whatever. In the rain, he's in a class of his own, looking for where the grip is, and immediately he has a feeling of the limit. Nearly everyone else has to find it, he is immediately on it. Ricciardo is quiet, smiling, but in the car, look at his overtakes. Ambush. His mascot is the honey badger – it's very dangerous but sweet looking. He isn't scared of anything. Senna was never as relaxed as Ricciardo and that for me – to be so competitive but to enjoy life – is amazing. Max is similar but there is more tension there.'

Ricciardo was an elite level driver at this time, fully capable of fighting anyone for the world championship with the right car. Now in his sixth season of F1, he'd built up a formidable arsenal of skills to support his great talent. Yet Verstappen arriving as his teammate with just one season of F1 behind him was able to compete immediately on level terms, sometimes slightly faster, sometimes slightly slower. In the 15 races in which a fair comparison could be made in 2016, Ricciardo qualified an average of five-hundredths of a second faster. He was right to be concerned about what Max might be able to do once he acquired more experience. He was also right to believe that's probably what Marko was thinking too.

A week after Hungary, at Hockenheim, Germany, Ricciardo demonstrated one of the skills Max still had to master: combining pace with tyre preservation when racing in the pack. Ricciardo was supremely skilled at this and used it to beat Max to third, overturning Max's dramatic around-the-outside pass of him in the race's opening seconds, wheels almost touching.

Max's occasional habit of making dangerous moves when up against it was on display again at Spa, after he was severely compromised within seconds of the start: Vettel squeezed

Raikkonen into him at the first corner, not realising there were two cars to his inside. After pitting for damage repairs, Max and Raikkonen were well down the field, but still racing each other. On the 12th lap, Raikkonen slipstreamed himself to the outside of Verstappen as they reached the braking zone for the tight Les Combes chicane. They banged wheels and the Ferrari driver was forced to take the run-off area to avoid contact, rejoining ahead but surrendering the position, as per the rules – you are not allowed to gain an advantage by leaving the track. On the following lap, Raikkonen tried again as they raced up the long straight at around 210 mph. Max positioned himself mid-track, waited for Raikkonen to choose a side, and then moved that way too. Raikkonen was forced to brake and jink left to avoid what would have been an enormous accident. Since it didn't actually break the letter of any regulation, it wasn't investigated by the stewards, much to Raikkonen's dismay. 'I'm fine with good hard racing,' he said afterwards, 'but if I have to brake on the straight at 340 kph so as not to hit someone, then something is not correct. For whatever reason the stewards said it was okay. There will be a massive accident some day. Maybe he needs an accident before things are more clear to everyone.'

There may have been an element of the new challenger laying down his arrival among the established top guys. It might have been partly an age thing – at 18, exactly half Raikkonen's age, Max's risk-assessment capabilities might not have yet been fully developed. But it was also a Verstappen thing: that absolute refusal to back down. It had been there throughout the careers of both father and son, but this was the most extreme example so far in F1. It was a strength in battle, but in F1 Max had redrawn the line in a way others weren't prepared to follow. This hadn't happened since the days of Michael Schumacher when new regulations had had to be written in response to some of his moves. The same would soon happen to Max.

This is when Niki Lauda made his famous, 'He needs to see a psychiatrist,' comment and Max made his cheery rejoinder of, 'Great, we can go together.' Max's grandfather Frans had a predictably Verstappen take on the whole incident, saying on RTL, 'Let's face it, Raikkonen is a cry-baby. I have always respected Lauda but it's insane what he's said. Since last week I am convinced that not only his ears have suffered in that crash, but also his brain. You can't say that my grandson has to go to a psychiatric institution. You're the loser who should go instead. Max never meant that he would push Ferrari drivers off the track. He meant that he will never give up without a fight. He would never intentionally crash into someone.'

Lewis Hamilton would get a little taste of the Max brand of brutal tenacity later in the season, in the closing stages of the Japanese Grand Prix. The Mercedes driver was making a recovery drive after a poor start had left him well back. Into the last lap, he was closing on Verstappen's second place and the one remaining passing place was at the chicane after the flat-out 130R. With Max again hovering mid-track, Hamilton moved for the inside. But Max simply took up his line into the corner, forcing Hamilton to run straight-on into the run-off area to avoid hitting the back of the Red Bull. This was a less dangerous breach of etiquette than at Spa, more just the usual rough and tumble of competition, and Hamilton wasn't unduly upset by it, but it gave him his first sense of how racing Max wheel-to-wheel could be tricky.

Sebastian Vettel was incensed with Max in Mexico, believing he had brake-tested him and later backed him into the other Red Bull of Ricciardo. Max hadn't impressed Nico Rosberg either, with a big hit into the Merc's sidepod at the first corner. Max was penalised five seconds for having gained an advantage by running off track in his dice with Vettel. The rage this triggered in Vettel was intense. 'He's a ****. That's what he is,' he raged over the radio about Max on the slow-down lap.

Raikkonen, Hamilton, Rosberg and Vettel: Max had made an impression on them all and got under the skin of at least one. He'd arrived on their big stage, wasn't going anywhere soon and they weren't sure how to deal with him.

Some of that was Max's hardcore racing attitude. Some was just part of his evolution as an F1 driver. But just as he was adapting to F1, so F1 would come to adapt to him. From Austin onwards, a new regulation specifically prohibited the driver ahead in the braking zone from changing their line more than once. Vettel was among the first to be penalised for falling foul of it in his Mexico dice with Ricciardo, which had happened mainly because he was so furious at Max's earlier moves. Oh, the irony!

There were other aspects of Max's game that still needed work; this was just his second season of F1, after all, and only his third season outside of karts. Although he'd conserved his tyres perfectly at Barcelona when running at the front, he'd over-used them at Hockenheim when having to fight wheel-to-wheel. At Singapore, his frustration at the slow pace being set by those ahead of him as they sought to make their rubber last, and the difficulty of overtaking, led him to burn through tyres in between pit stops, limiting him to a sixth-place finish on a day when Ricciardo was a strong second. It was a ragged, immature performance.

At this stage, his effectiveness depended upon the circumstances. When they demanded discipline and a slow pace, he often raged against it. We'd see this again in Austin when, warned by his engineer GP that his rear tyre temperatures were becoming too high, he snapped back. 'I'm not here to finish fourth!' It earned him a rebuke from his biggest supporter, Helmut Marko, who said afterwards, 'If you can't pass them, you can't overuse the tyres. Then you don't win races and certainly not championships. Compared to Daniel, Max had higher tyre wear.'

But when attack and verve were the order of the day, he was truly formidable. In Malaysia, the race after Singapore, he enjoyed a great gloves-off fight with Ricciardo for what was at the time second position. It went on for several corners and they both displayed supreme judgement at such close quarters. It was a different, less brutal, style of combat to that he'd used against Raikkonen, but still there were nervous faces on the Red Bull pit wall. Ricciardo eventually prevailed – and a lap later Lewis Hamilton's race-leading Mercedes blew its engine, handing Ricciardo the win, with Verstappen a resigned runner-up. He had at least enjoyed the opportunity to race in an uninhibited way rather than to a tyre temperature read-out.

The 2016 race that best rewarded Max's all-out attack and astonishing ability was probably Brazil, the penultimate event of the season. But as the F1 circus decamped there, the feathers Max had ruffled in Mexico had still not fully settled. After the race there, Mercedes boss Toto Wolff had called Jos to remonstrate at Max's wheel-banging with his driver Rosberg – leading the world championship at the time – at the start. He had also mentioned it in the Mercedes post-race media briefing, saying, 'As refreshing as it is, and how ruthless the great ones are, if you race the championship leader three races from the end, wheel banging is not what should happen.' He'd made much the same point to Jos, suggesting Max needed to calm down a little. Unimpressed, Jos related the conversation to Marko who in turn told Horner – unleashing a war of words in the Brazilian paddock in the days leading up to the race.

'I think Jos was a bit surprised when he put the phone

down to Toto that not only was he commenting on behalf of Mercedes but Ferrari as well, and that the way Max was conducting himself wasn't winning him any favours and he should wind his neck in, said Horner.

'I've not heard of a team principal calling up other drivers' fathers before, said Marko, 'but obviously, Toto felt the need to do so. I think it is total rubbish. If Toto wants to have a race for his drivers so they don't risk anything we can do that at 11 a.m., then we can have the grand prix at 2 p.m. where everybody can race . . . It's getting more and more absurd. I have never experienced such interference before. If Mr Wolff wants something from us, he should contact the people at Red Bull and not the father.'

Obviously, Wolff was asked to respond to these comments in Brazil and said, 'Max is spontaneous, exciting, just what the doctor ordered for F1. He contributes a lot and the last thing he should do is change his approach. I didn't say that he should move out of the way. What I discussed with Jos was two things: Jos has had a negative spin in some of the media, which is unfortunate, and I felt Jos being at all the races was important for Max.

'The second thing I said was that with two races to go to the end, if an accident were to happen with Lewis or Nico [as they fought for the championship] it would add to the negative spin in the media; so that is best avoided. So it was out of sympathy for Max. It was a private discussion that was dragged out in public.'

As he was saying this in the Mercedes media session, Horner happened to walk past outside, and peered through the glass to give Wolff a sarcastic 'phone me' hand gesture . . . All just part of the off-track warfare, soon to be rendered trivial by a quite spellbinding performance from Max in the rain of race day around the Interlagos track.

Visibility was appalling as the safety car pulled off to get the race underway, with Max already emerging out of Rai-kkonen's ball of spray to go third. Only the two Mercedes of Hamilton and Rosberg lay ahead of him as the race was red-flagged almost immediately to clear up debris from a big accident. When the safety car pulled off again, Max collected an enormous slide after the Red Bull aquaplaned at the top of the hill leading into the pit straight. Raikkonen's car did the same – and it bounced him hard into the wall. Another red flag ensued. As they started for the third time, Max was immediately stalking his prey Rosberg, and it was notable that he was using completely different lines on the wet track, finding the grip off line where there was no rubber build-up. It was just what you instinctively did when you had spent the previous decade pounding around wet kart tracks honing your skills, even when no one else was there, with just your dad at the side of the track.

Quickly, Max dispensed with Rosberg, getting better drive from his 'karting line' out of Turn 3 so as to pass before Turn 4. Ahead now was Hamilton, who was displaying much the same virtuosity as Max but in a faster car. For a time Max closed slightly, but thus informed, Hamilton stepped up the pace and the gap stabilised.

It was during this phase of the race that Max caught a moment that initially looked irretrievable as he again hit the standing water at the top of the hill, snapping the Red Bull sideways at enormous speed. He applied the opposite lock quickly enough to prevent a full spin and was able to scrub its speed off still within the width of the track, and he quickly pulled on the clutch paddle to disengage drive. As the car headed towards the left-hand barrier, most of the sting having been taken out of the moment, Max calmly released the clutch and induced a small power slide to quickly change its trajectory. 'Just like controlling a moment on the quad bike,' he quipped later. It lost him about four seconds on Hamilton but he retained the second place. He admitted over the radio that it had made his heart beat a little faster, but on his next lap he was over one second faster than Rosberg.

With the rain easing a little, Red Bull attempted to gamble Max a victory over Hamilton by bringing him in early for intermediate tyres. If the rain had continued to ease, it would likely have won Max the race. But when it started to pour once more, he was forced to pit for a corrective stop back on to full wet weather tyres after yet another safety car. This dropped Max back to 14th place, with 16 laps to go. He proceeded to drive a mesmerising sequence of laps, sometimes up to two seconds faster than anyone else, passing cars as soon as he came upon them, some quite outrageously at parts of the track never previously recognised as overtaking spots. He'd got himself back up to a remarkable third place by the time Hamilton took the flag.

'This felt great,' he said. 'Almost as good as my race in Barcelona. Every time my engineer came on the radio saying 'good job, keep going' I could hear the cheers from the crowd. It was amazing.'

'I think we just witnessed something very special,' said Christian Horner.

•

That spread between good and very special would continue to characterise Max's racing in 2017 as he sought to pull performances from another less-than-stellar car, the RB13.

Red Bull had been tripped up by the all-new set of aerodynamic regulations for this season, stipulating wider cars and bigger tyres. They would be significantly faster but, as it later transpired, Red Bull had failed to adapt its wind tunnel sufficiently to get accurate aerodynamic results on the new car. Not great news for the Verstappens: having become increasingly competitive in 2016, it would take most of the 2017 season to recover to that point. The early races were invariably fought out between Mercedes and Ferrari.

By the rocket-like standards of his career progress to date, 2017 was a treading water year for Max. Befitting his extra experience, he would deliver a calmer, cleaner performance through the season, still with the high-octane attacking style but with less controversial results. He would win two late-season grands prix, Malaysia and Mexico, in commanding fashion, but poor mechanical reliability and some lap-one incidents saw him finish only sixth in the championship, one place behind teammate Daniel Ricciardo, who managed just one win. From a small qualifying deficit to Ricciardo in 2016, Verstappen would establish a similarly small advantage in 2017.

Finding his car to be 1.2 seconds off Mercedes' pace in Melbourne wasn't the greatest way to start off the year, but Adrian Newey – an F1 engineer for Red Bull – would soon be hard at work clawing some of that back. In that original specification of car, Max took fifth, third, fifth and sixth in the first four races. For round five in Barcelona came the upgrade package and although it halved the deficit to the front runners, there would be no repeat of Max's fairytale victory here a year earlier. He was out just one corner into the race, as he, Raikkonen and Bottas failed to make it three-abreast and only Bottas made it through.

Fifth place in Monaco was followed by a starring cameo in Montreal: an aggressive start got him past Vettel's Ferrari and up to second, while a later safety car allowed him to put pressure on Hamilton's lead. But then the electrics died.

Though Montreal was a great piece of opportunism, the car first began to show some competitive underlying speed around the streets of Baku, and Ricciardo ended up winning a crazy, incident-packed race there. Max retired from the fray with a broken Renault engine. A Kvyat-Alonso collision took him out on lap one in Austria. The fast curves of Silverstone illustrated starkly that the car wasn't as competitive on that type of track as on the slow-corner ones, Max crossing the line almost a minute behind the winner Hamilton for fourth. In Hungary, he tried an optimistic move down Ricciardo's inside on the first lap but couldn't get slowed in time and embarrassingly took his teammate out. He apologised in person afterwards and Ricciardo accepted it. Electrical problems at Spa and a puncture at Monza (after clashing with Felipe Massa) continued the tale of woe.

Things began looking up at Singapore, another slow-corner track, after Max qualified on the front row. But he was out on the first lap yet again, the victim of a Vettel-induced collision between him and both Ferraris.

Then, in Malaysia, the waves of luck turned in his favour. Mercedes was out of sorts with an ill-balanced car and the Ferrari – the fastest cars around here – broke down.

Of all the circuits on the calendar, Malaysia's Sepang track featured the biggest spread of corner speeds. This was a particular problem for the low-rake 'diva' Mercedes W08 which in the words of its technical director James Allison, 'was too nervous at high speeds and too stable at low-speed.' Any set-up solutions for one of those problems would make the opposite problem worse. Only the Mercedes' powerful qualifying engine mode put Lewis Hamilton ahead of the Red Bulls on the grid. The other Merc of Valtteri Bottas was behind them. Vettel's Ferrari broke before doing a lap of qualifying and Raikkonen – who'd qualified on the front row, next to Hamilton – suffered an identical failure as he drove to the grid. That left just the two slower Mercs and Ricciardo for Max to beat – a much easier task than usual, especially now the RB13 had, at last, developed into a consistently quick car. Besides, Hamilton would surely be especially risk-averse as he was on the verge of sealing his fourth world championship.

Max dealt with Ricciardo through Turn 1 and the faster-starting Bottas into Turn 2. Ricciardo could find no way past the struggling Bottas, leaving Max to a private duel with Hamilton. It was immediately apparent that Max's Red Bull was able to track the Merc's every move. In doing so, Max was forcing Hamilton to use up his electrical energy store to stay in front and Max knew it would only be a few laps before that battery was empty and Hamilton vulnerable. With his own battery fully deployed, Max got a great run on to the straight to begin the fourth lap and simply hurled the Red Bull down the inside on Hamilton into Turn 1 from quite a long way back. It was a patented Verstappen move, aggressive but controlled. Hamilton resisted the urge to counter-attack. He had a title to win, his only rival Vettel was starting at the back and even if Hamilton had resisted

Verstappen at this point, the Red Bull would surely have passed later anyway.

So it was that on the day after his 20th birthday, Max Verstappen won his second grand prix. It wasn't anything like as hard work as his first, Max crossing the line 10 seconds clear of Hamilton who was fending off Ricciardo by the end. 'I could have closed that door, obviously,' said Hamilton to Max in the cool-down room before the podium celebrations.

'But you were fighting for a championship,' Max finished off.

'Yeah, I didn't want to risk it,' said Hamilton.

That conversation summarised the basic dynamics of the race but the bold way Verstappen had made his move clearly registered with Hamilton, as he referred to it a week later after winning the Japanese Grand Prix with Max right on his tail. 'I was kind of like – he won the last race, "I'm not letting you have this one." I was driving down the back straight at one point and I'm thinking "Jeez, the guy behind me is so much younger than me, I've got to make sure I kind of man-up and show my age, make sure that I stay ahead, show that I'm actually still very young at heart." That was kind of my thought process.' It sounded for all the world like Max had got into his head.

Verstappen relieved Raikkonen of third place on the last lap of the American Grand Prix but did so by missing out a chunk of the track – for which he was subsequently penalised, handing the place officially back to Raikkonen. Then it was off to Mexico. The super-high altitude of Mexico City suited the Renault engine particularly well and the Red Bull's high drag would not be punished so hard in the thin air. He qualified a strong second to Vettel's Ferrari, with Hamilton just behind them.

The stakes were vastly different between the first three drivers on the grid: a title to confirm for Hamilton who needed only a fifth place, the tiny sliver of a championship chance to eke out for Vettel who really needed a victory from his pole. For Verstappen, absolutely nothing to lose and motivated to hit back after the events of Austin – and in a Red Bull that was just made for this place. So as they fanned out three-abreast after the long run down to the first corner, something had to give and all that was certain was that Max was not going to back out of anything. For him, there was absolutely none of the ambiguity facing the other two – and that was a situation that suited his style and instincts perfectly.

He was either coming out of there with damage or – much more likely, knowing the other two had much more than he to lose – in the lead. It was the latter. Vettel unwisely tried to sit out the corner with Verstappen and lost a front endplate for his troubles. Hamilton and Vettel then made contact at the exit of the Turn 1–2 sequence, damaging their cars and releasing Max to a straightforward victory. 'This was one of the easiest races of my career,' he said. 'I felt I missed out on pole yesterday so I had a lot of motivation to get the result I wanted today.'

There were to be no repeats in the remaining two races in Brazil and Abu Dhabi, where he signed off with a couple of low-key fifth places.

Other than proving his debut win for the team in 2016 had been no fluke and that he could grasp the slightest opportunity of victory and never let it go, 2017 had been a plot-setting season for what was surely to come. The only question was: *when* would it come?

9

HEROES AND VILLAINS

'Dickhead. He needs to learn some respect.'
Lewis Hamilton

Having learnt from the mistakes of the previous year, Red Bull's 2018 car, the RB14, was perhaps the most aerodynamically advanced on the grid. But with 0.5 seconds worth of power shortfall in qualifying to Mercedes and Ferrari, it still wasn't made of the stuff to fight for titles.

Red Bull's resident technical genius Adrian Newey was despairing of the team's engine partner Renault. They'd promised him a lot for the 2018 engine but he'd heard it before. He would be monitoring the performance of the newly Honda-powered junior team, Toro Rosso and carrying out a direct comparison of the power units. At the beginning of the year, Horner confirmed that the Honda was only very slightly down on power compared to the Renault, with a lot more to come.

Newey was impressed with the ambitious attitude of the Japanese company despite its bruising three years with McLaren. Renault, he felt, lacked that ambition and was in it primarily for marketing reasons. Slowly but surely, Honda would come to form the backbone of Red Bull's mission to provide Max with a competitive car. This is what Horner was selling to the Verstappens as it dawned on them that 2018 would be another season of grabbing occasional opportunities, rather than dictating their own destiny.

As Jos and Raymond began to assess longer-term options, Max was going all out to compensate for the shortcomings of the new car himself. For the first few races of 2018 he was not the calm and measured performer of the year before, but more like the wildly determined disruptor of 2016. He seemed to have regressed.

In Australia, having lost out at the first corner, he ran the opening laps in fifth place behind the slower Haas of Kevin Magnussen, unable to find a way past. The Mercs and Ferraris ahead of him, meanwhile, escaped by up to one second per lap, and he became steadily more desperate in his attempts to find a way past the defensive Magnussen. He attacked with ineffective fury until eventually he clattered the car hard over the big exit kerbs of the fast Turn 12, damaging the car's diffuser. This lost him a lot of rear-end downforce, ensuring his rear tyres degraded even faster, playing its part in him spinning on the 10th lap and being passed by several cars before he could re-gather his momentum. He ended up sixth, 21 seconds behind fourth-placed teammate Ricciardo.

In Bahrain he crashed in qualifying, spinning into the gravel trap, and was unable to take any further part, leaving

him 15th on the grid. Hamilton had also suffered a compromised qualifying and they ran in tandem on the opening lap,
Hamilton ahead. Going into lap two, Max tried a marginal
move down Hamilton's outside into Turn 1. It was the sort of
move Lewis might have got out the way of when he was on
the verge of winning a title, but he had no need to accept it at
this stage of the season. Max seemed not to take into account
Hamilton's likely reaction and sure enough, the Red Bull
was bundled across the kerbs, puncturing a tyre, meaning a
long, slow drive to the pits for a replacement, his race ruined.
Hamilton continued unaffected and went on to finish third.
As the footage of the incident played in the green room before
the podium ceremony, a watching Hamilton could be heard
saying to teammate Bottas, 'Dickhead. He needs to learn some
respect.' In that comment was encapsulated the competitive
ego-driven pride involved in their contest. Verstappen had
pricked his attention in Malaysia the previous year and the
tension was only building. Max was surely fully aware of the
significance of how he chose to race Hamilton.

After this minor spat they publicly shook hands at the
beginning of the following Chinese Grand Prix weekend. But
the niggle on track was clearly still there.

All had looked like a routine 2018 race with Bottas'
Mercedes leading from Vettel's Ferrari and Hamilton's Merc,
the Red Bulls of Verstappen and Ricciardo a distant fourth
and fifth. But with no threat from behind, the sharp Red Bull
strategy team had delayed making their final stops, just in

case there was a late safety car they could benefit from. There was. The Red Bulls came in for fresh tyres, losing very little time as the pack was circulating slowly, joining right behind the lead three and on tyres way faster. It was all there for the taking. There was enough time left that they didn't need to risk much on a track where overtaking was relatively easy into the hairpin near the end of the lap.

Ricciardo had exited behind Raikkonen but he immediately picked off the Ferrari and sat himself on Max's tail as they both quickly caught the old-tyred Hamilton. The conventional thing would have been to wait until the hairpin to try any move, but Hamilton played Max. As they accelerated up to the fast sweep of Turn 7 – not a conventional passing place – Hamilton left a tempting gap to his outside. Verstappen, with the racer's impulse which in this moment he should have overrode, went to make the spectacular around-the-outside pass. All Hamilton had to do then was have a little bit of (an induced?) oversteer snap and Max was forced to take to the run-off area to avoid a collision. The following Ricciardo could hardly believe his luck as he zapped past them both into the next corner and then followed up with passes on Vettel and Bottas to win the race. Max did eventually get by Hamilton but then made contact with Vettel when trying to pass into the hairpin, spinning the Ferrari around and leaving Max back in fifth as Hamilton and Raikkonen repassed.

While the Hamilton incident could be put down to Max being suckered into it all, the one with Vettel was down to him. Even Jos afterwards was publicly critical. 'The overtake on Vettel really wasn't on,' he said. 'That wasn't possible. It was an error of judgement. In some circumstances, Max just has to think more.'

It was a brilliant win by Ricciardo but perhaps more significantly, an extraordinary little vignette of the pride of the pack and the young challenger whose thrusting energy had been de-railed by a cynical slap down. Was Hamilton surprised that Max had tried there? 'Yeah,' he replied. 'I've not ever seen anyone pass anyone there, certainly not a top driver. I'm surprised he tried it.' Leaving unsaid that Lewis himself had invited it.

Then Baku, a race that will live in infamy in Red Bull folklore, right up there with Istanbul 2010 and the collision of Vettel and Webber. The Red Bulls weren't as fast here as the Ferraris and Mercs and in the early stages Ricciardo and Max ran in tandem in fourth and fifth, having briefly had their races interrupted fighting the softer-tyred Renaults, with Max taking advantage of that to put a pass on Ricciardo. He was now the lead Red Bull and whichever was ahead would automatically get the first pit stop – which was usually an advantage. With the Renaults out of the way (Hulkenberg had crashed, Sainz had pitted) the Red Bull dice continued and it was at times quite a hair-raising one.

Ricciardo got the slipstream on Max (further aided by the wing-stalling drag reduction system which allows the car behind to be faster) down the long, kinking 'straight' parallel to the Caspian coast which sees the cars flat out for a mile, then pulled out and attempted to pass into Turn 1. Max sat it out, refusing to concede, and twice their tyre walls rubbed as they went side-by-side. Already there were anxious looks on the Red Bull pit wall but, they reassured themselves, the pair had raced like this in Malaysia last year and seemed to know where to draw the line. Still, rubbing tyres seemed a little too much . . . Finally, Ricciardo made the move stick and got ahead just before the pit stops and so came in first, with Max scheduled for the following lap.

Ordinarily, the car pitting first is at the advantage because it will be doing its out-lap on fresh tyres as the other car is doing its in-lap on old worn rubber. But sometimes the new tyres don't come up to temperature quickly enough and so it was here. On his out-lap Ricciardo could feel it. Meanwhile Max was making a stunning in-lap, aided by having got a big tow as he was lapping Pierre Gasly's Toro Rosso. Ricciardo's tyres were only just getting up to temperature as he completed his out-lap – and there was Max exiting the pits now in front of him again. 'You'll just have to do it all again,' Ricciardo's race engineer Simon Rennie advised, as if Ricciardo needed telling . . .

That was exactly Ricciardo's plan. He knew that on this lap Max would be suffering exactly the same tyre warm-up issues he'd just had and so would be vulnerable. This was the only lap on which Ricciardo would have a grip advantage and so he was already planning his move. Getting out of the final corner on to the long straight better, he timed the slipstream and the DRS perfectly. Max could see him coming and knew he'd be under attack going into the braking zone. Ricciardo would wait on the outside and try to dummy Max to cover that side then at the last moment swoop across to the inside. As he made that counter-swoop, Max was ready for him and also edged that way – which left Ricciardo, already hard on the brakes, no room. He hit the back of Verstappen's car hard, briefly lifting Max's rear wheels into the air and both Red Bulls slewed to a stop on the escape road, terminally damaged.

On the pit wall, Adrian Newey took off his headphones and threw them to the ground. Christian Horner, ashen-faced with anger, walked to the Red Bull unit in the paddock and waited there for his drivers. He wanted a word . . .

'Yeah, I was furious,' he recalls. 'I ripped them both new ones.' A couple of years after the incident, he gave Channel 4's David Coulthard a bit more detail of that meeting. 'I remember absolutely losing it with the two of them when we got back into the briefing room. Adrian was in the room as well, I remember he looked slightly shocked. And these two kids are looking at me as if I was some hugely scary-looking teacher or something. That was probably the last time I had an over-rev.'

Today, he sees it with the detachment of time. 'They raced each other closely for three seasons and only made contact twice, which isn't too bad considering the intensity of it and

how often they started alongside each other on the grid –
98 per cent of the time there was no issue. On this occasion
both drivers were at fault. Their interests suddenly exceeded
that of the team.' They were representing hundreds of people
at the factory who had worked hard to prepare the cars they
were privileged to race, Horner pointed out. To then have
them put their own interests above the team and leave them
with nothing was not acceptable. He demanded that when
they got back to base, both drivers would go through every
department in the factory and apologise to the workforce.
Horner threw in an additional penalty: they would have to
pay the drinks bill for the team Christmas party at the end
of the year.

'I got the impression that for Max it was all water off
a duck's back,' relates Horner. For Ricciardo it went rather
deeper. 'I felt I was being made to apologise like a naughty
schoolboy for something which I didn't feel was my fault.' Did
that play its part in him choosing to leave the team at the end
of that season? 'Yes, definitely. There were a few things, but
Baku was a big one,' he answered.

When Max was asked in the TV pen afterwards if he
accepted he'd made more than one move in the braking zone,
he simply disengaged from the question. 'I don't want to talk
about it,' he said. 'It's a bad situation for the team.'

That's how it is with Max. Things happen, then it's in the
past. There's little or no reflection. It's a quality which takes

the poison out of potentially vitriolic situations as he doesn't seem to hold grudges. Winning is all there is and everything else is subservient to that. As he phrased it in *Whatever It Takes*, 'Sometimes you even have to be a bit of a dick.'

'It was a racing accident between the two of them,' said Helmut Marko in the immediate aftermath. 'There is not one more at fault than on the other side.' Asked if the team could have prevented it, he replied. 'It's against our philosophy. We let the drivers race. We don't have a number one or number two. But we expect a responsibility from the drivers' side.'

'It is always a challenge when you have two very competitive drivers,' concludes Horner. 'Teammate is a fallacy because they are both basically dictating the value and worth of the other driver. Where you have a conflict, is between the team championship and drivers' championship. The reality is that it is the drivers' championship that means everything to them and winning races and that is what makes them so good.'

•

Fresh from his trip to Milton Keynes, Max was a solid third in the Spanish Grand Prix, far behind the two Mercedes of Hamilton and Bottas. But even then, he still made contact with another car, clipping off his front wing endplate as he lapped Lance Stroll's Williams. That made five consecutive races in which he'd had some sort of incident as the teams gathered for F1's most prestigious race: Monaco.

The personal devastation of crashing – in a near-identical repeat of his 2016 accident there – in practice and his consequent inability to even take part in qualifying was only intensified by how quick the car was around here. He and Ricciardo had been vying for the quickest time throughout the practices. Max knew he'd just blown a major, major opportunity and there was no one to blame but himself.

Max sat as a lone, crumpled, despondent figure in his room at the team's hospitality unit some time after qualifying had finished, with Ricciardo on pole (from where he would win the next day). Horner knocked on the door and stepped inside. 'So he'd already, in China, watched Daniel win a race that he should have won,' Horner recalls, 'and now he was about to be in that position again. It was a question of just sitting down with him to say, "Look, you have got all the ability to do this, you have got more talent than probably all the people that are out there, but you don't need to be the fastest on every single lap on every corner. Just think about it." And yes, he took it in, he listened, he turned up in Montreal on his own, without any people around him, and literally from that moment onward, bang, it was like a switch. He was like a metronome and he just got stronger and stronger and stronger. And I think he finally looked inwards. He had the ability to do that and realise that okay, there are areas that I can polish up and literally it was like a switch from that early part of the season to that Montreal race and then suddenly we were off.'

Formula 1 presents a complex set of demands and it's easy not to fully grasp how deeply this goes. For Max, endeavouring to maximise the outrageous talent that had always been so obvious, the crash down to earth in Monaco forced him to take responsibility for himself, to become more in charge of his own destiny. It allowed him to become a truly great driver every time he got in the car rather than just when circumstances aligned for him. From the moment of that crash, he became a world champion waiting for his car.

It's interesting also that he turned up at the next race without an entourage. Not even Jos. This de-coupling was probably necessary. He owed everything to Jos, but to focus fully on his own racing, now that he had all the tools in his box, he perhaps needed that distance. Helmut Marko had noticed the process beginning even before then. 'I'd say it had probably begun around the second year at Red Bull,' he says, 'so around 2017 some time. In the beginning, with only one year in F3, he was listening to and relying on Jos. But he's very smart. He found out a level where Jos cannot help and there were moments where Max has said quite clearly "this is your line". It was coming slowly, but it was a process you could see happening.' Monaco 2018 perhaps completed that process.

Not that he was prepared to talk about it coming into Montreal where on being asked in the pre-weekend FIA press conference if he was going to change his approach, having had an incident in all six of the previous events, he got irritated. 'Well, you know, I get really tired of all the comments of me, that I should change my approach. I will never do that, because it's brought me to where I am right now. After a race, it's not the right time to talk. So everybody who has those comments, I don't listen to it anyway. I just do my own thing. Of course, the beginning of the year so far it hasn't been going so well, not in the way I liked it. A few mistakes, I think especially Monaco and China, but it doesn't make sense to keep talking about it, because I get really tired of it. Yeah, it just feels like there are no better questions out there than to keep asking me about what happened in the previous weekend. So yeah, I'm just focusing on what's ahead. I'm confident that I can turn things around. You know the speed is there. I've always been quick, every single weekend. It would be much more of a problem if I was really slow, because that's a critical problem.'

A journalist tried to press the point, finally taking Max over the edge. 'Like I said in the beginning of this press conference, I get really tired of all the questions, so yeah I think if I get a few more I'll head-butt someone.'

He may not have shown much grace under provocation, but he had clearly drawn a line under Monaco, had looked inward to understand what it represented and had resolved to address it. Himself. Not with any further discussion – and certainly not in a press conference.

He was in effervescent form throughout qualifying in Montreal, nudging the Red Bull's tyres right up to the walls and qualifying third-fastest behind Vettel and Bottas but ahead of Hamilton. He'd finish that way in the race, max-imising what the car had to give. That's pretty much what he'd do for the next two and a half years. In France, he was second after Vettel and Bottas collided in front of him on the opening lap.

Occasionally circumstances would align and Max could now be relied upon to nail them – such as at the Red Bull Ring where the Red Bull itself was not particularly fast but where both Mercedes retired with mechanical failures. On the first lap Max diced wheel-to-wheel with Raikkonen's Ferrari, putting a wheel on the grass to stay alongside it on the run down to Turn 4, then going side-by-side, totally com-mitted through the fast kinks of Turns 6 and 7. Neither was prepared to concede and it was only settled as they rubbed tyres and the Ferrari twitched out of line, allowing Max to finally go ahead. In hindsight, that move won him the race, for Raikkonen was still right there at the end, coming at him on fresher tyres, Max judging things perfectly in not taking too much from his worn rubber while still forcing a hard pace on the chasing Ferraris. It was a perfect mix of aggression and control, way better than some of his frustrated tyre-destroy-ing races the year before. Career win number four.

Mechanical retirements in Britain and Hungary, a distant fourth in Germany, a third in Belgium half-a-minute behind the winning Mercedes, a fifth in Monza where the car was left breathless by the more powerful Mercs and Ferraris. These were races to be endured. But Singapore – with its emphasis

on low-speed handling and its lack of power sensitivity –
presented a chance to shine, especially after Ferrari messed
up the timing of its qualifying runs. Hamilton drove what he
reckoned was the best qualifying lap of his career to set pole.
Max drove what he reckoned was the best qualifying lap of
his career to go second – but it had been on course for pole
until late in the lap when a misfire cost him. That, essentially,
set the structure of the race, with Hamilton winning from
Verstappen and Vettel.

Back to normality in Russia (fifth behind the Mercs and
Ferraris) and Japan (third behind the Mercs). In Austin, a
driveshaft pulled itself out of the gearbox in qualifying as
Max rode too hard over a kerb. It left him starting 18th, but
in an incident-packed race he drove magnificently to finish
second, even pressuring Raikkonen's winning Ferrari.

Into the last few laps Hamilton was recovering from an
extra pit stop gamble Mercedes had made in trying to find a
way past Raikkonen. But before he could get to the Ferrari,
he needed to find a way by Max – who wasn't giving an inch.
With two laps to go on much older tyres than the Mercedes
he was slow out of Turn 12 at the end of the back straight,
giving Hamilton a run on him through the slow following turn
which they went through side-by-side. Verstappen refused
to surrender and the wheel-to-wheel dice lasted for the next
few corners until Hamilton used the run-off on the exit of
Turn 18, effectively surrendering rather than risk contact and
a non-finish.

'I thought you gave me a lot of room,' said an amused Verstappen later. 'Yeah,' said Hamilton, 'I never know with you. I didn't want a coming together . . .'

This result was the perfect run-up to Mexico, where the altitude was always very friendly to the Red Bull's Renault motor.

•

The Mexican Grand Prix would be Max's final opportunity to set the record of the youngest-ever pole-sitter (held by Vettel) and he was confident he could. So he was mortified when Ricciardo shaded him by two-hundredths of a second. As they pulled into the parc ferme at the end, Max knocked over the 'P2' bollard he was supposed to park behind. Jokey Daniel made a big thing of how delighted he was in the TV pen interviews afterwards, Max looking on with a face like thunder. It just seemed to rub salt into the wound. The little kid who'd thrown his game controller across the room after crashing out of the game was still visible.

'I saw his face when he turned up at the track today,' said Horner on the Sunday after Max completely dominated the race start-to-finish, 'and I could see there was absolutely no way he wasn't coming out of Turn 2 either with damage or in the lead. I didn't think anyone else stood a chance.' So it proved, Ricciardo retiring from a distant second with a power unit failure, Max taking career win number five. Meanwhile Hamilton clinched another world title, his fifth.

In Brazil Verstappen had the opportunity to make it two wins in a row as Mercedes were struggling with tyre usage. Having passed both Ferraris and both Mercs in storming fashion, Max was comfortably leading Hamilton when his old karting and F3 rival Esteban Ocon got in the way. The Frenchman had pitted his Force India for new tyres and was a lap behind but able on the new rubber to go faster than the two leaders. He'd already unlapped himself from Hamilton and was now slipstreaming Verstappen down to the Senna Esses. Max could have let him go at this point but as the leader he assumed the backmarker wasn't going to interfere with his race, that if he wanted to pass he'd do it somewhere risk-free and neutral – like under DRS on the run down to Turn 4 perhaps. Not by sitting out the apex of Turn 2 from the inside. Ocon, once he'd done the natural racing thing that's hardwired into a driver of claiming his piece of track, was left with nowhere to go as Verstappen turned in under the mistaken assumption that Ocon would no longer be there, that he'd have merged in behind to prepare a less risky pass. They collided, spinning in elegant formation. Before Verstappen could get going again, with much of the right-hand side of the floor missing, there was a flash of silver – and Hamilton was through.

Ocon had no real business fighting for track space with a car he was a lap behind. He simply assumed Max wasn't going to take issue, but shouldn't have. Max, in turn, was perhaps not wise in simply assuming Ocon would wait. But he wasn't in the wrong for the incident itself. In the post-race weighing-in area the drivers must visit, Max walked up to remonstrate with Ocon who said something to further irritate him. Max pushed him a couple of times.

In the green room afterwards, the microphones picked up him discussing with Hamilton the on-track incident he'd had with Ocon. Hamilton seemed to be offering advice, saying, 'Yeah, but he had nothing to lose. You did.' It was an expression of the different stages they were at in their careers, Hamilton talking from the perspective of someone who'd been annealed by years of success and was able to take a strategic view, Max still with it all to do and bursting with unfulfilled ambition.

But Max's charging, uncompromising style continued to make Hamilton wary of him on track. When Hamilton was doing a feature with Sky TV's Johnny Herbert, driving around the Austin track, Herbert had asked, 'Okay, imagine you've got Max Verstappen on your back coming into this corner, what do you do?' and Hamilton had replied, 'Well, that's the thing with Max, you don't ever know what he's going to do. I try just to give him room.' If he heard it, it would probably have been music to Max's ears.

The Ocon shoving incident in the weigh-in area would cost Max a reprimand and a bit of FIA 'community service' during the F1 off-season – he would attend the Marrakesh E-Prix in Morocco as an observer to the stewards. He took it in good spirit, saying afterwards, 'It's interesting to see it from the other side – normally you can't spend an entire day with the stewards. Everybody does their own job during the weekend, and it's good to really see what it takes to make these important decisions – sometimes a decision might not be nice for a certain person but it has to be taken and you have to follow the rules. I think it's good to experience different things in racing rather than just sitting in the car – to be here and do this kind of work has been a constructive thing for me.' It once again highlighted how his persona changes once he has his 'racing head' on.

Before then, though, was the final grand prix of the season, in Abu Dhabi where he was a distant third to Hamilton and Vettel. This confirmed his fourth place in the championship, meaning he wasn't obliged to attend the FIA prize-giving gala. 'Maybe I could do that as one of my community service days,' he quipped. Gesturing towards Hamilton and Vettel, the champion and runner-up, he suggested, 'I could help write the speeches for you guys.'

10

ALL THAT WAS NEEDED WAS THE CAR

Yet again Max did not have the tool with which to take on Hamilton . . .

There were two big changes at Red Bull for 2019: Daniel Ricciardo had left and Honda had arrived.

Ricciardo turned down the team's big-money offer and left for Renault, leaving a surprised Horner with the suspicion he was simply running away from the Max challenge. He'd won two races in 2018, the same as Max, but it could conceivably have been five for Max and none for Daniel had Max made smarter choices and in the qualifying battle Max's average advantage had increased. Replacing Ricciardo for 2019 would be the promoted Toro Rosso driver Pierre Gasly – and replacing him at Toro Rosso would be Max's old karting rival Alex Albon.

But while losing Ricciardo wasn't ideal for Red Bull, Max leaving would have been devastating – and there was a lingering concern about that. Helmut Marko confirmed there was a team performance clause in his driver's contract which, if not met during the 2019 season, could release him for the following year. With Mercedes, as ever, putting Valtteri Bottas on a one-year-deal for 2019, there would be an obvious place for Max in 2020 if he wanted to get on with fighting for championships. Ferrari, for certain, would also be keeping an eye on him.

'Max is an incredibly loyal person,' says Horner, 'as are the people around him and I think he really believes in this team. And I think that is why at any juncture to commit to the future, it was always a straightforward conversation. He always believed in the people, in our decision-making in bringing Honda into the team. His father had worked with Honda [in the late 1990s] so he knew their capability. So he trusted us. The missing piece for us was that engine and when Honda was able to start delivering, we were there.'

The big horsepower would be a couple of seasons arriving, but they were now building towards something more competitive each year rather than repeating the cycle of hope and disappointment of the previous few seasons with Renault.

There had been a significant technical regulation change for the new season, bringing simplified front-wing endplates, a limitation on under-nose guide vanes, a reduction in front brake duct sizes and a lowering of barge board heights. These seemed to combine to derail Red Bull from the fruitful aerodynamic path it had previously been on and had more impact on them than on Mercedes and Ferrari.

For the first third of the season the car was a handful, still very quick into the corners but with an inconsistent balance thereafter, as keeping the outwash airflow robust through different speeds and attitudes of roll and pitch proved impossible. The rear of the car would become progressively less stable through the turn, something which seriously hurt the confidence of the new recruit Gasly.

Although this would hurt both drivers, it tended to amplify the gap between Gasly and Verstappen, who was far more relaxed about the balance changes. This would come to have implications for both the team's driver line-up and also its development direction.

For now, the team concentrated on improving the RB15 and by mid-season it was good enough for Max to win at the Red Bull Ring for the second year in succession. Until then, he had been in the very familiar Red Bull no man's land behind the leading Merc and Ferrari drivers but ahead of the smaller teams: third in Australia, passing Vettel's Ferrari late in the race; fourth in Bahrain, China and Baku; a distant third in Spain. At Monaco, his skills and a good tyre strategy had him on the back of Hamilton's race-leading, older-tyred Mercedes for many laps and they even banged wheels at the chicane on the last lap. But his second place across the line became an official fourth because of an unsafe pit release penalty. In Canada, he was a distant fifth behind the Mercs and Ferraris.

Austria was different. The Mercs were in trouble with overheating and Vettel's Ferrari wouldn't start in Q3, leaving him starting the race down in 10th. Max's old karting adversary Charles Leclerc, now at Ferrari, was setting the tracks alight, especially in qualifying. Here he set his second career pole, a quarter-of-a-second clear of Hamilton's Mercedes, with Verstappen third ahead of Bottas. The orange army had invaded, despite the 10-hour drive here from Holland, and the campsites around the circuit were overflowing with Max's fans. The groans were audible as the start lights went out and Verstappen's car stuttered slowly off the line and dropped down to eighth place; he and the team had under-estimated the track's grip and set the clutch bite point too aggressively. But actually, that turned out to be the most wonderful blessing in disguise, since it made feasible a race-winning tyre strategy. Because he was the last of the group of fast cars – once he'd made his way through the slower runners – he had no undercut pressure from behind, this allowing him to run a very long first stint and putting him on much fresher rubber than the Ferraris and Mercs in his last stint.

There was magic in the hot air as he rejoined 12.9 seconds adrift of the leader Leclerc with 39 laps to go. Could he average 0.33 seconds per lap faster than Leclerc while also passing the two cars in between them? He was up for giving it a try – and so was Honda. He asked for more power. The reply came back: 'Mode 11 (selected by Max on his steering wheel). Run it to the end.' This was the engine's most aggressive mode. Honda's vice principal was here, the whole fanatical crowd was behind them – and Max was in the mood.

Vettel was his first scalp and as he passed the Ferrari the crowd could be heard above the engines. Next: Bottas. Just as he was almost up with the Mercedes, he suddenly fell back. 'I'm losing power,' he radioed. It was merely an exhaust sensor playing up and with some guidance from the pits about how to reset it, he was soon back to full power and scything up the inside of Bottas to go second, with Leclerc now just five seconds ahead.

With six laps to go Max was within DRS range of the Ferrari – and the crowd was going crazy. A lap later and he was alongside at both Turns 3 and 4, but Leclerc was defending perfectly. Saving his energy for a lap, Max relaunched his attack on the 68th, slicing up the inside of Turn 3 to take the lead – only for Leclerc to switch to the inside and get the tow up to Turn 4, where he was able to get back ahead.

Lap 69, two from the end, Max went yet deeper on the brakes into the inside of Turn 3. At some point between turn-in and mid-corner Max had the place, the Red Bull's nose clearly ahead. Leclerc refused to surrender though and opted to stay side-by-side, around the outside. Max held firm, the wheels banged – and Leclerc went off the circuit, losing vital momentum.

'What was that?' questioned Leclerc for the benefit of the stewards. 'He pushed me off the track.' The stewards looked at it later and didn't agree. For them, the pass was legitimate – and just like that, Max gave Honda its first win since 2006.

As he stood beaming on the top step of the podium, he was pointing to the big 'H' on his overalls.

'I don't think the second overtake was done correctly,' said Leclerc afterward, 'but I believe that anyway the end would have probably been the same. But it's just not the way you overtake.'

'It's hard racing,' countered Max. 'Otherwise we have to stay home . . . if those things aren't allowed in racing, then what's the point of being in Formula 1?'

•

In one of the press conferences earlier in the weekend Hamilton had been asked about the rumours of Verstappen joining him at Mercedes for 2020 and he was a little taken aback. 'I think the team's pretty happy with Valtteri and me,' was his initial response. But, bravado building, he followed up with: 'I do know Max is definitely interested in opportunities . . . Maybe. If there is a chance, then great.' Turning to Max, he said, 'Sure, I don't mind driving with you. I'll drive against whoever.'

I asked Max about that at the following British Grand Prix. 'Yes, well he had to say that,' he replied with a smile. 'I'd have said that in his situation. He's not going to say, "Oh, I'd hate it." But I don't think about these things. Also, I'm not purely focused on Lewis. There are other great drivers in the paddock who can achieve similar things.'

At Silverstone, the Verstappen-Leclerc dice continued

where it had left off in Austria, albeit only for third position this time as Mercedes dominated. Their wheel-to-wheel dice had the crowd cheering wildly and this time it was Leclerc who emerged on top. Max was later barged into the gravel trap after Vettel misjudged an out-braking move into Vale corner. He got going again but the delay left him back in fifth place at the flag.

Max bounced back hard at the next race, around Germany's Hockenheim circuit. This event had been financially moribund for years but the insatiable ticket demand from Max's fans had extended its life for at least another year. His following was now a phenomenon, unseen since the days of Michael Schumacher's in Germany, but in Max's case extending everywhere else too. They were not to be disappointed on this late July weekend. The car was becoming steadily faster – or it was for Max at least. His teammate Pierre Gasly, still wrestling with its demanding aerodynamic traits, was nowhere near Max's pace and already Helmut Marko was looking at promoting the rookie Alex Albon from Toro Rosso in a re-run of the Kvyat-Verstappen swap of three years earlier.

Max qualified on the front row, helped by mechanical issues for both Ferraris. Heavy rain greeted the crowd on race day, setting in place a festival of drama out of which Verstappen would emerge victorious. Initially in third place behind the two Mercedes, he eventually made it to the front after both Hamilton and Bottas suffered incidents in the slippery conditions, as did Leclerc who crashed out in the Ferrari when looking set to take the lead. Then all Max had to do was stay there, looking totally in control through the comings and goings of safety cars both real and virtual. It was a superbly judged performance and further confirmation of his now all-encompassing skill.

'An unbelievable performance from Max and the team today,' said Christian Horner afterwards. 'It took five pit stops to win that race. Max kept his head in tricky conditions, he had great pace when he needed it and he made that win happen.' Horner also reserved praise for his old driver Daniil Kvyat who had finished third in his Toro Rosso. 'Massive congratulations to Daniil, who in addition to this became a father last night.' The mum was Kelly Piquet, daughter of triple world champion Nelson Piquet.

Although it was Kvyat who scored the podium for Toro Rosso thanks to a late gamble on tyres, for most of the race the lead Toro Rosso had been that of the rookie Alex Albon, who in the tricky conditions was running an impressive fourth from very early in the race. Given that Gasly had crashed out – ironically while dicing with Albon – that rather decided things in the minds of Marko and Horner. Plans were made to swap the two drivers from the Belgian Grand Prix: Gasly would return to Toro Rosso and Albon would be promoted to Red Bull in his rookie season.

At Budapest's Hungaroring the week after Hockenheim, Max finally took the first pole position of his F1 career. He led the race from Hamilton who attempted a pass around the outside of the Red Bull at the fast Turn 4. Verstappen held him out over the kerbs and thereafter Hamilton was running out of tyre grip. In a tactical masterstroke, with a big gap back to third place, Mercedes decided to pit Hamilton again to see if he could use the extra grip of new tyres to catch and pass Verstappen before the end, thus trapping Red Bull into trying to hang on (as Hamilton's 'undercut' would have ensured Max coming out behind if he'd responded by also pitting). Three laps from the end, with his tyres almost dead, Max had to surrender to the inevitable and accept defeat.

It was thin pickings for the next few races, with retirements and power unit grid penalties, with only a third in Singapore and a fourth in Russia to show. In Spa, he was hit by Raikkonen and in Suzuka by Leclerc, both on the first lap. At his old happy hunting ground of Mexico, he set the fastest time in qualifying but was demoted three places for having not slowed for yellow flags for Bottas' crashed Mercedes when exiting the last corner. In the race, he made heavy contact with Hamilton at the first corner after running the Mercedes out wide, knowing Hamilton would need to be cautious, with a title to clinch.

Hamilton got as far over as he could in avoidance but as he applied the power with his outside tyre on the painted white line, he got a snap of oversteer at just the part of track that pinches the cars together for the left of Turn 2. They touched – and both took to the grass and lost many places.

'I was surrounded by a bunch of cars,' related Hamilton.

'I braked into Turn 1 and all of a sudden Max is alongside me. If you've seen races before, I always leave Max a lot of space – it's the smartest thing you can do. But there wasn't a lot of space for me to give him . . .'

Max was still clearly very much in Hamilton's head. Whenever he was around, Hamilton was not racing naturally. Max was later taken out of contention entirely after puncturing a tyre attempting to overtake Bottas.

In Austin, he finished a close third to the Mercs despite floor damage.

And then, out of the gloom of this late-season slump came a superb victory in Brazil. The Honda was impressively potent by now and after a technical directive in Austin had limited the Ferrari's power, it was probably the strongest engine of all. Verstappen set pole, burst into the lead from Hamilton, and though he was briefly undercut by the Mercedes at the pit stops he reclaimed it almost immediately. A late safety car gave Red Bull strategy chief Hannah Schmitz the agonising dilemma of whether to surrender the lead for fresh tyres or leave Max out there at the front ready for the restart but with Hamilton likely on new tyres right behind. The car's pace and the aggressive racecraft of Verstappen gave her the confidence to opt for the former. And she called it perfectly: Hamilton, who had stayed out on his old tyres in response to Max pitting, was mugged by the Red Bull on the restart.

Another safety car for the crashing Ferraris led Hamilton to pit and rejoin behind Gasly's Toro Rosso and Albon's Red

Bull. After passing Gasly on the last lap, he made an ill-judged move on Albon, spinning the rookie out and costing himself the runner-up spot which was instead taken by Gasly, giving Honda a 1-2.

•

The race strategy group of any F1 team numbers dozens of people, with a large proportion of them feeding information in real time from the 'operations room' back at the factory. But it's the chief strategist on the pit wall who has to make the calls. Usually, they are simply dictated by the numbers and there is a whole lot of sophisticated predictive software, ana-lysing millions of scenarios in a fraction of a second, behind those numbers. But sometimes, as in this case, it's a case of gut instinct and belief. The former Hannah McMillan has a Masters degree in mechanical engineering from Cambridge University and specialised in statistical modelling, opti-misation and regression analysis. She'd just returned from maternity leave as she sat on that Brazil pit wall making the crucial call. But she made it partly based on the absolute certainty of Max being able to pull the pass on Hamilton if she gave him a new set of tyres. That confidence his ability instils in her helps her to help him. She would come to be instrumental in other Max victories in the future.

Just a few days after the Brazil race, grandfather Frans – where much of the essence of Max's story had begun – finally lost his battle with cancer. 'Joy and sorrow are often close together', Max said in a brief statement read out by Dutch broadcaster Ziggo Sport as he cancelled his planned appearance on their show.

Max signed off the 2019 season with a second to Hamilton in Abu Dhabi. It had been a very promising start to the Honda partnership, three victories and third place in the championship for Verstappen. But it still wasn't 'The Car', the one in which he could conquer the world. Would that car ever arrive for him?

The Red Bull RB16-Honda might have been that car. Turns out it wasn't. The Red Bull technical department had changed the aerodynamic concept around the front, adopting a Mercedes-like slim nose with the aim of enhancing underbody downforce. But testing in Barcelona suggested possible problems. It was reasonably quick, albeit not as quick as the Mercedes. But more worryingly, both Verstappen and Albon spun the car frequently. It wasn't easy to pinpoint what was making it so unpredictable.

We'd find out more at the opening race in Melbourne, we assumed. But aerodynamic niceties turned out not to be the topic of conversation around Albert Park. The F1 bubble was no protection against the new Covid-19 virus. After two mechanics tested positive on the Thursday, the whole meeting was cancelled, the Australian authorities not wishing to have a 'super-spreader' event on their doorstep. The move was fully supported by the automotive manufacturers Ferrari, Renault, Mercedes and Alfa Romeo, if not by all the teams.

As the world closed down in the face of the global pandemic, Liberty Media, the recent new owners of F1, looked on with horror at what might be about to happen to their investment. One after another, races on the calendar were cancelled. Meanwhile sim racing's popularity took off as bored F1 drivers, denied the real thing, made high-profile entries into online racing competition. Max had already teamed up with his friend Lando Norris in the previous year to win the virtual Spa 24 Hours with Redline Racing. Now, others joined – notably Leclerc and George Russell.

The F1 management arm of Liberty Media looked at the problem of how to restart the F1 calendar in a time of a global pandemic and lockdowns in much the same way F1 approaches any problem: with analysis, innovation and determination. The barriers were removed one-by-one until a way had been found to run the races behind closed doors without spectators but still with the massive global TV coverage. Teams, logistics people, media and broadcasters were each assigned their own bubbles to limit any spread. On-site Covid testing centres were introduced together with an automated phone app which ensured only those testing negative could gain entry, and then only within their own designated areas. Formula 1 made agreements with the relevant national governments and their border forces after satisfying them of the robustness of their systems. Deals were done with various circuits and the calendar looked nothing like that of any in recent history – but a way was found to hold 17 races during an unprecedented pandemic. F1 was the only global sport that found a way of continuing.

As the F1 management was discussing how their plan would work, Red Bull owner Dietrich Mateschitz was the one who gave motion to the whole idea, volunteering to open the season with two grands prix on consecutive weekends at his Red Bull Ring circuit in Spielberg, Austria. So the season started there in June rather than at Melbourne in March and the calendar was improvised along the way.

This had an indirect impact upon Max's competitive circumstances, in that it wasn't until racing began in June that the limitations of the car were fully evident. Had the season begun in March, there'd have been more time to develop it than in the compressed season the pandemic dictated.

The car had an inconsistent handling balance between fast corners and slow. In slow corners requiring lots of steering lock it tended to oversteer despite a general understeer balance in fast corners. It put Alex Albon in much the same position as Gasly the previous year, unable to live with Max's ability to let the rear of the car float around him into slow corners.

It would lead to Red Bull replacing Albon for 2021 with the experienced Sergio Perez. Being paired with such a phenomenon as Max in his rookie and sophomore seasons, in such a car, did not give a representative reading on Albon's ability. 'Max is a very difficult teammate,' says Christian Horner, 'because it must be soul destroying that you are looking at a piece of data and he's three quarters of a second up the road and you are thinking how the hell has he done that? And it's not just at one race, it's at every race.

'Yet he doesn't demand number one status, he doesn't have anything in his contract that stipulates he has to have all the best bits, the newest bits, the developments; he is very fair in that respect, but the team will always gravitate around the driver that has the best chance at the end of the day.'

Helmut Marko addressed the same subject: 'Teammates compare their cars with his: "Do I have the same material?" they think. "How can I overcome him?" They can't, so they try to change the set-up on the car or adapt their driving style. Of course, you can't accept that you're simply not as good as him. At some stage, you have to recognise, "bah, there is someone who is special and it's just not possible to beat him". It's sometimes my job to make them understand that. Is that cruel? I don't think so.'

But while the tricky RB16 exaggerated the gap between Max and his teammate it also meant that yet again Max did not have the tool with which to take on Hamilton. For most of the year, at least.

At the Red Bull Ring for the first spectator-free grand prix in history Max was running second, in between the Mercs of Bottas and Hamilton, in the opening stint of the first race when his car broke down. The following weekend at the same venue he qualified second-fastest to Hamilton in heavy rain but in the dry of race day was caught and passed at the pit stops by Bottas. His distant third place pretty much pre-viewed what his season was going to look like. Wet weather would give him an occasional opportunity to nip at Bottas and sometimes beat him, like at the third round, in Budapest. But Hamilton was invariably out of reach.

There were two consecutive races at Silverstone, the second of which Max won but only because the Mercedes cars suffered terrible tyre blistering. In Spain, he split the Mercs after Bottas blew his start. In Belgium, the top three of Hamilton, Bottas, Verstappen remained unchanged through-out. In Monza, he retired early from a lowly position with a blown engine and a week later at Mugello was taken out on the first lap by Gasly's Toro Rosso. This was the anti-clock-wise circuit, never previously used for a grand prix, where Verstappen had refused the 'pussy pad' to support his neck. In Russia, a double penalty for Hamilton allowed Max to take runner-up spot to Bottas. At the Nurburgring he had Bottas beaten for second even before the latter retired. In Portugal, he was a distant third to the Mercedes one-two. In the cold of the rebooted Turkish Grand Prix the car's inability to switch on its tyres limited Max to fifth.

But between that race and the next (in Bahrain), a break-through was made at Red Bull and for the last three races Max was able to compete on more or less equal terms with the Mercs, qualifying on the front row in Bahrain and win-ning the season finale in Abu Dhabi from pole.

The team's technical director Pierre Wache explained

how Verstappen's talent had played its part in leading them astray, until they realised what was happening and were able to reverse their development direction.

'He has an ability to control instability that would be impossible for some others,' he said. 'We know that sometimes, making a car on the edge in this way can create a quicker car. So we went in this direction and Max was extracting lap time from it and so we *kept* going in that direction. But it was only because he has so much talent that he was still getting lap time from it. We realised after a while that we had reached the ceiling with the car in this way and also you saw with the other drivers, with Pierre [Gasly in 2019] and Alex [Albon], they struggled to extract the best from it. We had gone too far in this direction. In an F1 team the system is so big, to revert back is quite long and painful. But we had got there by the end of the season when we were fully competitive with Mercedes. It was frustrating because if we had known at the start what we found later, Mercedes was beatable.'

Max's teammate of that year, Alex Albon, gave further background to this story when he talked with *The Players' Tribune* in early 2023 about his time in the senior Red Bull team in 2019 and 2020 when he drove as Pierre Gasly's replacement after the Frenchman had been judged too far adrift of Max's speed. 'When I got in the car and had a few sessions under my belt, I thought of Pierre. I get it. I get it, mate. The car is set up in a unique way that is built around [Max]. And I totally get why. When all is said and done, he might be the greatest driver of all time. But he has a very distinct style of driving and he likes the car set up a certain way and it's a way that's hard for a lot of drivers to synch with. . . . I like a lot of front end [response], a lot of 'nose'. I've been teammates with George [Russell] and Charles [Leclerc] and I've always had way more nose than them. Basically, think front end sensitivity. And then when I got in the Red Bull . . . I mean there was so much nose on the thing that if you blew on the wheel it would turn.'

As Wache and his team reversed that direction, Max got closer to the Mercs and Albon began qualifying closer to Max. But it was too late to save him from being replaced as Max's teammate for 2021. Too late also for Helmut Marko's dream of Verstappen beating Vettel's record of the youngest ever world champion. The 2020 season had been his last opportunity to do that.

But that late 2020 upturn in competitiveness was the early sign that after seven years in the relative wilderness, Red Bull was ready to take the fight to the Mercedes team which had won every world championship since the hybrid era began in 2014. The learning process of that 2020 season and the understanding it gave Red Bull of where the optimum car balance lay was part of the foundation for the world titles that followed.

Maybe it just isn't possible to combine Max's level of innate driving ability with deep technical insight of the sort that can help engineers create the optimum car, because he can make very similar lap times no matter how the car is behaving. Certainly, this appears to be the view of Guillaume Rocquelin, who made his name at Red Bull as Sebastian Vettel's race engineer and was by the time of Verstappen's time there in more of a technical overview role.

Speaking in the *Les Fous du Volant* F1 podcast in November 2022, he said, 'Max has always been a boss. He has enormous self-confidence, he knows what he wants and he has a very direct style of communication. But I'll be honest,' he continued controversially, 'at a technical level, Max is a bit weak compared to other drivers that I've worked with and I think he's still got a lot of progress to make.'

That seemed a harsh judgement. Being critical, seemingly, of Max's ability to mask technical shortcomings partly by the vastness of his talent is a very engineering-centric view.

Christian Horner sees it slightly differently and draws on comparison with Red Bull's previous star Sebastian Vettel. 'Sebastian was a very deep-thinking person that needed to feel very secure; he was studious in his attention to detail. That's where he got his security and confidence from. Max in many respects is much more binary, more straightforward. You bolt him in, you know you're going to get 110 per cent. You know if he feels he isn't getting 110 per cent back that pisses him off and he is going to voice it. But that is it. He doesn't carry it out of the car.

'But then, he is not going to be the guy that is going to be in a debrief for two and a half hours. He is very specific about what he needs from the car in order to go quicker, he has a very good feel for what he does need, for where the limitations are, but he is not going to take 25 minutes talking about a formation lap and the clutch-biting points and temperatures and so on that Sebastian would do even before he got to the debrief. Max is just very focused on this is what I need to go faster, give me that and I will sort the rest out.'

All he needed was the car . . .

11

LONG LIVE THE KING

'Yeah, I think I'll make him nervous if he sees me in his mirrors.'

Max

Before charting Max's first two world titles of 2021 and 2022, it pays to fast-forward to the first race of 2023, the Bahrain Grand Prix. He has dominated the whole weekend, running free and undisturbed from his pole position slot, leaving the others in a different race. He could go faster, but there's no need. Yet he is still lapping faster than his race engineer is comfortable with. 'Just bring it home, Max,' says Gianpiero Lambiase on lap 39 with 18 still to go, Max leading by 11 seconds from teammate Sergio Perez and 25 seconds ahead of the third-place Ferrari of Charles Leclerc.

But the engineer's request to 'just bring it home' is too ambiguous to slow Max significantly and by lap 43 he's going faster than when the request was made. Lambiase is going to have to get more specific and actually define the lap time he wants to see: 'Thirty-seven-zeros, please mate,' Lambiase specifies. 'Leclerc's doing 37.2.' Max doesn't say anything but responds with a 36.3 . . .

'So, the target is 37.0,' repeats Lambiase. Eventually Max talks back. 'Erm . . . I'm happy to go slower, but everyone's going slow.' The clearly exasperated engineer replies, 'There is no race at the moment, Max. So, target 37.0 please. 37.0.' Max reels off a couple of 36.3s. Cue Lambiase on the radio once more, Max surely delighting in the mischief of it all. 'So, you are looking for plus point-seven, Max. Plus point-seven on the dash. I'll get bored of this, so just please do it.'

Bickering over how much to slow down while pulling away from the field – that's how dominant Max and Red Bull have become. It brings to mind the line from the 1970s cult film *Vanishing Point*: 'The question is not when he's gonna stop, but who is gonna stop him.'

But such dominance has built steadily. In something as technologically complex as F1, the competitive cycles turn slowly. Once an advantage is found, it tends to endure. Hence the Ferrari Schumacher era of the early 2000s, Red Bull's four consecutive titles with Vettel 2010–13, or Mercedes' dominance 2014–20. The principle of entropy always prevails, though, as the energy dissipates and the names made by success are coaxed away by rivals; a steady erosion of the advantage over the team in the ascendant, in this case Red Bull. If we're lucky, there will be a season or two of overlap where the titans go at it; if we're really lucky, the generational shift of the teams will play out between the king and the pretender in the cockpits. So it was in 2021, a truly epic contest, one of the greatest the sport has ever seen.

For the last few years of Mercedes/Hamilton domination, it was obvious there was a pretender in the wings and that it was Verstappen. Hamilton himself had clearly identified this from, at the latest, Malaysia 2017. It's a recurring storyline in the history of F1: think Ayrton Senna laying down the gauntlet to Alain Prost in the 1980s; Michael Schumacher doing the same to Senna until Imola 1994 brought that to a tragic end; Fernando Alonso taking it to Schumacher in 2006; Hamilton coming along as the star rookie a year later to challenge Alonso.

Because F1 is a machinery-dependent sport, these challenges require the right equipment and in 2021 Red Bull finally gave Verstappen a car with which he could fight tooth and nail with Hamilton's Mercedes. As a generality, the Red Bull had the edge in the first half-season, the Mercedes in the second – and they arrived at the showdown finale in Abu Dhabi equal on points.

It was a season which cast the two combatants in elemental roles, accentuating the contrasts in their make-up. Hamilton is more emotionally driven, has worked hard through his racing life to put a lid on the cauldron and to direct his feelings. His competitive self – the intimidating warrior – is quite separate from his persona outside the car, which is a sometimes vulnerable, questing one, wrestling with the big questions. Then there's the showman within him, the guy who will crowd-surf at Silverstone or do smoking burn-outs on his motorbike in the car park for the fans at Monza, the fashionista, the musician. He's all these things and more. The social justice and race equality campaigner, the LA scene face who mixes in Hollywood circles, and still, sometimes, in off-guard moments, the boy from the Stevenage council estate.

In Hamilton, you can sense the immense pride at having achieved against the odds. There's a keen antenna for criticism, which he's had to work hard at concealing. When the pride is pricked, he'll fire back with steely conviction, the underlying intensity of his self-belief seeming to ooze from his being. There's also a need for recognition, though, for external validation. This is someone who still carries the scars of having forced his way into a sport that looked unattainable for reasons of both finance and race, and who hasn't forgotten what it felt like to be fearful that it could all be taken away.

For Max – someone who was injected direct into the veins of F1 – it's much simpler. He's a lighter, sunnier, less complex personality. Neither criticism nor praise appears to make the slightest impression. He really isn't interested in validation and has what appears to be almost a disdain for his success, like it has always been, for him, his destiny. It isn't so much carried with arrogance as just matter-of-fact realism, hardly something even worth pondering. There are just the realities of what he is facing at any given race weekend. He'll communicate with the team with sharp, sometimes searing, honesty but expects exactly the same back. He doesn't need emotional support from them, just that they do their jobs as well as he does his. Occasionally, in the heat of the competitive moment, you get a glimpse of the sulky kid who threw his game controller across the room when he didn't win. Outside of racing, however, he doesn't have campaigns to fight but just a private life to live.

Although Verstappen and Hamilton are near-neighbours in Monaco, the chances of them hanging out are close to zero, not because of any animosity – they are neither of them poisonous characters – but simply because their wavelengths do not resonate in either frequency or amplitude. The only time that happens is on the track.

•

In 2021, Hamilton and Verstappen were the two greatest racing drivers on the planet. One of them had been around long enough for that reality to be converted into career numbers and had almost forgotten what it was like to lose, even though he knew it would come one day. The other had been starved of that winning feeling for too long, had been waiting years for this opportunity of racing where he knew he belonged – at the very front, all the time, fearless and ready to battle all-comers, but especially the man with all the titles and plaudits.

The Covid pandemic's financial impact on the sport had led the governing body to postpone all-new technical regulations for a year. Instead, for 2021 the existing 2020 cars would run, but with a crucial difference: the area of the down-force-creating floor was reduced, ostensibly to reduce strain on the marginal rear tyres. But this impacted the long-wheel-base Mercedes more than the shorter Red Bull. Together with the fruitful engineering direction Red Bull had found towards the end of 2020, this had the effect of rebalancing the scales.

Testing at Bahrain in the lead-up to the opening race of the 2021 season suggested Red Bull had the edge, and it was confirmed in qualifying as Verstappen took pole position, 0.4 seconds clear of Hamilton, the gap exaggerated a little by Hamilton locking up his brakes. This was new territory for the previously all-conquering Mercedes team and it seemed a little shell-shocked. 'We don't really have any strengths relative to them,' said Merc's track engineering chief Andy Shovlin after forensically looking at the data. 'We aren't taking any time out of them anywhere. There were a couple of corners they really took chunks out of us, in qualifying, the high-speed sections. In qualifying we're bang on their pace in our best corners but they're quicker in the others.'

But being the chaser can have its strategic advantages on race day – and so it was for Mercedes here in Bahrain. Verstappen eased away from the start but, guided by his team, set a pace at which his tyres could live around this abrasive track. Hamilton ran a couple of seconds back before Mercedes pulled a bold stroke, pitting its man very early for the first stop of what was a two-stop race. Such an early stop

– which necessitated an even earlier second stop – was a gamble only the chaser could make. Because the performance of the tyres degrades so fast here, it would have the effect of undercutting him ahead after Max stopped three laps later but then committed him to a final stint on much older, slower tyres which may not even be able to make it to the end.

Max rejoined from his second stop 8.8 seconds behind Hamilton with 17 laps to go, but on tyres 11 laps newer than Hamilton's and vastly faster. The battle of the titans F1 had craved for so long was finally on. They'd had their skirmishes before, but never for an extended campaign. Here was Max Verstappen in the first race of a genuine world championship fight, a project which had been building for all those years. He chased down his nemesis even while being advised by his engineer, GP: 'Make sure you've still got some tyre life left by the time you get up with him.'

With Verstappen's pace putting him on course to catch Hamilton before the end of the race, the latter was asked to up his pace, 'I can't do that and still have the tyres to fight him when he arrives,' he replied. Max was coming to get him and Hamilton steeled himself. Radio silence in both cockpits. It was down to them now, king and pretender.

On the 51st of the 57 laps, Hamilton locked up into the Merc's bogey corner, Turn 10 (just as he had in his final Q3 lap the day before), and ran wide on the exit. That brought the gap down to under one second, now giving Verstappen the benefit of the wing-stalling DRS function. On the 53rd lap Max got partly alongside the Merc on the pit straight, the skid blocks of the two cars cascading sparks into the evening darkness as they sped, inches apart. Hamilton remained calm, making Verstappen go the long way round into Turn 1. Lapping Antonio Giovinazzi between there and Turn 4 made things a little awkward for Hamilton as Verstappen slip-streamed him. Max hung on around the outside with more momentum and looked like he'd made the move, but he ran all four wheels well off the track in completing it, obliging him to hand the place back and try again. Launching a new attack going into the fast-uphill Turn 13, he slid wildly out of line – his rear tyres were finished, overheated from the chase and now out of grip. Hamilton was off the hook.

Round one to the old guard, but they'd needed stealth and a gamble to pull it off. On raw pace, Verstappen and Red Bull had them on the run. This was fascinating opening fire. Bahrain established beyond any doubt that Red Bull had finally provided Max with the means to fight for the sport's biggest prize. The next round, in Imola, would establish another crucial theme of the contest.

But before we got to the critical moment on the opening lap where Hamilton naively tried a move which would have required Verstappen's co-operation to succeed and didn't get it, the weekend build-up brought out some interesting differences between their two cars. Many of these would come to be significant in their seasonal contest.

Mercedes had improved its car in the three weeks since

Bahrain. Furthermore, the surface of the fast Imola track didn't trigger the Merc's tendency to overheat its rear tyres and oversteer, so improving its balance. But in the cool, damp conditions that prevailed for the weekend, getting the front tyres up to temperature in qualifying and at the beginning of race stints was the crucial challenge – one which the Red Bull met better than the Mercedes. But the track's traits brought its difficulties for Red Bull too. Even though the team had backed away from the extreme front-end responsiveness of the 2020 car – as outlined earlier by Pierre Wache – it was still a snappier car than the Mercedes. This would make it faster into slow corners (especially with Verstappen's amazing ability to let the rear of the car move around him on corner entry) but more nervy through high-speed bends – and Imola is nearly all high-speed bends. So it was a quick car, but one that required the driver to be a little busier than did the more stable Mercedes.

This would play out with both Verstappen and his teammate Sergio Perez making crucial errors on their final qualifying laps, putting Max only third and Perez second while Hamilton took pole. The other Mercedes of Valtteri Bottas –unable to get his front tyres up to temperature until part-way through the lap – was back in eighth. That two Red Bulls versus one Mercedes dynamic at the start of the race – the opposite of Bahrain – played a crucial part in what happened down at Tamburello a few seconds after the start. Hamilton couldn't defend from both Red Bulls as they swarmed him in the spray – and in defending from Perez on his right he made the mistake of allowing Max through on his left. From the second row of the grid Max was leading already – but Hamilton decided to fight it out by staying around the Red Bull's outside as they turned left. As the car ahead, Verstappen was entitled to take up his line so it was at Hamilton's own risk if he decided to sit it out and bank on the other guy giving him space. He was in much the same situation as Leclerc had been in Austria 2019 – and he made the same choice. With the same outcome. Hamilton had required Verstappen's mercy to make the move – and, predictably, there was none. The Mercedes bounced high over the kerbs, taking a piece off the front-wing endplate as it did so. Verstappen was pulling away, as the Mercedes took around 10 laps for its front intermediate tyres to come up to temperature.

In trying to cut into Verstappen's lead, Hamilton later ran off into the gravel trap but was rescued from the penalty of that by a red flag on the next lap for a big accident between Bottas and the Williams of George Russell. This meant Hamilton did not go a lap down and began the restarted race ninth, with only seven slower cars between Max and him, cars which otherwise would have been a lap ahead. He was able to recover to a distant second.

But that was a mere detail. The bigger point had been made at the first corner by Verstappen: he would continue to race in the same merciless way he'd always done, and Hamilton would have to tailor his approach accordingly. Hamilton, who had several times over the previous three years admitted that he didn't really know how to handle Verstappen's aggressive style wheel-to-wheel and would instead just give him room, had evidently realised that was a policy he could no longer afford. If he was going to be fighting out the world championship with this guy, he reasoned, he was going to need to toughen up. He had tried it at Imola and come off second-best.

Thus was formed a crucial theme in the psychology of the duel. It was an unsettling thing for Hamilton: the spotlight was now on how he, with the pride of being multiple world champion, was going to handle this seemingly unstoppable force. It was all part of the Max effect.

The first two races had established the competitive and psychological foundation of the thrilling season to come. The next few passed by in a blur of competitive see-sawing between the protagonists. Hamilton prevailed in Portugal and Spain, the Merc's tyre usage giving a crucial advantage in the latter event. Ironically, Verstappen's aggressive start at Barcelona – from the inside, he went side-by-side with Hamilton into Turn 1, refused to back out of it and rubbed tyre sidewalls, forcing Hamilton to concede – trapped him into a strategic dead-end. Once in the lead and free to choose the pace (because of the big 1.2 second advantage needed to overtake around here), Verstappen chose to run far harder than was feasible for a one-stop in a Red Bull which was more aggressive on its tyres than a Mercedes. Hamilton went with him – and together they pulled out such a big gap on the field that it created the track space behind them for Mercedes to throw the dice with a second stop. That trapped Verstappen in a nightmare re-run of Budapest 2018, leading but with far too many laps left to hold on against a much fresher-tyred opponent.

At Monaco, Max was dominant, putting him in the lead of the world championship for the first time in his career. He was helped by two things: first, the repaired pole-position Ferrari of Charles Leclerc breaking down on the way to the grid (he had crashed in a re-run of Verstappen's 2016 and 2018 incidents as he was about to improve on the pole lap he'd already set). Second, on a track that exposed the Merc's difficulty in getting its front tyres quickly up to temperature, Hamilton was nowhere.

Max looked even more dominant in Baku until a rear-tyre explosion at around 200 mph smacked him hard into the wall (shortly after Lance Stroll had suffered a similar failure in his Aston Martin). The race was red-flagged and the restart – with just two racing laps left – was from a standing start, with Perez on pole from Hamilton. This was a huge opportunity for Hamilton to score big, given that Max was on zero points from the weekend. The potential championship implications were enormous. Unknowingly, however, Hamilton had knocked the 'brake magic' switch on his steering wheel on the reconnaissance lap, meaning only his front brakes were working as he tried to slow for the first turn attempting to pass Perez. His front wheels instantly locked up and he slid up the escape road as the rest of the field flew by. It was a particularly costly error: Verstappen lost nothing by scoring nothing. Perez won the race, doing the perfect back-up job for Red Bull with Max out of contention.

Red Bull and Verstappen appeared to be on the back foot around the Paul Ricard track in France after Mercedes turned up with a more powerful engine. But to the surprise of both teams Max undercut himself ahead at the pit stops, with Mercedes later tracing the crucial time loss to the positioning of its pit box immediately after a curve in the pit entry lane, requiring Hamilton to awkwardly manoeuvre to line himself up.

It was a great and important victory for Verstappen – and he followed it up with two more on consecutive weekends at the Red Bull Ring, for the Styrian and Austrian grands prix. 'Absolutely clinical,' Christian Horner radioed his driver after the first of those victories, with Hamilton a distant second. 'Keep turning that screw.' Because the French, Styrian and Austrian races had been held on consecutive weekends it meant Max became the first driver in the sport's history to win grands prix three weeks in a row.

•

The Red Bull was getting ever-faster thanks to constant development work and Mercedes was getting left behind in the development race. Throughout the two weekends in

Austria, a steady stream of Red Bull trucks were arriving, carrying freshly minted new parts from the factory. Mercedes boss Toto Wolff was very aware of how much resource was going to be needed in creating the 2022 car for the all-new regulations that were coming. He conceded that while there would be an upgrade for the next race, at Silverstone, there-after the development tap of the 2021 car would essentially be switched off. Red Bull, on the other hand, chasing its first world title in eight years, was more gung-ho. When would their 2021 development stop, Horner was asked. 'At Abu Dhabi,' he replied, referring to the final race of the season.

But two important things happened during the British Grand Prix weekend that completely altered the pattern of the championship fight, neither of them in Red Bull's favour. This was the fulcrum on which the whole season pivoted, its tone hardened to something more intense and emotionally gripping. Mercedes brought its promised update – and it was a very powerful one indeed. Not so much during the Silverstone weekend, when the team was still fine-tuning the new specification, but in the subsequent races. It meant that Mercedes was set to be the faster car for much of the season's second half. But at Silverstone, which car was faster depended on track temperature. At higher temperatures it was Red Bull, at lower temperatures Mercedes and that threshold was being crossed constantly during the three days. At anything below 40 degrees C, the Mercedes was in its happy place, anything above and it struggled.

With conditions relatively cool for Friday qualifying, Hamilton took pole. In the sprint race the day before the main event, however, conditions were super-warm and Verstappen left Hamilton well behind, putting him on pole for the main Sunday race. As the 2.10 p.m. start time approached, the track temperature was 49 degrees C: Red Bull territory.

Hamilton knew he had to pass on the opening lap to have any chance of winning this race in front of his home crowd – and even then, it would be a struggle. He was 32 points behind in the championship and now was not the time to play it cautious. Aside from that brief skirmish at the first turn in Barcelona, he'd not had to go wheel-to-wheel with Verstappen since the bruising Imola incident. They'd passed and repassed as their different tyre and pit stop strategies played out in Spain and France, but they weren't true battles. This one looked like it might be.

It was evident from the body language of both cars as soon as the lights went out that this race had an extra intensity, that emotions might be running a little higher than normal. Hamilton made a slightly better start from the inside and was actually ahead into Abbey, the fast Turn 1, but Verstappen hung on around the outside and kept coming, making the pass as he kicked up the dust from beyond the exit kerb, the Red Bull giving a menacing little snaking movement as he took up his place ahead of the black Mercedes. Around the Village loop, Hamilton placed his car to get maximum momentum out of there on to the Wellington Straight so as to slipstream Verstappen. It was timed perfectly: Hamilton was able to pull alongside and they raced with their wheels almost touching all the way down to the approach to the left-hander of Brooklands. Hamilton was ahead but on the outside, trying to squeeze his rival into conceding by moving across to begin taking the corner, Verstappen refusing to budge, obliging Hamilton to back out. This was a desperate last lap-style dice being fought out on the opening lap of the race. It was not normal and it couldn't last.

One reason why Hamilton may have decided not to force the issue into Brooklands was what he knew about the Red Bull's power delivery at the piece of track – the Wood-cote kink – that was coming up seconds later. All weekend, Mercedes had monitored on the GPS traces that the Honda engine would de-rate through there, reducing its electrical power deployment slightly to be used elsewhere on the lap where it was more advantageous to lap time. In response, Mercedes had set up its electrical deployment to give full power through there. Hamilton knew this and, sure enough, as they raced through there the Red Bull's acceleration reduced a little relative to the Merc's and Hamilton came out on to the old pit straight gaining, gaining, gaining, forcing Verstappen to defend as they headed up to the almost flat-out Copse Corner.

The day before, Hamilton had tried for a pass on Verstappen on the outside, which Max had closed off even before the turn, causing Hamilton to inwardly curse to himself that he should have made the move down the inside. This time, he'd decided that was what he was going to do. But he would feign first for the outside as a bluff and then make a counter-move down the inside. At the speeds they were going here, the margins for pulling this off were tiny, but Hamilton was resolved: he was not backing off and he squeezed into the tiny gap between the Red Bull and the pit wall. They got into the corner side-by-side, Verstappen ahead, Hamilton's front-left wheel alongside Verstappen's rear-right.

For Max, there was no choice: he would race exactly as he always had and if ahead he'd take up his line and leave it to the other guy to get out the way. Still flat-out – the telemetry shows he literally didn't lift the throttle, such was his level of commitment – he began turning, saw Hamilton was still there, then eased the turn slightly as if to give the Mercedes a little more time to back out. Hamilton – who was well wide of the normal apex by now, such was his entry speed from a compromised angle – could not back out of it as the Red Bull kept coming across. At the very last millisecond Hamilton tried to back out but it was too late and as the Red Bull's rear wheel hit the Merc's front, so Verstappen spun at horrifically high speed across the gravel trap and into the tyre barriers. It impacted, partly sideways-on, with a force of 51g.

'Max, are you okay?' asked GP over the radio.

There was a worrying three-second silence. Then, only slightly less worrying groans from Max, as if he was just coming round from unconsciousness. Then the pained, groggy exclamation, 'Oh fuck!' And nothing further.

Such are the safety advances made in previous decades that Verstappen was winded and had a possible concussion. He'd be helicoptered to the local Northampton hospital for precautionary checks and released later that night.

Meanwhile, the impact had checked Hamilton's momentum, allowing the following Ferrari of Leclerc to pass for the lead before the race was put under a safety car. As Hamilton circulated behind, he doubtless had time to reflect on the possible consequences. 'Just turned in on me. I was ahead going in there, man . . . I was fully alongside, it was my line.' The safety car took them past the scene of the accident and it can be seen quite clearly from Hamilton's cockpit camera how deep into the tyre barriers the Red Bull is.

The race was then red-flagged, with everyone instructed to return to the pits. As he was making his way into the pit lane, Lewis finally asked: 'Is Max okay?'

'He's out of the car,' replied Hamilton's race engineer Pete Bonnington.

Hamilton won the restarted race after serving a 10 second penalty for the incident.

It's the most controversial accident in recent F1 history – and blame was quickly being assigned. Red Bull, predictably, was furious and even months later Adrian Newey described it as, 'a deliberate foul'. Christian Horner was straight on the radio to race director Michael Masi, saying, 'That corner, every driver who's ever driven this circuit knows that you do not stick a wheel up the inside at Copse. That's an enormous accident and it was 100 per cent Max's corner. As far as I'm concerned full blame lays on Hamilton who should never have been in that position . . . Thank God [Max] has walked away unscathed so I hope you're going to deal with it appropriately.'

On the Mercedes side, Toto Wolff was also campaigning Masi and had emailed him a steward's briefing guidance drawing for such situations, specifying if the car on the inside has its front wheels ahead of the rear axle line of the car on the outside (as was the case in this incident) the car on the inside has the right to the corner. 'As for the incident between Lewis and Max,' he said in his media briefing later, 'it always takes two to tango and these two competitors were not giving each other an inch. It's a high-speed corner and that's why these things are nasty to look at but there is a clear regulation and that is something that is black and white on paper that if the front axle is over the middle of the car on the outside, it's your corner. Now you can say, is that a corner that is equivalent to any other? Maybe not. But again, an accident involves two drivers.

'This is a championship where the greatest driver of all time, a seven-time world champion is fighting with a tool that is maybe not as good as the other car, driven by an up-and-coming star who is trying to make his mark. And they collided and crashed. We have seen that in days before and with all the great rivalries in history, and this is what happened today.'

But even away from the directly affected parties, there was split opinion. Jenson Button: 'Max left enough room, but at that speed, it's difficult [for Hamilton] to get around the corner on the inside. He had to back out and misjudged the apex, which is fair enough because he's coming at such a speed from a new angle. It's a difficult one to have a definitive answer on who was wrong. I get the penalty [for Hamilton] because he put someone in the wall but it's a tricky one.'

Sky's Damon Hill: 'Max knew he was there and he didn't make enough of an allowance for that perhaps. Two cars shouldn't come together. If they were young and inexperienced, you'd tell them to calm down. It was a high-risk move, Lewis has stated his intention, he's not going to let this go to win back the advantage.'

The following day, on being interviewed by talkSPORT, Hill said, 'The level and intensity of it reminded me of Senna and Prost and the way Senna used to terrorise Alain Prost. I was surprised by Lewis' aggression. I think it was predominantly a racing incident but I do think that Lewis was the aggressor in that sense, but he was trying to pass him. He was trying to put a move early on in the race, which he knew he had to. He had straight-line speed advantage with their set-up, so was able to attack aggressively on Max and Max had to defend. It always looked like it was going to happen on that lap.'

The BBC's Jolyon Palmer: 'Lewis is actually pretty much completely alongside Max – and then you've got two championship challengers gunning for the inside line at Copse, and one of them had to back out. Lewis was completely alongside – obviously, he misses the apex slightly and moves into Max, but Max also keeps turning in, and he's taking a huge risk doing that at Copse corner. It's a tough one, a really tough one. I could have seen it as a racing incident, both racing each other so hard.'

Sky's Karun Chandhok's take was: 'Max gives him the space, Hamilton is up the inside, but at no point . . . has he moved in front of Max. Max is coming in and Lewis does appear to be wide of the apex. When they're making contact, his trajectory is heading wide of the apex. Max has given Lewis racing room, but he's also, I think, expected Lewis to back out of it. That's the critical thing. I think Lewis expected Max to back out of it, and Max expected Lewis to back out of it. Max could have given Lewis more room, but Lewis equally could have gone more to the kerb on the right-hand side . . . If you ask me, they could have both done more to avoid the incident, but I would put it down as a racing incident.'

Elder F1 statesman Jackie Stewart, a man who worked tirelessly on safety during and after his racing career, believed both drivers were out of order. 'Lewis' incident with Verstappen was very disturbing for me,' he told talkSPORT. 'Frankly, if that had been in my day and well after my day, Verstappen would've been killed. The race track has been made so safe, the run-off areas so big, and the structures that he finally came to a stop on and even then, the g-forces were enormous. I think that was a great example of what Silverstone have done to make the track safer. Now it's so safe I think people are taking too many chances. The early laps at Silverstone was a good example of that because I think both drivers were overdriving, particularly when you think about it being only the beginning of the race. We've got to re-address that and sadly it sometimes takes a big, big action or even a life to make that come to real understanding.'

Hamilton won the restarted race but his spirited celebration afterwards brought a bitter reaction from the Verstappens. 'Glad I'm okay,' Max tweeted from his hospital bed. 'Very disappointed with being taken out like this. The penalty given does not help us and doesn't do justice to the dangerous move Lewis made on track. Watching the celebrations while still in hospital is disrespectful and unsportsmanlike behaviour but we move on.'

'You don't celebrate your victory with such euphoria when your colleague is still in the hospital,' father Jos told F1-insider.com. 'And as for Toto Wolff: we have had good contact for years, he kept calling and smeared honey around our mouths. I think everyone knows why. He didn't get in touch yesterday. Now he no longer needs to call.'

Later, in an interview with the-race.com's Scott Mitchell, Max gave his take, a few months on. 'I will continue to race like I did. I felt like I didn't do anything wrong in that fight. I gave him more than enough space but he completely mis-judged the cornering speeds, and especially the angle he went into that corner there was no way he was going to make the corner with the speed he entered it. When you go so close to the inside wall, on the entry to Copse and then still try to do the same speed as I am doing while opening up the corner again and then giving him more than a car width space, you're going to run out of road. But this time he ran into my right rear and caused me to hit the wall. I was very well aware where I was positioning my car and I also know that you go in with such a tight angle, especially from his side, from entry to mid to the exit you have to open up the corner, to give him the space. But he still ran out of space. From my side, I continue to race like I did. And I think he will also learn from what happened there.'

'I dummied him,' said Hamilton in the press conference after the race, 'moved to the right for that gap and I was pretty far up alongside him but I then could see he wasn't going to back out, and we went into the corner, and we collided. When someone's too aggressive, these things are bound to happen. There's not really much more for me to say – hope he's okay, because of course I would love to have a wheel-to-wheel battle for the whole race, I enjoy racing with him and I'm looking forward – but I will never back down from anyone and I will not be bullied into being less aggressive.'

A few months on, Hamilton gave me his take on it. 'If I was in that position, I would do the same thing again. That's how I view it from my racing experience – and I think I have a pretty good track record generally of overtaking and where I position my car and spatial awareness. But it has just been different scenarios. I wouldn't say I have necessarily had to change my approach but I would say definitely there has been a need to gain points and you have to get a little bit less willing to give up too much because bit by bit you are losing more points as the season goes on. I was quite far behind in points at that time.'

From the pure racing point of view, a driver is not obliged to make space for a challenging driver. By standard racing etiquette in this situation, neither was obliged to back out of the move, but neither could have been surprised when it led to an accident – and it will always be the driver on the outside in this situation who is more vulnerable. Verstappen raced that corner exactly as he's always raced. What was different was Hamilton's refusal to accept that. Whether a different judgement should have been made because of the possible serious consequences of choosing such a high-speed corner to put his non-acceptance into action is a question outside of the regulations of racing and very much a personal call. The competitive imperative of the moment overrode all.

As Valtteri Bottas, who had watched it all from two cars back, said: 'I had a feeling something was going to happen. Obviously, they were fighting hard. That kind of thing happens – that's racing. It can happen when you fight hard, when you don't give up.'

One small moment Verstappen recalls of the whole episode came hours later, as he returned from hospital to a near-deserted track after all the fans and teams had left. Waiting for him by his motorhome was Sebastian Vettel, who said he just wanted to check that Max was okay. It meant a lot.

The impact destroyed Verstappen's engine, actually cracked its block. Coming into Silverstone 32 points up, Verstappen left only eight ahead and minus a power unit, which would almost certainly mean a grid penalty in a coming race. Relations between Red Bull and Mercedes were hardly improved in the following Hungarian Grand Prix where, in a wet track start, Bottas' misjudgement of his braking into the first corner resulted in a skittles-type multiple accident which involved both Red Bulls and destroyed Sergio Perez's engine. Bottas had sent McLaren's Lando Norris into the side of Verstappen's car, taking out much of the Red Bull's floor. Hamilton had got through unscathed but the team blew his chances in the race by restarting him from the grid while everyone else pitted for new tyres as the track was drying.

This limited him to third on a day when Verstappen was able to limp home only 10th, putting Hamilton back into the lead of the championship.

The Belgian Grand Prix was rained out, the Spa track never drying enough to be considered safe for anything other than a few laps behind the safety car. But half-points were awarded based on the qualifying outcome, meaning Verstappen got 12.5 for setting pole and Hamilton 7.5 for third-fastest time.

But the sun was shining for the reborn Dutch Grand Prix at Zandvoort, a race which Max's success had made happen. There hadn't been a grand prix here since 1985, but such was the devotion Max had inspired in his vast army of followers that it was almost wished back into existence. Magically, a particular tweak to the circuit – a heavily banked Turn 3 – played perfectly into Red Bull's hands as the long wheelbase Mercedes cars could not get around there without grounding out their noses. They lost almost all their lap time deficit to Verstappen in that one corner and although Hamilton gave chase, Max was in control throughout, to the delight of the orange crowd.

What they didn't know was that shortly after the race Jos had to be helicoptered to hospital, after suddenly falling ill with severe abdominal pain. Inflamed intestines were diagnosed and he was treated with antibiotics. Max's celebrations were therefore more muted than they might otherwise have been.

Although the Mercedes qualified as the fastest car at Monza, a bad start for Hamilton in the Saturday sprint race limited him to fifth, with Verstappen taking second. With sprint winner Bottas taking an engine change penalty for Sunday, that put Verstappen on pole for the main event and Hamilton fourth. A pit stop delay for Verstappen put him and Hamilton on a collision course yet again. As at Silverstone, it was another case of neither being prepared to back down. Mercedes had responded to Verstappen's 11 second delay – caused by a procedural error from a mechanic – by bringing Hamilton in. The Mercedes exited just in front of the Red Bull but with Max going faster. They funnelled into a point of conflict at the right-left of the first chicane. Verstappen stayed on the outside of the first part, ready to go for the inside of the second but Hamilton refused him the room, their wheels interlocked and the Red Bull reared over the top of the Mercedes, both coming to a halt in the run-off, with Verstappen's car perched on top of the Merc's roll hoop and halo. Game over for both. Verstappen remained five points ahead in the championship.

After being held responsible for the Monza accident, Verstappen was handed a three-place grid penalty for the following race in Sochi, Russia. Red Bull decided to combine this with the engine change penalty which had been hanging over him since Silverstone – and he started from the back, with Hamilton on pole. Taking advantage of a late-race rain storm, Max came through in brilliant fashion to finish second to his rival in a great display of damage limitation. His decisive call on when to pit to change from slick tyres jumped him several positions. Hamilton's win put him back in the lead of the championship by two points.

In Istanbul, it was Hamilton's turn to take an engine penalty, but Verstappen was unable to capitalise fully because Valtteri Bottas' Mercedes was decisively quicker and won comfortably, Max second and Hamilton fifth. Verstappen retook the lead of the championship by six points.

The Circuit of the Americas in Austin hosted a beautifully poised United States Grand Prix, with Verstappen using his new-found tyre whispering skills to maintain the advantage over Hamilton, who had led the early stages. In response, Red Bull took a leaf out of Merc's Bahrain book and gambled on a very early first stop to gain track position but knowing that would mean a very defensive late race.

'That was just brilliant,' recalls Christian Horner. 'It meant he was really exposed for the last 10 laps and he just let Lewis cruise up to the back of him but ensured that he got that grip for those last laps. You've got to have a lot of self-confidence to do that, especially when you have got Lewis Hamilton stuck on your exhaust pipe.' It made for a startling contrast with his tyre-chewing performance here in 2016. Verstappen was now 12 points ahead in the championship with the last few races counting down.

In Mexico, the team was caught out with its tyre preparations by a sudden increase in track temperature just before qualifying, leaving Max on the second row behind the two Mercs. He corrected that in brilliant fashion within seconds of the start, anticipating where a gap would open up on the run down to Turn 1 and standing on the brakes about 20 metres later than either of the Merc drivers. From there, he was never challenged and won comfortably from Hamilton. Verstappen led the championship now by 19 points.

For Brazil, Hamilton took another engine change. Being able to run it much more aggressively now it had to last only three races gave the Mercedes a spectacular performance advantage around the Interlagos track and Hamilton qualified on pole for the sprint race by over 0.4 seconds. However, he was then thrown to the back of the sprint grid after the DRS slot gap of his rear wing was found to be 0.2 mm too big on one side. Verstappen started this Saturday race from second to Bottas and stayed there. Hamilton vaulted from 20th to 5th which after taking his engine change penalty had him starting the main race from 10th.

Within seconds of the start of the main event, Verstappen deprived Bottas of the lead while Hamilton set about continuing his recovery from the day before, quickly passing the slower cars, then being waved through by Bottas so that he was in third place behind the two Red Bulls after just five laps. It took some time for Hamilton to wear down Perez and by the time he did so, Max had a useful four second lead. So here were the two gunslingers duking it out yet again, but on this day the Red Bull just didn't have the Merc's pace. The new power unit had given Hamilton a big performance boost and he was so much quicker in the straightline sectors of one and three that Max was having to push hard in the corners of sector two, giving his tyres a harder time than Hamilton's.

After the second stops, Hamilton had the gap down to a couple of seconds. He kept the pressure on and each lap as they crested the rise, Verstappen would demand to know the gap. If it was one second or more, he didn't need to use his full battery deployment. If it was under, he did. The urgent radio messages were the battle sounds of a tense championship fight and it ran like this for a few laps, Verstappen driving to his tyre temperatures, Hamilton's car clearly more than comfortable at this pace.

With 23 laps to go, Verstappen's tyres were fading. He was slow through Turn 3 and Hamilton was able to slipstream him down the back straight to Turn 4, getting ahead alongside on the outside approach to the corner. Max trod the line between tenacity and penalty very finely in this moment. He backed off very late from a shallow angle and the car began to understeer. He could have driven through the corner at the speed the understeer was dictating in which case Hamilton's extra momentum would have carried him past. Instead, Max maintained his speed and simply drove off the track on to the tarmac run-off, forcing Hamilton to do the same to avoid contact. This was Max shrewdly using his points advantage, knowing Hamilton could less afford a non-finish. But he was playing with fire – as the stewards could easily have penalised him for forcing another driver off track or gaining an advantage by leaving the track.

Hamilton spent a few laps regrouping and after 10 more laps Max's front tyres were so worn that Hamilton this time was able to complete the pass even before Turn 4. Verstappen's tenacity had made a fight out of it but the Merc's new-found pace had allowed Hamilton to close the points gap down to 14.

This Mercedes advantage carried through to the first Qatar Grand Prix where Verstappen was a distant second to a dominant Hamilton, reducing his points lead to eight.

Both drivers were ramping up the pressure on the other off-track at this time. Hamilton even made reference to it as a way of applying some to Verstappen. On being asked whether he believed the collision between them at Monza was a manifestation of the stress Max was under, Hamilton replied: 'Obviously, Max won't admit to it, I'm not going to make an assumption! But I remember my first title battle was difficult. It was intense. I was going through a lot of different emotions. I didn't always handle it the best. And that's to be expected, it's a lot of pressure.' The unspoken inference of course being that Hamilton had faced this level of tension nine times already (and had come out on top seven times).

Obviously, Max was asked about that comment. 'Yeah, I am so nervous, I can barely sleep!' he replied with sarcasm. 'It is so horrible to fight for a title, I really hate it! If someone actually knows me, they know I am relaxed about those things and I cannot be bothered. I am very chilled. Those comments show that he doesn't know me, which is fine because I don't need to know him. I just focus on myself and I enjoy it at the front and hope to be there for a long time.'

In an interview with the *Dutch Telegraph*, Max didn't just respond to Hamilton but got on the offensive. On being asked if he thought he made Hamilton nervous, he replied, 'He would never admit that. At least I'm not afraid of him. Yeah, I think I'll make him nervous if he sees me in his mirrors. He's a different driver than me, less aggressive. He doesn't know how to race like I do. I can't blame him for that, either, because he was never able to learn that like I did from my father.'

F1's former uber-boss Bernie Ecclestone, a man who had witnessed just about every F1 title fight there had ever been, gave his take. 'Max is a kid compared to Lewis and the worst thing is Lewis has a massive publicity campaign working for him. [Mercedes] have been pushing down all the time on Max and then the race directors have been looking in because Toto goes to the race director. So Max has more than a race to confront as he has them too on his back because they are bullying him and not playing fair. It is psychological game-playing.

'Max has had a few years of racing but has not had years in the streets like Lewis. It has built character in Lewis, and knowing he would win the race with Mercedes being the dominant force over the past few years has made him a much stronger character than Max.

'For Max, this season is the first one he has had a car capable of winning regularly whereas before it was nothing like competitive.'

Dr Riccardo Ceccarelli had a different view: 'In my opinion mentally Max is a little bit stronger than Lewis,' he told the *F1 Nation* podcast. 'Max is the kind of character who is only focused on himself. He has huge self-confidence.

'Lewis is just looking for external support. He's that kind of person. You can see by the team radio how much he talks. He is looking for security, asking what the strategy is. Max never does this.

'Or he [Lewis] is trying to have the support of the people, the fans. We saw with the Brazilian flag and he has a physio who is always with him. Nobody knows who the physio is for Max.

'Lewis is the one that needs to create a familiar environment that will protect him. Max is the type of driver who doesn't need anyone around him. He needs himself. They are two different people, so we have to respect how they are.'

Indeed. Different people with different histories at different stages of their careers. That's what was making this intensely fought championship so fascinating.

•

Max arrived at the penultimate race – the newly-inaugurated Saudi Arabian Grand Prix – with the pressure very much on: only eight points clear of a rival whose car seemed now to be quicker and with two races to go – and therefore 52 potential points available. Regardless of how he tried to deflect it, those around him noted how he seemed not his usual laid-back self out of the car. He carried himself in an untypically surly and self-protective way all weekend, in contrast to his usual open and relaxed manner.

'It's the first time I've seen him like this,' commented F1 boss Stefano Domenicali. 'Usually, he doesn't seem to feel pressure.' Perhaps it was the enormity of what might be about to fall from his grasp after striving so long and hard for it.

'I don't know how it felt in the Mercedes camp,' related Helmut Marko, 'but from here the tension of that season was terrible. Max said afterwards he couldn't have stood that for long. I felt the same thing. It was so on the limit with everything, the politics, the animosity.'

That was the backdrop to a highly controversial weekend as Max tried absolutely everything in his power to thwart the continued Mercedes advantage. He came within one corner of stealing pole position off Hamilton with one of the most outrageously committed laps of his career, skimming the walls to within a coat of paint. As Fernando Alonso and Daniel Ricciardo – who'd just been eliminated from qualifying at the Q2 stage – stood in the TV pen being interviewed, they were unable to remain focused, their attention diverted as Verstappen's incredible performance unfolded. Alonso nudged Ricciardo and pointed him to the adjacent big screen. They stood in open-mouthed awe – until Max finally overstepped the mark and hit the wall in the final corner. He'd be starting from third on the grid, behind the two Mercedes, with Hamilton on pole.

Running behind the Mercs and staying out as they made their first tyre stops, Max's first big break came when a Mick Schumacher accident brought out the red flags. With the race stopped, he could get his tyre change for free and would thus be lined up on pole for the restart. He'd got ahead of both Mercs without having to overtake them. And here's where it started to get fruity. As Hamilton got a better start, Verstappen drove with all four wheels on the run-off to retake the position at the first left-right. There wasn't time for race control to instruct him to surrender the place because there was almost immediately another red flag as Perez and Leclerc collided, triggering a big accident further back.

Race director Michael Masi gave Red Bull the option of either accepting a two-place grid demotion to third for the next restart (as Max had also passed Esteban Ocon's Alpine in his off-track manoeuvre) or to hand it over to the stewards after the race and so have destiny out of their hands. Accepting the demotion, Max immediately countered it with a beautifully committed out-braking move inside Hamilton at the first corner, using his softer tyres to maximum effect. But with his tyres degrading faster than Hamilton's harder compounds, the Mercedes came back at him and with the aid of DRS, Hamilton passed on the pit straight. Max again refused to surrender, going all four wheels off track again and rejoining aggressively in front of Hamilton who had to swerve to avoid contact. If they'd both gone out, Max's eight-point cushion would have been preserved. It was not a legitimate move and Max was ordered to give the place back. He slowed just ahead of the DRS detection point before the final turn, obviously intending to get DRS on Hamilton so he could repass. Hamilton, seeing what Max was trying to do, also slowed. Max attempted to force the issue by standing on the brakes, slowing the car at a rate of 2.4g – and Hamilton couldn't avoid rear-ending him. 'Brake-testing Hamilton was a bit silly,' said Adrian Newey in the nearest he has ever come to a public criticism of his driver.

Hamilton's car was only superficially damaged from the collision and they continued their dice, with Hamilton eventually going definitively ahead just as the stewards were awarding Verstappen a five second penalty. As Hamilton passed, he held Max out wide, forcing him off track, for which he received a black and orange 'warning' flag. Hamilton won and afterwards was visibly drained at the mental stress of this hand-to-hand combat with Max. Things were getting acrimonious and the war of words continued in the press conference. They were now equal on points with only the title-decider to go. If neither of them finished in Abu Dhabi, Max would be champion on account of the countback system (the driver who has the greater number of the highest places).

In Abu Dhabi, Verstappen took a superb pole position against the faster Mercedes with his final qualifying lap. But despite his softer tyres he lost out at the start to Hamilton. He got a run at the Mercedes into the Turn 8–9 chicane, getting down Hamilton's inside. Hamilton took to the run-off and rejoined still ahead. 'He has to give that back,' radioed Verstappen. The stewards ruled otherwise and Hamilton proceeded to pull out an increasing margin in the lead for the next hour or so.

And that looked to be that. Jos certainly thought so, as he recalled in an interview with David Coulthard the day after the race: 'I left the pit and went upstairs to sit quiet, I had my television and lap times because I didn't have the feeling it was going to happen and I didn't want the cameras on my face all the time.'

Meanwhile out on the track, Max was cleaving to his father's advice, internalised down the years, to never give up, never stop pushing – even if in that moment, Jos seemed unable to practise what he had preached. As Max related to David Coulthard, 'Well of course it didn't look great throughout the whole race, they were clearly faster but I said to myself, "I am just going to push regardless and I'm not giving them a big gap". And basically, because of that they never had a free stop and that always gave us the opportunity to put new tyres and different tyres on. At the end, I was on the soft and he was on his old hard tyres, and so it did give us that flexibility. Although we were too slow, we were still within that pit window. And yeah, so I kept always hoping for a miracle – and that came.'

It came six laps from the end, when Nicholas Latifi, his brakes fading, crashed his Williams into the barriers at Turn 15, triggering a safety car. This presented an agonising choice for the Mercedes pit wall. Watching at home with Victoria, Sophie made a plea to the angels. Jos, having been joined in his upstairs bolthole by Raymond Vermeulen, now jumped up and started shouting at the TV for the safety car to get out of the way so his son could get on and race for the championship. 'You know, it was, yeah, I can't express it, it was so emotional,' Jos said.

With just six laps to run, would the incident be cleared in time for racing to restart? Upon that judgement Mercedes had to decide whether to pit Hamilton for new tyres – in which case Verstappen would surely stay out and assume the lead – or leave him out there in the knowledge that Red Bull would then surely pit Verstappen. If Mercedes did the former and the race stayed under the safety car to the end, they would have given the world championship away. If they did the latter and the race did restart, with Max right behind on fresh tyres which would be around three seconds faster than Hamilton's old tyres, they would have given the world championship away. They gambled that the race wouldn't restart and left Hamilton out. Red Bull accordingly brought Verstappen in.

It was taking some time to crane the crashed Williams to a safe place and re-pack the impact-absorbing material behind the barriers. Red Bull sporting director Jonathan Wheatley was on the radio urging Masi to get the race underway, followed by Christian Horner doing the same. It is at the race director's discretion whether to allow lapped cars to unlap themselves before the restart. Doing that and waiting for them to line up at the back of the pack – and then having the safety car do the regulation extra lap – would likely take more laps to achieve than were available. But not doing that would leave five slower lapped cars between Hamilton and Verstappen, taking any sting out of the closing stages.

What Masi decided to do, under immense pressure, was allow only the lapped cars between Hamilton and Verstappen (and none of the others) to unlap themselves – and to bring the safety car in immediately afterwards. Neither of these options was catered for in the sporting regulations, but he actioned them nonetheless.

The race was underway again with one lap to go. With a massive tyre advantage, Max dived down the inside of Hamilton into Turn 5. The watching Jos couldn't believe what he was seeing. As he said to Coulthard: 'Everybody knows if Max is behind on the last lap he will try, whatever happens, and we were just thinking where will he do it, and he did it in corner five, what I didn't expect because then you have two long straights coming.'

This would surely give Hamilton the opportunity to slip-stream him up the following straight into the chicane. But Max, harnessing at the crucial moment all that steely confidence in his own racing abilities, knew the sooner he made the move the greater his grip advantage would be and that all he would need to do then was defend the braking zone once – after that he'd pull away. It also had the advantage of taking Hamilton completely by surprise.

Just like that, Max Verstappen became 2021 champion of the world. Mercedes protested the result on the grounds of the restart procedure, the stewards threw it out. Hamilton stoically offered his congratulations to his rival and later said, 'Max did nothing wrong. He just did what he needed to do, what any racer would have done in that situation.'

Even Toto Wolff, despite his intense conviction that his team had been wronged, did not let that extend to begrudging Verstappen his victory. 'Toto sent me a text,' said Max, '[Saying] congratulations on the season and that I deserve to win it. So that was very nice of him, of course. Emotions run very high to that last lap from both teams. It is what it is.'

For all that he'd once said F1 was just karting with more spectators, this was different. 'My goal when I was little was to become a Formula 1 driver. You hope for wins, you hope to be on the podium and that, when they play the national anthem, you hope one day they play yours. And when you stand here and they tell you, you are the champion, it is something incredible.'

'Especially also my dad, some of the special moments we had here. All the things come to your mind, all the years we spent travelling for that goal and then everything comes together in the last lap. It's insane.'

There was no question that race director Masi made an

invalid call. You can argue he was under time pressure but was also responsible for safety, that he was endeavouring to comply with an F1 request not to end any race under the safety car if possible, and that he had the frenzied campaigning from both leading teams in his ear as he tried to make his decision. But there was nothing in the sporting regulations that permitted him to do what he did, on two counts. Consequently, a few months later, before the new season started, he was removed from his post and later left the FIA altogether. An investigation by the governing body (under the new presidency of Mohammed bin Sulayem) found that, although Masi had not acted in bad faith, there were 'human errors' in how the restart had been handled.

This wasn't just the view of fans rooting for one driver and against another, or some British-held conspiracy theory. Here's the view of Kees van der Grint, a Dutchman with close links to the Verstappens: 'What happened – and I say this as a Dutchman with big admiration for Max and Jos – in Abu Dhabi '21 was a terrible part of F1 history. Lewis was by rights the winner and without the mess with the way the rules were applied he was the deserving champion. But of course, the mess wasn't Max's fault.'

Interviewed for TV at the FIA prizegiving, Nyck de Vries, a Dutchman and friend of Max's (though also a Mercedes-contracted driver at the time), said: 'There's little doubt that Max is a worthy champion. He deserves it without a doubt; he had a fantastic year. He was very strong. I just think there . . . Lewis had it taken from him because the rules were not followed in the way they are described in the rulebook. In sport, we assume that things are fair and square. I was really astonished because I couldn't understand what was happening.'

Asked if he felt caught in the middle as a Mercedes-contracted driver but also a Dutchman, De Vries replied: 'No. I feel I was a neutral. I was watching as a sports fan who loves to watch our sport. But I'm neutral in this. It has nothing to do with me.'

It is true that there had never been a title showdown quite like this one. But there had been at least once before a final-race battle in which the championship outcome was determined by an invalid interference in the result – and on that occasion Hamilton had been the unwitting beneficiary. The deliberate crash of Renault driver Nelson Piquet Jr in the 2008 Singapore Grand Prix – which won his teammate Fernando Alonso the race – cost Ferrari's Felipe Massa a likely victory. Had Massa won that race, his victory in the final race in Brazil would have made him – and not Lewis Hamilton – that year's champion.

On this occasion, however, the official error did not go in Lewis' favour. F1 is a competition with many variables, including luck – and on this occasion the luck had fallen with Max. Without the Latifi accident, without the erroneous way the race was restarted, he would not have won this title. But that would have had somewhere between little and nothing to do with merit. Both Hamilton and Verstappen had performed well enough for the title, regardless of the controversies through the season.

Max's ex-Toro Rosso race engineer Xevi Pujolar summarised it like this: 'If we were only looking at the Abu Dhabi race until the safety car came out, Lewis was dominating, without question. But if we look at the season as a whole, Max deserved the title. He had a tough time in F1 in the first few years, but he deserved the top spot by showing all his improvements.

'He is the right winner for the 2021 World Championship because he drove very well, making fewer mistakes – both he as a driver and his team, behaving great also in the strategies. Max has faced bad luck and several penalties.'

Verstappen isn't one to reflect for long on any of this. Things happen and it's in the past. His title was hard-won, the culmination of many years of intense slog and, as he said in his moving TV interview with Sky, the reward to his family for the way his racing had disrupted their lives, how they had all – his mum Sophie, sister Victoria and of course Jos too – lived for him getting to this moment. And this was all that mattered to him. That some external controversy contributed to his win was neither here nor there. It wasn't a case of right or wrong, only what actually happened. Max Verstappen, 2021 world champion – and no one was taking that away from him.

12

UNBEATABLE

'You have to be aware of the situation . . . I've seen him just edging off a little if it's not for the championship or the race win . . . and I've seen him not going nuts. That, I think, is the overview a champion has.'

Alex Wurz

'Can we do this for many, many years?' were Max's words to his Red Bull teammates as he rode the high of his slow-down victory lap in Abu Dhabi 2021. These words would trigger the pre-2022 season signing of a new contract with Red Bull, running to the end of 2028 – quite feasibly the final one of Max's F1 career.

Speaking to *De Limburger* at the end of 2022, he said: 'I have often said that [the F1 season] is too much, too many races. It's the main reason why I will not continue to do this until I turn 40. This much travelling and activity is just not healthy. I still really like it now, but you have to give up a lot for it as well. That sounds crazy because driving in Formula 1 is of course a dream for many people. But you are always very far from home and from the people you love. There comes a time when you are done with that. But that's how it really is. When I'm done with it, I'll stop. It's that simple.'

He alluded to it again at the team's 2023 launch, saying, 'The problem is that we are travelling so much and it's getting more and more. Basically, the question is, "Is it worth it to spend so much time away from family and friends by chasing more success?" I already achieved everything I wanted in Formula 1. But I know I have a contract until 2028. I'll be 31. It's still pretty young, but like I said, I also want to do different things in life.'

That 2021 world title was the goal achieved, the dream made true. Everything that came afterwards would be a bonus. This is how he looks at it – and it just might have made him even more formidable. It's also possible this contract comes to be the springboard for records he's never even stopped to imagine as he chases around the globe.

The new contract effectively laid down the challenge to the rest of F1 for the next few years. It finally aligned Red Bull and Verstappen for the long-term where previously there had always been loopholes. Red Bull now had its power unit destiny in its own hands while Mercedes and Ferrari seemed to have already instigated their own long-term succession plans with George Russell and Charles Leclerc respectively. This deal effectively said: 'You ain't seen nothing yet,' and in 2022 Max and Red Bull set about proving as much, wiping away any lingering doubts created by the way the 2021 title had been decided.

They were about to dominate a season in a way few had ever managed before. The worrying thing for the rest of F1 was they may barely even have started, that these two consecutive titles were quite possibly just the opening chapter of a whole new era now that Red Bull and Max were firing on all cylinders and with their respective power strokes in full harmony.

The postponed all-new aerodynamic regulations came into force for 2022, creating cars that had a very powerful underfloor capable of generating massive downforce at high speeds, but which could be tricky to balance.

Another problem with such 'ground effect' cars – which rely on a venturi shape within the floor to create a massive pressure drop as the lowest point gets close to the ground, effectively sucking the car down – was 'porpoising'. As the downforce builds, the rear of the car sits down, blocking the underfloor airflow's passage, stalling the whole process, causing the car to rise up on its rear suspension and for the process to begin again, at high frequency. As Red Bull's technical guru Adrian Newey describes: 'If you have an aero map which as you get closer to the ground generates more downforce, eventually the flow structure breaks down and loses downforce – and then it's going to porpoise. With these regs, you could see that was a possibility but whether they would and how you model that, was the difficulty.'

Ground effect aerodynamics, regulated out of F1 for the previous four decades, turned out to be way more complex than anyone had envisioned. With the possible exception of Adrian Newey – who had arrived in F1 direct from university at the tail end of the previous ground effect era.

The Red Bull RB18-Honda was essentially immune to the porpoising problem – or at least could run with a higher level of downforce, enough to beat the others, without triggering the dreaded phenomenon. The Mercedes, driven by Verstappen's 2021 rival Lewis Hamilton and Hamilton's new teammate George Russell, were badly afflicted and would no longer be Red Bull's main competitors. That turned out to be the Ferrari driven by Verstappen's old karting rival Charles Leclerc

In fact, as the season began, with the Red Bull as much as 25 kg overweight, the Ferrari – with its more responsive chassis balance and a new engine which delivered great acceleration out of the corners – was the faster car. Between the beginning of the season in March and eight races later in June, the Red Bull was stretching to keep up. But the Ferrari was unreliable and its strategy team not as sharp as Red Bull's. That and Max's tenacity allowed him five victories in the first eight races. Thereafter, with the Red Bull on a diet and the Ferrari's engine restricted in the interests of reliability, the Red Bull became the fastest car, sometimes by a huge margin. With a weapon like this beneath him, Verstappen set a new seasonal victory record of 15 and sealed his second championship with four races to go. The competitive tide had turned.

•

The season began with two Middle East races, Bahrain and Saudi Arabia. This highlighted once again F1's awkward partnership with regimes so at odds with the values of equality F1 claimed to stand for. The discussion around this also shone a light once again on the contrast between Verstappen and Hamilton. Hamilton had taken on the cause as part of his wider campaign for social justice. It was he who had private discussions with Bahrain's ruling Prince about hunger-striking activists in jail and who was willing to talk to the media on the subject if asked. Verstappen was there to race his car. This echoed a schism between F1 fans: those who felt sport and politics should always be separate and those who believed that was unrealistic, that F1's very appearance would be used for political purposes. Many of Hamilton's supporters agreed with his view that F1 could not exist in a bubble and should use its profile to highlight wrongs in a troubled world. Many of Verstappen's fans rejected that stance and felt their enjoyment of the sport was being compromised by Hamilton's insistence on bringing real-world problems into their leisure time. Verstappen is supportive of the Hamilton-led campaigns of equality. But as a younger person with quite different life experiences, and his racing blinkers still very firmly on, he's simply not interested in initiating them. He's much more of an old-school racer in that sense, even though he's the younger generation.

But on-track, it was no longer about Max versus Lewis, as the latter's car was the thick end of one second per lap slower than Verstappen's. Max's on-track problem was now Leclerc, who in Bahrain qualified on pole, 0.1 seconds faster, and proceeded to lead the race, with Max in chase. Max was being told to lift and coast to bring his brake-disc temperatures back under control as early as lap three. He would be allowed bursts of attacking driving, strictly rationed. 'Impossible to race like this,' was one of his many frustrated complaints over the radio.

After the first pit stops, Leclerc calmly repelled Max's three out-braking moves on the Ferrari. After that, Max's brakes and tyres were too hot and Leclerc had the race won even before Max's engine died with a few laps to go (just as teammate Perez's would) because the new fuel system could not pick up the last few litres of fuel in the tank.

In Saudi Arabia, Max at his tenacious best won a brilliant race-long dice with Leclerc, but qualifying had seen the highly unusual occurrence of him being out-paced by teammate Perez, who secured pole position ahead of Leclerc and Verstappen. The Mexican led the first stint of the race and was only taken out of victory contention by the unfortunate appearance of a safety car just after he'd pitted, allowing Leclerc and Max to leapfrog past him by pitting while the field was at a reduced pace.

What was noticeable about his thrillingly close dices with Leclerc in both Bahrain and Saudi was that there were none of the ruthless, zero-compromise moves he'd so often used against Hamilton. He denied there was any difference, but others saw it. 'I think,' says Christian Horner, 'that it's very much a status thing. You don't see it with any driver, the way he races Hamilton. I think they race each other harder because they recognise in each other that they're both exceptional and both at different stages of their career and don't want to concede.'

Helmut Marko agrees. 'Let's put it the easy way. He and Charles are of the same generation, raced each other in karts. Whereas whenever he lost against Mercedes, it was always excuses. This competition is more sportive, less politics.'

'I think it was a bit of an ego thing for both guys,' says Giedo van der Garde. 'Their ages, the two best drivers on the grid, Lewis is the guy who won a lot of championships and Max was trying to prove he could beat the big guy, I think that is why things were sometimes tough and hard. I think now Lewis has a lot of respect for Max and Max now has more respect for Lewis. When they are together there is a bit of a tension, the energy between them is sometimes too high and I think that is why they crash. Sometimes it goes wrong.'

Alex Wurz, long-time chairman of the Grand Prix Drivers' Association and party over the years to many behind-closed-doors discussions among the drivers, has a very nuanced view about Verstappen's racing style. 'When Max joined, he was testing the limits of regulations – and individuals. On track, equally perhaps in the stewards' office. But I think it's a two-sided approach where a) the rules are continually being adapted and changed. [On] whether this is a good thing or not we probably need a book. b) But equally he has changed. Some of this comes with maturity but also now [he is] in a car where he has the outright pace to win so you don't always have to go for that one move to win, which you do when you have a deficit in car performance. So the faster car makes it appear a little more controlled because you can wait for another move and another move rather than that one chance only. But he's definitely a person who explores the grey areas. I think that's what he as a driver has to do and he's doing it right. It's an interesting process to observe from the outside.

'At times, he gives nothing. So you have to be aware of the situation and who you are to fight him. I've seen him just edging off a little if it's not for the championship or the race win and he knows maybe the other guy is on a different strategy and I've seen him not going nuts. That I think is the overview a champion has and that's needed to win.'

In Australia, Max was running a very distant second to Leclerc when his Red Bull stopped with a fuel leak. Forty-six points behind Leclerc after just three races, Max was not shy about putting some pressure on the team, saying: 'We need to be quicker, which we are not at the moment, and we need to be reliable, which we are also not. So there's a lot of things to work on.' Asked about his title challenge, he replied, 'I don't even think about it. At the moment, there is no reason to believe in it.'

When asked about this moment later after winning the title, he gave a little bit of behind-the-scenes insight: 'Everyone is of course upset [when it happened] but then we also tried to really quickly fix it and be super-motivated to try and turn it around. So yeah, it's maybe a day where you're a bit upset, or two days, but then you're on calls, and talking to people: what can we do? what can we fix? And how do we move forward? And you get to the next race, and everyone is smiling again. And we all have the same goals. So that's the thing, the nice part of the team. You always stay quite neutral in success and disappointments . . . you have to just keep being focused.'

The cool and damp of Imola for round four saw the beginning of the Red Bull comeback. Leclerc led the Saturday sprint almost to the end but as his front tyres began to grain, so Max was able to pounce for the win, putting himself on pole position for the main event. From there – and with Perez slotting immediately into second, controlling Leclerc – Max took his second win of the season.

The Ferrari's harder use of the front tyre played its part in Miami too, Leclerc at the front initially but Max in swashbuckling style out-braking him for the lead. A restart from a safety car allowed Leclerc to renew his attack but Max had him covered, withstanding the pressure until his tyres came up to temperature and he was able to pull away to victory.

Around Barcelona, however, front tyres were not the limiting factor and so Leclerc's Ferrari resumed its early-season advantage. Max was following on until a gust of wind took him through the Turn 4 gravel trap, losing him a lot of time and a couple of places, one of them to Perez. That seemed to have secured Leclerc a straightforward victory but after 27 of the 66 laps the Ferrari's power unit died. Because his DRS was not working, Max had to be put on a two-stop strategy to get himself back ahead of George Russell's Mercedes (which had passed as Max went through the gravel) and this in turn required Perez's co-operation in getting Max to the front. Reluctantly, Perez agreed but made plain his feelings about it. Four wins from six for Max.

But it was all a little harder than it should have been, he felt, particularly against his own teammate. This is where the slightly lazy front end of the overweight Red Bull was allowing Perez to be way more competitive than with the more alert and demanding car of 2021. As recalled earlier, this reached a crisis point next time out, at Monaco, where Perez won – assisted by his own qualifying crash preventing Max from completing the lap which would have otherwise put him ahead on the grid – and Max was a disgruntled third. Cue Jos and his tirade against the team on Max's website.

Two weeks later, in Baku, Perez again outqualified Max and was leading the first stint of the race, with Max pressuring Leclerc for second but unable to find a way by. Staying out under a safety car as Leclerc pitted, Perez lost position to the Ferrari and after everything had played out, Leclerc was leading from Verstappen by quite a margin but on older tyres. We didn't get to find out how that contest would have resolved itself, though, as the Ferrari blew up another engine, just as the sister car of Carlos Sainz's had done a few laps earlier. Max thus took another victory.

Perhaps of greater significance was the catastrophic mechanical failure on the Ferraris which forced the team to run the power units in detuned form for the rest of the season. It would cost them around 0.2 seconds per lap. When this coincided with the new lightweight Red Bull from the next race – in Canada – the performance tables were decisively turned.

Furthermore, the weight taken out of the Red Bull had been mainly towards the front of the car, so it was no longer limited by understeer. This meant Max could work his shamanic magic, leaving Perez far behind and firmly back in the support role. Races then just surrendered themselves to Max, rendering the second half of the season just a blur of pummelling superiority. Canada, France, Hungary (from 10th on the grid), Belgium (from 14th), Holland, Italy, Japan, USA, Mexico and Abu Dhabi all fell to the Red Bull with the number one on its nose.

If he didn't win, it was because something had gone wrong. In Britain, he'd just relieved Sainz's Ferrari of the lead when he clattered over some debris left from an AlphaTauri collision on the previous lap and it ripped his floor away. In

Austria, they got the set-up wrong and the car ate through its tyres, allowing Leclerc to pounce for the win. In Singapore qualifying came the team's only serious error of the season, igniting such fury in Max that he couldn't even bring himself to attend the team debrief and stormed back to his hotel. Even Jos was taken aback, commenting he had never seen Max so angry.

It was all about fuel levels on a wet but drying track in Q3. There is a requirement still to have one litre of fuel in the tank at the end of qualifying or race, so that the FIA can take a sample if it wishes. If you are found to have less than that amount, the penalty is invariably disqualification from all of qualifying behind closed doors and a back of the grid start.

Max was in the middle of a lap that would have stood as pole had he completed it when the team called on him to abort, because it could see that on the following lap (when the track would be even drier and faster) he was on schedule to be baulked by traffic. Having guided him into backing off to create the necessary gap, they then realised he would have less than one litre of fuel if he completed that lap, and so that one was aborted too. All of which left him relying on a time he had set when the track was much wetter, putting him only eighth on the grid. To rub salt into the wounds, Perez took P2 with Leclerc on pole and won after a race-long battle between the two, again doing a perfect stand-in job with Max indisposed.

All this was forgotten a week later in Japan, however, as Max clinched his second world championship. (Fittingly, Suzuka had been the scene of Max's first participation in an F1 session seven years earlier.) Though totally dominated by Max on a wet track once he'd made a bold, off-line pass around the outside of Leclerc at the first corner, the race did not reach even half-distance because of weather-induced delays to the start. The assumption even among the teams was that only half-points would be awarded – in which case Max's points tally could mathematically still have been over-hauled in the remaining four races – but a small change in the sporting regulations since the previous season meant full points were awarded. Hence Max only learned of his championship from Sky's Johnny Herbert just before being interviewed. 'Are you sure?' Max asked. It took a few attempts at persuading him before an FIA representative finally confirmed it to him, allowing him finally to believe it. 'I found it all quite funny, actually,' he said later of the confusion.

He could afford to. This wasn't a marginal, tense situation like at the end of 2021; the outcome had not been in doubt for months. 'Yeah, I began to believe it around the time of France [in July],' he revealed in the champion's press conference.

It was a very different, more resounding title win than his first. But also quite different in the type of racing the new generation of cars had made possible. Max reflected on the 'beautiful side' of these cars. 'Before you [would] really focus a lot on qualifying, because you knew that it was very hard to pass a car. Now even if your qualifying is not amazing, if you have a good race car, you can still fight and you can still actually pass people.

'I think we wouldn't have won the amount of races as we did this year because, yeah, this year, pole was nice, but it doesn't always mean that you're going to win the race.'

'It's really been an enjoyable year . . . The highlight? I think I have to go for the Spa weekend. Because I think that was just total dominance, which, yeah, these kinds of weekends, they very rarely happen like that. And especially when I came home that night, you know, you start to reflect a bit on the weekend. And you realise that was, yeah, pretty crazy and pretty special.'

He was in relaxed, open mood, seemingly happy to answer questions indefinitely. Asked if racing as reigning world champion had made any difference to his season, he replied, 'Yeah, probably people expect a little bit more of you. But at the end for me, that doesn't really change. It's just you always look at yourself and say, what can you do better, right? I don't think necessarily I became a faster driver, because I don't think at this stage of your career that you suddenly find a tenth or two-tenths in your driving. It's all about learning from previous seasons and just trying to apply that. And probably that just sometimes, some situations can make you a little bit faster . . . Can be the car, can be the tyres, just track experience. But yeah, besides that, of course, we didn't have the fastest car over one lap for most of the season, I would say. Just – I don't know – it just didn't really suit our car, the one-lap pace. And being a little bit overweight, of course, in the beginning, quite a bit. That doesn't help over one lap performance.'

He also reserved special praise for Honda. It was, after all, especially fitting that he'd sealed this title at the track owned by Red Bull's engine partner – especially as its racing department was still trying to change the minds of the corporate arm about remaining in F1 in the long term.

'It feels so perfect,' he reflected, 'because it's not just that we are driving with Honda power. We've been really working together with them for a few years – and it's also where we came from together. I think everyone, or most people, told us we were crazy when we started to work with them back in the day, is it going to work out, you know, because they had a tough time at that time. But you see, never give up and full dedication to make it work, and that's what happened. Of course, already last year, we were very competitive, but even better this year. And that's why I'm really proud of the whole team and I'm also very proud of everyone within Honda for that mentality. Because it's hard when you have a lot of criticism on you. And there's a lot of pressure, because people are demanding a lot and you need to perform, and you need to show results. But I think they stayed calm and they knew what they had to do, eventually, and look where we are now.'

'He's a different driver this year,' Marko said in Japan. 'Look at Spa, Hungary, the first lap from poor grid positions.

Very controlled and patient. I was thinking it was a different driver in the car. Who is in there? That would never have happened last year. Also, his tyre use is just exceptional now. He has a great feel for the tyres and this is still developing. Sergio was supposed to be the tyre whisperer but it's moving towards Max now.'

Marko's old friend Dietrich Mateschitz, by now very ill, was nonetheless following events in Japan closely. It would be the last race he'd ever see. He passed away on the Thursday of the following United States Grand Prix a couple of weeks later.

This was the race at which the FIA confirmed that Red Bull was to be penalised for a budget cap breach in 2021, with a fine and a restriction of wind tunnel time and other simulation restrictions. Discounting the incorrect input of a corporation tax rebate, the actual excess spend was just over £400,000 (around $485,000) on a budget cap of $145 million (around 0.3 per cent).

Verstappen batted away questions about this as he took a dramatic victory in Austin, coming back at Hamilton's Mercedes after being delayed for 11 seconds in the pits. The Mercedes was becoming increasingly competitive and was also Verstappen's closest challenger in Mexico. In Brazil, George Russell was able to grab himself a win after Red Bull had got itself into a corner with its set-up, just as in Austria earlier in the season. Max was a distant fourth after the almost inevitable collision with Hamilton as they reprised the 2021 season. 'I went around the outside, and I immediately felt he was not going to leave space,' related Max. 'It cost him the race win. For me it cost a five second penalty. It wouldn't have mattered anything for my race, because we were just way too slow. But it's just a shame, I thought we could race quite well together, but clearly the intention was not there to race.'

'You know how it is with Max,' countered Hamilton. Clearly, their uncompromising attitude towards each other when their cars were competitive was still there, one year on.

But that wasn't even the biggest Max controversy to take place in Brazil. That came on the last lap as he was instructed to allow Perez – who had earlier moved aside under instruction so Max could have an attempt at passing Leclerc, Perez's rival for runner-up in the championship – back ahead for fourth. Max didn't respond. When GP asked why over the radio, his response was sharp. 'I told you already last time, in the summer, you guys don't ask that again to me, Okay? Are we clear about that? I gave my reasons and I stand by it.'

He seemed to be referring to Perez's Monaco qualifying crash, for which he was clearly still holding a grudge. 'It shows who he really is,' snapped Perez. Grievances became heated in an emergency post-race meeting but afterwards, both insisted everything had been sorted and they were now happy. Whether the rift had been healed or just given a sticking plaster, only time would tell. But if the two did go to war, it was difficult to foresee any other winner than Max. In the grand scheme of Red Bull's overwhelming success, it was a niggle, but it underscored the emotions that were running in the cockpit.

Former Red Bull ace Mark Webber gave a view on it: 'Team principals are always managing dynamics between the drivers, and it is very easy to handle that when you're not battling for wins or championship position,' he said on Speedcafe.com's KTM Summer Grill. 'For the top four or top five, there's generally no real friction between the drivers and management have an easier ride on it, but it changes when there's championships or championship positions at stake between the two drivers. The team principal goes on a journey too – they haven't got all the answers. In our day, it was the first experience of it for Christian, Sebastian, myself and Red Bull. They were some challenging times, but that is the nature of the beast. In hindsight, there are decisions that you could do differently and better for the team or one driver in particular, but F1 is great at hindsight. The team can't press the pause button in the middle of the race. The communication with Max in Brazil seemed to surprise him somewhat. It was dealt with internally post-race. Trying to talk to the driver with the helmet on in the last laps of the race to try and get the full picture of what was going on is not always easy.'

Normality returned with a resounding Verstappen victory in Abu Dhabi – a normality which continued even more emphatically into the beginning of 2023. Max says he isn't chasing numbers, isn't targeting records any more. He is just happy to have doubled down on the achievement of the goal that he and his father set their faces towards all those years ago.

Yet the numbers are mounting regardless. Red Bull is at the very top of its game in a way that may even exceed that of its Vettel-era domination. Certainly, Christian Horner believes so. 'This is by far the best Red Bull team we've ever had. There is so much strength in depth and I believe that, in Max, we have the number one driver, the best in the world.'

But even as Red Bull has clawed itself to the front after years of rebuilding to finally give Verstappen the machinery to prove Horner's point, Max himself has also developed, believes Marko. 'He's a much calmer driver today than he was in yesteryear,' he says, 'when he was close to freaking out if he was not at the very top of the timesheets on Friday. We would be working hard for the race, which bothered Max a lot a year or two ago. He just always wanted to be P1. But what is most important, of course, is victory.'

Victories. So many of them they begin to blur into one another. And as those numbers rack up, the records Max says don't concern him begin to appear on the horizon. With Max's contract running for another six years at the end of 2022, there were six more possible titles there for the taking to add to the two he already had.

As Max had prevented Lewis Hamilton from breaking Michael Schumacher's seven-title record at Abu Dhabi 2021, the question being asked was when Hamilton might next be able to take that record-breaking eighth.

Perhaps we were looking in the wrong place.

13

IRRITATIONS VS REWARDS

'I'm not here to be second.'

Max

Max had waited all those years for a competitive F1 car, but once Red Bull finally achieved that threshold it only got better. After his record-busting 15-victory 2022 season, even he probably didn't expect a still bigger competitive advantage in 2023, but that's what he got. Now his career would surely be plain sailing, a smooth run to a third consecutive world title with a further five years on his contract after that. It was everything he dreamed of, right?

Maybe. But there was an undercurrent of dissatisfaction in many of Max's voiced opinions in the early part of this season. Not about the car or the team, necessarily, more just a general malaise. It was as if he was losing patience with the peripheral superficialities of F1 in its aggressively expansionist phase. The American ownership of the sport was bringing unprecedented income but also squeezing the calendar. That and the general razzmatazz didn't sit well with Max and he tended to give full and frank answers when asked about it.

In the Australian Grand Prix press conference, for instance, he was questioned on the changes to the Sprint format of races in 2023. 'I hope there won't be too many changes,' he replied, 'otherwise I won't do it. I won't be here for long.'

This threat to leave F1 echoed that which he'd made after the social media abuse he and his family had received in the aftermath of the Brazilian Grand Prix controversy with teammate Sergio Perez at the end of 2022, when he'd commented, 'When your own sister tells you that you have to do something about it because it's too much, that says enough. Of course, that does something to me, because you shouldn't touch my family . . . It's not only related to that, to be honest, but I won't be here when I'm 40, that's for sure.'

It was ironic that the driver who was talking most about leaving F1 was the one with the longest-running contract. But his dissatisfaction was real.

Between the moments of irritation, he looked to be well on his way to a third title, despite occasional inconveniences. After dominating the opening round in Bahrain, a broken driveshaft in Saudi Arabia left him starting 15th and paved the way for Sergio Perez's victory, as Max came through to second but couldn't quite get close enough to threaten his teammate. In customary fashion, Max wasn't shy of letting his displeasure be known: 'I recovered to second,' he said, 'which is good. And of course in general, the whole feeling in the team, everyone is happy but personally, I'm not happy.

Because I'm not here to be second, especially when you are working very hard also back at the factory to make sure that you arrive here in a good state, and basically making sure that everything is spot on. And then yeah, you have to do a recovery race, which I like – I mean, I don't mind doing it – but when you're fighting for a championship and especially, you know, when it looks like it's just between two cars, we have to make sure that also the two cars are reliable.'

Late in the race, he asked Lambiase what the fastest lap time had been. 'We're not concerned about that,' replied the engineer. 'Yeah, but I am,' said Max. Taking the fastest lap from Perez would mean a two-point swing in his favour. He harvested his electrical power for his last lap assault – and duly delivered it. The point he took for it was the one by which he led the championship. It was a performance of great merit considering he was ill at the time. 'At home in the days before the race I was really ill, like I could barely just walk around and I felt like I was missing a lung. And yeah, I got to the weekend really believing that it was gone, because normally when you get sick, like, two or three days after you are normally alright, you can just do your workouts. But then when I jumped in the car in FP1 . . . Even just one performance lap, I felt like I had to recover for two laps to be able to breathe normally. So yeah, it definitely did affect me throughout the weekend, which I didn't like, because it was one of the first races where I just felt like I was physically limited.'

He was fine by Australia two weeks later, retaining control of the race despite several red flags which wiped away any gap he'd established up to that point. Baku followed a similar path to Jeddah with Perez holding off immense pressure from Max to win. Around a street circuit at which Perez always excelled, Max was not as well attuned as usual. He'd lost his early lead through the timing of a safety car, Red Bull bringing him in just as Perez had seemed set to try for a DRS pass on him, but with 'Checo' then able to leapfrog himself ahead by pitting while the field was slowed by the safety car. Max was gracious in defeat. It wasn't a team failing. 'You were unlucky there,' Perez commented of the safety car timing. 'Yeah, it happens,' Max said. 'It happened to you last year in Jeddah.'

Miami was another super-tight struggle between them: Max had been left only ninth on the grid, having over-committed through a corner on his first Q3 run, then been denied a second attempt by a red flag. Though Perez started from pole, it didn't take Max too long to be in place behind him. With the teammates on opposing tyre strategies, it then became all about who could get the best combination of speed and tyre degradation. In this, Max's mastery in the slow corners of the second sector was decisive. It forced Perez to claw the time back through the fast sweeps of the first sector and eventually that hurt his tyres, allowing Max to DRS his way past his teammate to victory.

•

IRRITATIONS VS REWARDS

As the marketing-led direction of the sport ramps up, it seems Max increasingly struggles to shut off that inbuilt Verstappen impulse to dismiss what he sees as stupid and irrelevant, and it eats into the energy reserves that keep him doing F1. There was a revealing moment in the official press conference that preceded the Miami Grand Prix weekend, after Max was asked a particularly vacuous question, when a look of irritated exasperation flashed across his face, before he then composed himself to give a suitably bland answer. These giveaway micro-expressions seem all of a piece with his growing disenchantment with the sport he has come to dominate. How big those reserves are and how much they are replenished by the rewards of racing are something only he could know – and even he probably doesn't. Not yet.

Speaking to *Sport Bild* early in the season, he was back on the subject of the finite timescale of his career. 'Sometimes, this sounds very weird for people on the outside . . . you're in Formula 1, you are winning – I would have probably said the same when I was in their position but when you are in it, it is not always how it looks or what people think. Yes, it is great, it is amazing and you can do a lot of things, but there is always a limit to certain things.'

This constant tension between Max's irritation at the demands of F1 and the clear rewards it brings – the big dopamine hit of being so brilliantly accomplished and demonstrating his mastery – seems set to characterise his remaining time in the sport. However long that might be:

to the end of his contract in December 2028? Before then? After?

In the weighing scales of what keeps him in F1, an important factor will probably be his judgement of the finances, of whether there is enough to keep himself plus all those he feels responsible for in the style to which they've become accustomed. Forever. That's a big burden to shoulder for one so young. When that is met – if it hasn't been already – all that will be keeping him here will be the energy trade-off between the irritations and rewards. Not the record of accomplishment. He's repeatedly said that's of no interest, as if he doesn't want to be enslaved by numbers which only mean anything to those outside. When that time comes, the unstoppable Max – on his own terms, at a time of his own choosing and not that of any contract – will stop.

Acknowledgements

Thanks to Jonathan Taylor at Headline for conceiving the book and David Luxton at David Luxton Associates for co-ordinating the project. Thanks to journalist Linda Vermeeren for her translation skills and Verstappen anecdotes. Thanks to my friend Ernst Berg for making valuable contacts.

Also thanks to all who have contributed with their time, in particular Frans van Amersfoort, Kees van der Grint, Allard Kalff, Giedo van der Garde, Michel Vacirca, Christian Horner and Helmut Marko.

Index

INDEX

INDEX

INDEX

INDEX

INDEX